Why We Write

Conversations with African Canadian Poets and Novelists

Interviews

edited by H Nigel Thomas

We acknowledge the support of the Canada Council for the Arts for our publishing program.

We also acknowledge support from the Government of Ontario through the Ontario Arts Council.

Library and Archives Canada Cataloguing in Publication

Why we write : conversations with African Canadian poets and novelists / edited and with an introduction by H. Nigel Thomas.

ISBN 1-894770-34-X

1. Canadian literature (English)--Black-Canadian authors--History and criticism. 2. Canadian literature (English)--20th century--History and criticism. I. Thomas, H. Nigel, 1947-

PS8089.5.B5W49 2006 C810.9'896071 C2006-903021-9

Printed in Canada by Coach House Printing

TSAR Publications
P. O. Box 6996, Station A
Toronto, Ontario M5W 1X7
Canada

www.tsarbooks.com

For Harold Head, Ann Wallace, Lorris Elliot, whose labours were crucial in establishing a foundation for African Canadian literature; and the Black pioneers who wrote mostly in oblivion.

Contents

Introduction
Facing the Challenge

I'll employ this brief introduction to outline a few of the issues affecting African Canadian literary production: issues such as the Canadian writing environment, the language we write in, publishing, marketing hurdles, critical reception, and even the implications of the African Canadian label. I am well aware that the issues raised here could be applied to First Nations writers and even to some writers whom others and I might consider to be part of the Canadian literary superstructure. Before tackling these issues, however, I'll offer a few comments on the genesis of this project.

These conversations came about for several reasons, most important of which was my need to meet and chat with fellow Black writers living across Canada. No doubt, the isolation I felt from living in Quebec City, cut off from Anglophones and particularly from Black writers, was a contributing factor. This need grew keener after 1997. In the summer of that year, at the CELAFI Conference held in Toronto, where African Canadian artists in all areas of the arts came together, I was one of three panellists charged with opining about the African Canadian aesthetic. Frankly, I did not know what it was, and I said so. The other panellists—George Elliott Clarke and Rinaldo Walcott—gave fascinating presentations and engaged in a lively discussion with the audience, but they did not state what the African Canadian aesthetic was. I left the discussion wondering if such a phenomenon as a definable African Canadian aesthetic were possible, and promised myself to continue reflecting on the topic.

In the fall of that same year, two African Canadian writers and an African Canadian book illustrator won Governor General Awards. Moreover, it became clear to me then that this was the amplification of a process of African Canadian literary works winning or being nominated for national and local prizes (George Elliott Clarke offers a lengthy account of this in his interview).

It was evident to me as well that in a few years Black writers living in Canada had produced a significant body of work, due in part, as Lorris Elliott had remarked in 1988, to the increased immigration of Blacks to Canada primarily from the Caribbean (4). These works were worth studying to see what, if anything, distinguished them from the cultural production of Euro-Canadian and other variously labelled writers. In short, I wished to see whether they embodied anything that might be called an African Canadian literary aesthetic. But beyond ascertaining whether such an aesthetic exists, something else was needed: the ancillary documents that bring texts into the fold of literary studies, that relate them to other texts, that make them resonate beyond the impressionistic comments of book reviewers. This collection of interviews evolved into being a modest attempt in this regard.

An issue affecting African Canadian writing is the context in which it is done. Initially, it was clear that the Canadian literary superstructure was uninterested in this literature. In the 1960s and '70s Austin Clarke was the only Black writer being published by a mainstream publisher. Harold Head, a Black immigrant from South Africa, established Khoisan Press to publish the many Black writers who had no publishing outlets for their work. Dionne Brand was one of the writers he published. By 1980, Ann Wallace, initially from Jamaica, established Williams-Wallace and created a space for many Black writers. Her list of authors included NourbeSe Philip, Claire Harris, Dionne Brand, and Makeda Silvera. Makeda Silvera's Sister Vision Press enlarged the publishing possibilities for Black writers, as did Horace Goddard's Afo Enterprises.

By the end of the eighties resistance to African Canadian writing changed from casually ignoring it to openly resisting it. Something resembling a backlash emerged in the hostile reactions to the "Minority Caucus" and in the marginalized treatment the 1989 PEN Canada Conference accorded non-White authors. In the 1990s the resistance consolidated even as African Canadian writers were garnering awards. To what extent this resistance is linked to the deep-seated notion of Canada as a White country, i.e., a country of transplanted Europeans, is impossible to tell. But, in 1992, Bhausaheb Ubale, drawing upon knowledge gained while working as a Human Rights Commissioner and as Ontario's first Race Relations Commissioner, observed that "mainstream white English Canadians define themselves as Canadian and all others as immigrants or non-Canadians . . . Thus, ethnocultural and, in particular, racial minorities are seen as different, as non-Canadian, and therefore as less acceptable and less worthy of holding the same positions as true Canadians." (Qtd in Huggan 126). Cecil Foster, in *A Place Called Heaven: The Meaning of Being Black in Canada* (1996); and Joseph Mensah, in *Black Canadians: History, Experiences, Social Conditions* (2002) are two of the several scholars who've examined the impact of such attitudes on Blacks living in Canada. Foster's more visionary, later study: *Where Race Does Not Matter* (2005) takes these analysis further in its examination of the historic vision of Canada as a country of transplanted Europeans vis-à-vis today's expressed wish for a multicultural Canada.

It would have been naïve to think that Euro-Canadian writers would be exempt from the racist ethos that has characterized European belief and practice for centuries. As Smaro Kamboureli observes in a comment on Joy Kogawa's *Obasan*, "the cultural terrain is related to that of politics and . . . history should not be seen as a silent archive that has been packaged away" (xii). Of course, it was no longer necessary nor was it in good taste for the Euro-Canadian writing establishment to state outright (at least not in places where their views might be recorded and broadcast) that Canada's reality is a White one. Its members knew that they ruled the cultural kingdom. Instead, race-neutral literature became their mantra-like duplicitous phrase as they blocked attempts by Blacks to enter into the cultural domain. The literary establishment viewed every attempt by non-White writers to meet and discuss ways of enlarging their space in the cultural domain as evidence that some sort of coup was afoot.

A decade and a half later we can look back at the silliness inherent in much of the reaction. We knew then and know now that those privileged with power are never very good at examining why they exclude others. If anything, wielders of power invest heavily in preserving and justifying their power. Employing strategies similar to those of capitalist manufacturers or service providers, the Euro-Canadian literary establishment has sought to devalue the works of African Canadian writers. Literary agents transmit to Black writers the message from publishers that there is no market in Canada for books dealing with Black themes. A CBC broadcaster, in her role as host of CBC Radio Noon, confidently asserted that she was pleased that Thomas MacMillan, the protagonist of André Alexis' *Childhood*, did not feel Black. Montreal writer Dany Laferrière says that his literary success is due to the title of his first book: *Comment faire l'amour à un Nègre sans se fatiguer*. He added that unless he wrote about sex, he would be forced to earn his living working in a factory (1993, 19–25). We know too that not only do publishers offer their Black writers the lowest advances, they spend least on promoting their books. In this respect, publishers' behaviour reflects the racist attitudes in the larger society, where non-Whites earn significantly less than their White counterparts (Mensah 159; Peter Li 162). It is therefore not surprising that, in its attempts to discredit and restrict Black literary production, the Canadian literary superstructure began to refer to Black literature as victim literature. Manuscripts by Black authors began to be evaluated in terms of whether they were more or less victim art, whether the groaning was humorous or grim. Such statements are not usually made in places where they can be debated; they come to the writers in the form of comments by anonymous reviewers on the submitted manuscripts. Of course, by categorizing much of what Blacks write as victim art, the superstructure implicitly defines its own art as conquerors' art, aptly illustrating Chinua Achebe's observation that when lions write history antelopes fare badly.

The history of racism has long alerted us to how those who seek to oppress us would perceive our writing. The paradigm, which was created early in the seventeenth century, coincided with the beginning of British New World colonization; it is expressed in Prospero's impatience with "cursing," complaining Caliban, to whom he claims he has given language (colonizers would later change language to civilization). A century after Shakespeare, Thomas Jefferson was sure Phyllis Wheatley's poetry could not be more than aping, because, for Jefferson and his slave-holding ilk, it was impolitic to acknowledge that a Black woman, a slave to wit, could write poetry. And some half a century later, in an era when it was illegal to teach Black slaves to read and write, John Calhoun was absolutely certain that Blacks could never learn Greek and Latin and were therefore uneducable. Today J. Phillipe Rushton numbers in his ranks the long line of prominent thinkers from antiquity to the present day who've supported his view that Africans constitute a subspecies of intellectually challenged, oversexed beings with a criminal predisposition (5; 91–111). We wrote and resisted, even when death was the penalty for doing so and we still write and resist. We've never been and we never will be Philomels—our enslavers', colonizers', exploiters' fantasies notwithstanding.

How does all this relate to an African Canadian literary aesthetic? In some small way it does. As a result of reading the corpus of the writers whose opinions are expressed in these conversations and the corpus of many whose opinions are not, I think I have a clearer notion of what could be called an African Canadian aesthetic. I am loathe, however, to attempt to define it; for, inherent in definitions is the very notion of boundaries; moreover, a definable aesthetic is usually a decadent aesthetic. I can nevertheless say that there is an ethos that readers encounter in the works of Black Canadian writers; it is an ethos rooted in identity; and it is there whether the writers' sensibility was shaped in the Caribbean, Windsor Plains, Montreal, Ottawa, Newmarket, Petrolia, Calgary or Vancouver. Those who desire explanations for why such an ethos prevails in African Canadian writing would find them in these interviews, but also in NourbeSe Philip's *Frontiers and A Genealogy of Resistance*, Dionne Brand's *A Map to the Door of No Return*, and in Cecil Foster's *A Place Called Heaven* and *Where Race Does Not Matter*. They would also find them in the race theories of Philippe Rushton (op. cit.), Richard Hernstein, and Charles Murray (1994), among others—today's race theorists; and in the race theories of Arthur Jensen (1998), and H. J. Eysenck (1971)—yesterday's race theorists. No one with visibly African characteristics escapes the sullying such race theories deliberately or inadvertently produce. It's a sullying that goes to the heart of our identity, and from our resistance comes that ethos that tinctures our literary works. If one replaces "the novel" with "literature" in Toni Morrison's statement—"My sense of the novel is that it has always functioned for the class or the group that wrote it"(340)—one gets a clear sense of the relationship between literature and group identity as it applies to African Americans. It applies also to African Canadians. Beyond this, it would be impossible, I think, to speak of an African Canadian aesthetic. Our preoccupations are the preoccupations of humanity everywhere; and how we employ words comes down to individual talent, preferences, and temperament. At this level we are like writers everywhere.

Very noticeable in the works of many of these writers is their preoccupation with history: history transformed into narrative, history distilled into tropes. In the interviews, Lawrence Hill, George Elliott Clarke, Afua Cooper, NourbeSe Philip, Wayde Compton, and Cecil Foster all state that they employ history consciously. I'll aver that in doing so they inscribe their ontology into the Canadian "historical [and cultural] narrative" from which it has been excluded (Rinaldo Walcott 36). In this, they are like other members of the African Diaspora for whom literature was/is a privileged site to debate and counterattack the demonizing, devalourizing discourse engendered and disseminated by those who've sought to oppress Blacks and diminish their place in the human species.

All the writers interviewed here state explicitly or implicitly why they write. Althea Prince is adamant that she writes to clarify things for herself or because an inner force compels her to do so, and she is oblivious of her audience. She and Afua Cooper perceive writing as a noumenal phenomenon: a gift of the "spirit." Explicitly, Austin Clarke perceives the act of writing as an escape from quotidian obligations. But, from his answers to other questions, I infer that he, like Prince, writes to make sense of the world. Indeed it can be argued—and Lawrence Hill states this forcefully in relationship to himself—that making sense of the world is a major force that drives most creative writing. Prince and Austin Clarke excepted, all the interviewees overtly or covertly acknowledge the millennia-old notion that serious writing is both educational and entertaining. Mordecai, Hill, and Cooper comment unabashedly on how this influences their choice of language and genres. NourbeSe Philip laments what she feels is her failure to function effectively in the demotic, with the consequence that she in part fails to reach her desired audience. George Elliott Clarke exults in the self-recognition Black audiences encounter in his works.

In my own case, I write because reality mystifies me, and my temperament pushes me to explore it via the imagination. I know that my senses apprehend little more than the masks of reality. My desire, then, is to strip away the mask and send probes into the darkness beyond, and I can attempt to do so only by way of the imagination. *Spirits in the Dark* began with the question: Who—perhaps What is more precise—is a West Indian? But, post facto, I can see the numerous psychological needs that creation—in this case, *Spirits in the Dark*—might respond to. I can see, too, that *Spirits in the Dark* is aimed at a Caribbean audience and is inadvertently educational, and this in spite of a narrative structure that makes it inaccessible to most Caribbean readers. None of this was planned, and so I concur with the dictum: trust the tale not the teller.

Those interviewees whose formative years were spent in the Caribbean face the issue of linguistic politics frontally. They're unequivocal about why they employ Caribbean English (sometimes referred to as nation language) and the adjustments they may or may not make to render it accessible to an international audience. All of them are aware of the political and economic consequences of their choice. George Elliott Clarke, who on occasion employs a Nova Scotia-based Black vernacular (most noticeable in his novel *George & Rue*, which was published after this interview was conducted), adds a proviso to this: in addition to giving "back the voices of the community in the community's own terms, Black audiences expect us to be able to handle standard English because we're writers . . . We have to be able to do both, and it's a challenge." I am disappointed that I was unable to interview, on the one hand, Makeda Silvera, whose novel *The Heart Does Not Bend* is written almost exclusively in the Jamaican vernacular; and on the other hand, André Alexis, who eschews Caribbean English in his novel *Childhood.*

On the subject of "nation language," I was struck by how frequently the name Kamau Brathwaite was mentioned. His seminal influence on Vancouver writer Wayde Compton, whose roots are as far removed from the Caribbean as the Circumpolar Inuit are from the Kalahari San, impressed and surprised me. Brathwaite is a prolific poet and scholar and a master of two academic disciplines: history and literature; to these, one might add his informal studies of popular and folk culture as well as linguistics, all of which he draws from to establish theoretical bases for the creation and study of Caribbean and African Diasporic literature. His essay "History of the Voice" deals extensively with the concept of "nation language." Brathwaite's understanding of how place shapes language and the artefacts of language motivated Wayde Compton to uncover the writing that Blacks in British Columbia had produced since colonial times, and deepened his awareness of how place affects his own aesthetics. We hear too Brathwaite's echoes in NourbeSe Philip's narrator's lament in "Discourse on the Logic of Language" that she has no tongue to mother her (55–59); and we see Brathwaite's aesthetic practices at work in the poetry of Afua Cooper and Pamela Mordecai. Does this establish African Canadian literature as quintessentially Diasporic? I think so.

A question that I removed from the list of questions asked—but one that I asked NourbeSe Philip when I interviewed her fifteen years ago—is: How do you feel about the issue of voice appropriation? Interestingly, Austin Clarke, in his answer to a question about the literary marketplace for Black authors, stated that writers must at times write about things they're ignorant of. I agree. But he also said that he had been asked to write a book that would exclude West Indian reality, and he wondered out loud how he could be expected to do that. He thereby acknowledged that it is via the known that we negotiate the unknown. Put another way, our depiction of the unknown is whatever we project out of our own experience and imagination onto it. In 1991, when I asked NourbeSe Philip this question, she gave as an example her own creation of the character Livingstone (43–44), which, given the fact that she is neither male nor nineteenth-century European, would violate the injunctions against voice appropriation. A female professor of African American literature once objected to the fact that several of my short stories have female protagonists. She was particularly peeved, she said, by "Death of a Murderess." I might have answered that I had a mother and one grandmother I was deeply attached to, a sister I am close to, and that my two closest friends—I refer to them below as de facto sisters—are women. But it was with humility that I accepted her chiding. I may add that as someone who is constantly told by heterosexuals that I chose my sexual identity and should be punished for doing so, I cannot be indifferent to the complex issue of voice appropriation. Nevertheless, I chafe at the thought that one might put restrictions on the creative imagination. I think it is this impulse that made me remove the question.

And what about attaching racial or ethnic labels to authors and their works? Some of the interviewees—Ayanna Black, Lawrence Hill, and Bernadette Dyer come to mind—expressed discomfort with the label African Canadian. My use of the term excludes the boundaries that the cultural critic Rinaldo Walcott draws around it (XV). Suzette Mayr prefers to be called a Caribbean Canadian writer. In a sense, these are old disagreements that have already taken place in other parts of the African Diaspora and that have only now come to Canada because there is now a substantial African Canadian literature. Langston Hughes and Countee Cullen quarrelled about this during the Harlem Renaissance some eighty years ago. Cullen rejected the label "Negro" poet, and Hughes castigated him in print for doing so. Even more contentious is how Blackness is depicted in, or why it's sometimes excluded from, writing by Blacks. To this day, African American literary critics continue to snipe at each other from two diametrically opposed camps over Zora Neale Hurston's portrayal of African Americans. Such sniping has occurred in the Caribbean as well, where, for a while, it seemed as if writers there were divided into Derek Walcott and Kamau Brathwaite camps. A product of this quarrel is Walcott's essay "What the Twilight Says: An Overture." That we too are now having such debates reflects the diversity that now characterizes our literature, a diversity that brings to African Canadian literary criticism the divergent viewpoints employed to critique the literature created elsewhere in the African Diaspora.

But the quarrels over labels originate in part because of the way literary products are commodified: how they are marketed to a book-buying public, especially one that has been conditioned to devalue Blackness. Insofar as book publishers are part of a merchandising structure, they are obliged to assess the value of the African Canadian brand. Moreover, African Canadian literary works fall into that muddy swirl of multicultural Other, where they might well be made to perform sinister functions. Suzette Mayr has observed that some of her Black creative writing students erase race from their texts, convinced that it would be a marketing impediment. In doing so they reify the belief that White connotes greater value. Dany Laferrière mines the African brand, plays to the debased stereotypes it embodies, and seeks post facto to deconstruct his motives and those of his readers. Do we have any control over how our literature is consumed? What happens when, to paraphrase Graham Huggan, it is marketed "as a form of wilful exoticist discourse" in order to deflect "attention away from social issues—discrimination, unequal access [and] hierarchies of ethnic privilege"[?] (126) The history of African American literature provides a few cautions in this regard. In 1950, Zora Neale Hurston informed her readers of what "White Publishers Won't Print." In 1993, in *Cette grenade dans la main du jeune Nègre est-elle une arme ou un fruit?* Dany Laferrière tells us what today's White publishers will print and why White readers will enjoy it and Black readers will loathe it; and the motives, as he describes them, are exactly the same as those of publishers and readers during the Harlem Renaissance of eighty years ago.

Still on the subject of labelling, a Quebec City friend, Malcolm Reid, asked me if by African I also meant Algerians, Moroccans, Tunisians, Egyptians. To which my answer was yes, provided the Canadians of Algerian, Moroccan, and Tunisian origin consider themselves African Canadians. Whatever I have said before, I still believe that it's up to the individual to define him—or her—self. I have no difficulty calling myself African Canadian. As regards the Canadian, apart from holding a Canadian passport, I've come to love winter, pine forests, and snowshoeing; I embrace what I hope are the best of Canadian values: for example, the right of children to grow up in safe environments free from the fear of violence, a failing I frequently note about the country of my birth, where children are routinely flogged by parents, teachers, magistrates, and even older brothers and sisters; and I love the works of Margaret Laurence, Alice Munro, Timothy Findley, Alistair McLeod, Jane Urquhart, David Adams Richards—writers the superstructure deems quintessentially Canadian and therefore never tags with race or ethnicity. Concerning the African, I am often asked by White Canadians not only "Where are you from?" but also "Why did you come?" On occasion (when I fail to suit some predetermined plan they have for me), they tell me angrily to go back where I came from. All three reactions are linked to the rich melanin Africa has given me. What's most African about me however—and First Nations too—are the oneness I feel with all nature and my strong belief in the value of community. Conjoin them all and I am African Canadian: right? Identity isn't so simple. At least mine isn't. Factor in a same-sex orientation, which has led many Africans, African Canadians and Euro-Canadians to cast further doubt on my humanity—some even think that I should be put to death. And what happens when I add my Carib (First Nations) and British colonial heritage to the mix? The latter was emphasized in the home in which I grew up. This identity phenomenon is by no means simple (that's both a blessing and a curse): it foregrounds much that is arbitrary—and suppresses/represses much that may or may not be salutary. And here's something that isn't arbitrary: Canada is/was a "settler colony," and Whites who live here are de facto Euro-Canadians; and the prefix carries, for better and worse, a ponderous and partly insalubrious history, the consequences of which First Nations and usurping nations are currently wrestling with.

All this, if we choose to examine it as I do here, merely affirms the infinitely complex creatures we are, a complexity that needn't disappear from the literary art we Canadians, however pigmented or acculturated, create. It is essential, therefore, that we, labellers and labelled, share our feelings, our fears, our sense of things, our meditations on reality. If allowed unrestricted circulation, the literatures, hyphenated and unhyphenated, produced in this multicultural country could be mutually enlightening and enriching. Far from complaining, far from being "victim art," enlightenment, enrichment—entertainment too—are what African Canadian writing proffers.

Most of these interviews took place in the fall of 2002, and, consequently, the interviewees' post-2002 works were not discussed. The exceptions are Robert Sandiford (2004), Pamela Mordecai (2005), and Austin Clarke (2006). As regards the choice of authors, I had hoped that this would be a two-volume collection, but for various reasons this wasn't possible. Concerning the missing authors, some of them declined the offer to be interviewed; some I could not locate; others did not respond to my telephone messages and e-mails. I am especially conscious of the fact that the playwrights, dub poets, and the many authors of children's books, memoirs, and other nonfiction works aren't included here. Nor are Francophone African Canadian writers. I have read enough of the work of Francophone writers to know that their identity concerns are similar to those of Anglophone African Canadian authors. However, inasmuch as the overwhelming majority of Francophone African Canadian writers are of Haitian origin or descendants of Haitians, I felt that my ignorance of Haitian Creole and Haitian culture disqualified me from undertaking the serious engagement with the literature that a project of this nature requires.

Several individuals and groups contributed to making this project a reality. I am indebted to them all and I apologize to anyone who might be overlooked in the list that follows: Université Laval gave me a paid sabbatical in 2002 and funded my travel expenses. The Centre for Research on Latin America and the Caribbean (CERLAC) at York University—and Professor Patrick Taylor, in particular—arranged for me to spend the fall of 2002 at York as a visiting professor. York University's extensive holdings on African Canadian literature facilitated my task immensely. David Crean subletted his apartment to me. Althea Prince and Ayanna Black helped me find the writers. Makeda Silvera gave me very valuable advice. My childhood friend Edson Huggins, his wife Jennifer Bynoe, and their children: Colleen, Monique and Nicholas, helped to make my Toronto stay a pleasant one. So did my friend Jean Jubénot. Professor Esmeralda Thornhill greatly facilitated my Halifax stay.

In 2003–2004, when illness forced me to put all my writing projects aside, several friends helped me return to a productive phase: they include those I have already mentioned, but also Shirley Small and Jeanette Keane, who are my sisters in everything but biology; Elsie Sutherland, Lebert Gayle, Cynthia and Maurice Conliffe, Horace Goddard, Julia Carter, Marie-Michèle Brutus, Aylene Sutherland, Junia Wilson, Viola Daniel, Malcolm Reid and his wife Rejeanne Cyr, Louise Gauthier, Dr Nalini Warriar and her husband Dr Manjapra Variath Govindan, Debra DeSouza and her husband Denis Tremblay, Debra Jones, Denise Peter, Michael Okeefe, and my ex-partners Bruno Deblois and Sylvain Giguère. Claudine Auger transcribed some of the interviews. The interviewees generously gave me their time and patiently replied to my nagging queries. I apologize to you for the delay in completing the project. Nurjehan Aziz and TSAR Publications expressed a strong interest in the project from the moment they heard of it, and gave me the final, necessary push to complete it.

Ayanna Black

Ayanna, would you please tell us something about the places where you've lived and how they might have influenced your work?

I was born in Jamaica. While attending school there, I had a teacher called Frazer who was very passionate about literature, mostly the classics—Shakespeare, Tennyson and William Blake. I was fascinated too by the stories of our own Jamaican icon and storyteller: Miss Lou [Louise Bennett-Coverley]. And there was my grandpa George, who was an avid storyteller. He told me many stories about ghosts and horses.

In my early teens I immigrated to England. There I began to think more and more about my absentee father. In those days, I kept a diary to put my feelings to paper in order to deal with the need I felt for my absent father. I enjoyed England very much. I was able to see in the landscape some of what I had learned in the literature about England. During the seven years I lived in England, I learned a lot about Canada mostly from National Geographic and television. I found the Canadian landscapes enchanting, and so I came to Canada.

From earliest childhood, I knew I wanted to write in order to explore several issues; but it never came to fruition until I came to Canada. I remember vividly when it happened. I was living near Bloor and Rusholme here in Toronto. One evening I was watching the sunset from my balcony, and it was so beautiful that it sparked a poem. The whole experience was like an awakening. My writing began with that Canadian sunset.

Around that time I became interested in the feminist movement and began attending Freda Foreman's brown-bag lunch lectures on feminism at the Ontario College of Art, now the Ontario College of Art and Design. Simone de Beauvoir's *Second Sex* was the feminist bible then. There I met like-minded women that validated some of my ideas on feminist issues. I incorporated some of these ideas in my early writings, especially in my first book, *No Contingencies.* I think really and truly that Canada is where my formal writing began. But it has been profoundly influenced by the Jamaica of my childhood. Jamaica's culture is rich and organic, and I deeply enjoyed it. I remember the pleasure I felt listening to the street musicians playing improvisational music. I still hear the drums and saxophones in my memory.

In your essay, "Silence," you point out a relationship between your writing and the silence in your life where your father should have been. Would you like to comment?

I never knew my father. While growing up I invented a father, because growing up without one was painful, disempowering, and, at times, embarrassing. My friends had two parents and talked constantly about them, so I invented a father, and told my friends stories I'd made up about him. Later I got to the stage where it got boring and problematic, because I did not remember the last story I had told them.

You created fiction in order to cope with reality.

Right. But this was during my younger days, when I was bothered by my father's absence. For me, it felt like violence, violence that left bruises in the heart. This is what I'm referring to in the essay. After I dealt with the issue in the poem "I Write Imaginary Stories," I made my peace with it.

At the time I had no idea that this was happening. Following my reading of the poem at Harbourfront, a few women came up to me crying, and I could not figure out why. Later, a friend explained to me that it was because the poem expressed feelings they had been grappling with and needed to hear expressed. I reread the poem and realized that the absentee father was a sort of ongoing psychological violence in my life. I'm told that women who had been sexually abused create images to block the horror of what they'd endured. Finally, after therapy, most are able to heal and move on. What I did to deal with my absentee father was similar. In essence, the child bears the burden of the parent's absence. In those days it was difficult for single parents, mothers, to register their children in some Jamaican high schools. Mothers were snubbed if their children did not have fathers. Today some women go to extremes, even to sperm banks, to be able to have children (don't get me wrong; I'm not judging anyone). In the poem I question such practices; the anonymity of the process bothers me. I think it is important to know one's father. Among other things, fathers influence their daughters' choice of mates much like mothers influence their sons' choice.

Quite clearly, then, you see creative writing as some form of healing?

Definitely. I believe that authentic writing can help others overcome their problems. The important thing is to write from one's inner core.

Your preferred form of creative writing is poetry. Why poetry and not, let's say, the short-story?

I am not quite sure why yet. At the moment I feel comfortable writing poetry. That may change because I can see that narrative is prevalent in my work. I like poetry for its sound and imagery. I've always seen a link between poetry and avant-garde jazz—the jazz of composers such John and Alice Coltrane, Cecil Taylor, Art Ensemble of Chicago, Sun Ra and John Cage. It's the world presented in sound and images.

Your poems range between very short graphic poems such as "California Skies" and the renga poems to your very long poem "Freedom Dance." Most contemporary poets avoid the long poem for all sorts of reasons, including those Poe gave more than a hundred and fifty years ago. What are the advantages of either form?

One should just let the muse be. When I am writing I never think about the number of lines or stanzas or the length of the poem. If I can do something in four lines and I am comfortable with it, then I end it there. If the energy extends to a hundred lines, then I'll go with it. Poems have their own internal energy.

What were your objectives in creating "Freedom Dance"?

It was an expression of the systemic oppression and injustice meted out to non-White South Africans. At the time I created it, the antiapartheid struggle was at its zenith, and I was very much involved in it—attending demonstrations and doing things that highlighted the issue. The poem came out the way it does because of the energy in the anger I felt about what was happening in South Africa. I wrote that poem until it stopped. It was part of my protest.

You seem to have wanted combinations of word sounds that approximate musical instruments. "Stanza 12," for example, seems to imply a medley of drums. How challenging is it to make the voice perform thus?

The way the poem is on the page is how it came out. I wanted to reflect some of the images, and to capture my feelings in sound, hence the suggestion of drums. I have always wanted to write poems in an avant-garde jazz mode. The poem did not come out in a jazz mode but rather more like Jamaican street music.

You took part in an unusual poetry writing exercise, the writing of renga poems. Would you explain what renga is?

The Japanese borrowed the concept from the Chinese and turned it into a literary form, and made it a central feature of their culture for centuries. It's similar to a call-and-answer pattern; it functions like a conversation piece. One person writes a stanza or line and the other person reacts. It's done between two or more persons writing one poem simultaneously, connecting metaphors, images, or concepts to construct a sequence. We decided to do it two persons at a time because we were more comfortable with that format. We spent a week living with each person, and then we created out of that experience together. Each person makes an offering to the other, who can accept it or refuse it if it is not up to his or her standards. Both then talk about it and make the adjustments.

It seems to me that it's an exercise that values orality.

You are right, because that's how the project began. Dôre Michelut, an Italian Canadian writer, was living at the time in Toronto, and we discussed extensively the relationship between writing and orality—Furlan, her language, is dying—and decided to make a go at writing renga.

To produce the renga poems, you worked with three different poets of different backgrounds; and it seems to me that the personalities of the poets, and maybe their cultural backgrounds, facilitated in some cases and hindered in others the poetic process. Comment.

For example?

From my reading of the poems, the exercise with Lee Maracle and Paul Savoie were more successful. With Maracle you found a language of metaphors in ancestral traditions, with Savoie in nature and its creatures and in healing past wounds. With Michelut, you struggled to find a language of the body and weren't always, I think, successful. It seems to me that there was a conflict between you both that comes out in the poem.

Yes. Your perceptions are correct. I think that our being in Merida, Mexico affected the writing. We worked in the city and observed the landscape, the tourist attractions, the Mayan culture, etc., and spoke a lot about them. I agree that we had some tension, which is expressed in the poem. She felt that our piece was incomplete, but I think we did the best job we could.

It made me wonder if people do not need something cultural to link them before they undertake a renga exercise.

I don't think so. There's the anticipation of entering unknown territory. More important is having the openness necessary to build a bridge or a link to the unknown. In Lee's case it was easier. She is a First Nations writer. The colonizers have travestied and tried to destroy her culture much like they've treated Caribbean culture. Our history provided a link. In Paul's case, the absent father and the need to heal this breach played a key role in our debate. The fact, too, that Paul is French, but lives in English, alienated from his language, must have helped. I think that with Dôre, a link came after our struggles over cultural politics. She does not think that political issues are pertinent to writing. I think, however, that even language itself is political—which languages are dominant, which marginal, are the results of political acts. Politics is how the world operates. Not to understand that would be a disservice to myself.

Would you engage again in writing renga?

Yes, I would. After I finished that exercise I wanted to work with a visual artist. You have to be careful whom you work with though. Some personalities do not work productively well together.

Does renga hold any possibilities for teaching creative writing?

I think so. One of the writers I work with uses it online and in the classroom. Sometimes I myself use it in my poetry workshops in the schools. I discovered that it's a good technique to use with students of different cultures because it helps to create links among students of different cultures.

Some of your poems are written in Jamaican "nation language," and I would argue that to do so in Canada is to make an implicit political and cultural statement. Your approach, I infer from "Inglish: Writing with an Accent," emphasizes accommodation of what's called standard English and the Caribbean nation languages. Would you like to comment?

The poem you're referring to is based on a real life story of a woman I'd met on a bus. Another strand of the story came from a woman who called me from an employment office. I wanted the poem to reflect who she was, the language she spoke as well as her life. In Jamaica I understood patios but was discouraged from speaking it. At the time when I needed to write the poem, I called Lillian [Allen] for her opinion about what I was about to do. Lillian advised me to use my own techniques. It was difficult to write it, but it was something everyone could understand. It is a popular poem with high school students who were born in Jamaica or whose parents are Jamaican. For them, it is empowering to hear their language valorized in poetry.

You conclude "Inglish" with a citation from a Louise Bennett poem—a poem in which the narrator wonders how England would respond to reverse colonization; but I have thought of another poem of hers where she castigates the English for calling her language dialect while they ignore the dialects in their own country as well as the very fact that English began as a dialect. Comment.

That's how colonial powers cheapen the cultures of those they've conquered. I arrived in Toronto at a time when there was a passionate debate taking place about the Jamaican vernacular, much of it centering on the subject of illiteracy. In England there's cockney, and in Quebec there's joual. Nobody calls these dialects.

Louise Bennett was a great influence while I was writing this poem, and even beyond. The few times I saw her in Jamaica she appeared larger than life. There was enormous energy in her performances, and I like that kind of energy. And I would say too that her work conferred dignity to the Jamaican language. What others disparagingly call dialects are people's mother tongues, and you can see the difference when they are using it, as opposed to formal English.

How conscious are you of challenging stereotypes in your writing?

I am very political and very proactive in fighting stereotyping. I remember that ten, fifteen years ago, whenever I saw stereotyped advertising on television, I would complain about it to the advertising companies or organizations. I still do. Stereotyping is so embedded in the culture that one has to be always vigilant against it.

While I was growing up in the Caribbean, I was aware of stereotyping based on race and colour. It was an unavoidable feature of my growing up. In my own writing I stay away from stereotypes, unless of course I am creating a character that sees things in stereotype. But as an African Canadian woman, I know the extent to which we are stereotyped. I'm making the distinction here between stereotypes and traits that are representative of our heritage.

You are touching on something here that I might link up with the ROM exhibit, "Into the Heart of Africa," and also with Showboat. *Would you like to comment?*

I think that what happened at the ROM was very unfortunate. A great opportunity for education was missed—for the schools and for the general public. I think the title doomed it from the start. "The Colonization Experience in Africa" might have been a more honest title.

For me, the ROM exhibition evoked Conrad's Heart of Darkness. *But that's how a lot of people, including educated people, feel about Africa. A colleague of mine was astonished when a student told him that Conrad's depiction of the Congo was racist. He was upset with me when I told him I agreed with the student.*

The Canadian media establishment, even a programme like "Sunday Morning," sided with the curator and demonized the protestors.

I felt bad that this happened to the curator. The protest surrounding the show demonstrates that our major institutions such as the Royal Ontario Museum are still struggling with systemic oppression. In this case the ROM made some crucial mistakes that are still being debated—and I feel that this is a very good thing. So much has stamped us with the pathology of colonialism, and we relive it in the images that the colonizers have passed on to their children.

I saw raw power operating in the ROM fiasco. The ROM and the curator felt they had already done what they thought fit to accommodate Blacks, and adopted a put-up and shut-up demeanour.

It is quite fair to say it was a done deal. They invited the Black community to a reception to announce the exhibition and that was when voices of dissent began. Consequently, the ROM arranged for focus groups to offer comments. But this was after the exhibition was conceived and packaged. The focus groups felt that they were being sounded on how to market and promote the exhibition. I was part of one of the focus groups. We made suggestions regarding the depictions and captions of some of the images. A couple of us were paid to look at the texts, including the rewriting of some of the captions. But the changes made were not enough to neutralize the stereotypical constructs.

Apparently the curator felt that she was the scholar, not the focus groups. In a panel about the ROM fiasco some years later, a curator from MOMA stated that she had gone to Toronto to see what the quarrel was about, and immediately saw that there was no debate in the way the artefacts were arranged. The European perspective, she said, drowned out the African voice. As far as I am concerned, that show, however well intentioned it was, could not cut loose from an ongoing discourse that attempts to exculpate Europe for its atrocities against indigenous peoples worldwide.

In your interview with James Berry [a British poet of Jamaican origin], he pointed to writing as being one of the sites where stereotypes might be challenged. But I will counter that if the writing is never published, or publicized, or distributed, and consequently debated, such challenging never happens. This brings me to the problem that we in Canada have of getting our works published, distributed, and reviewed.

To change the system, we really cannot depend on established publishing houses. We have to develop a strategy to get our own works out to the public. My first writing experience began with the Women's Writing Collective, at a time when there were not many women's voices, especially women of colour. We had to publish our own work and develop our own reading ventures. We started out writing about feminist issues. I'm not sure that this was a conscious decision.

The problem for writers in this country is distribution. Most publishers take on well-known writers. Very few will take chances on unknown authors. It's no longer a colour thing. Writers have to understand the dynamics of book publishing and marketing. A writer like Nikki Giovanni had to do a lot of the marketing herself before she became known. Writers have to understand that they have to build an audience, and that they must begin by publishing in magazines before publishers would be interested in them. It's the work that will open the gateway to a larger publishing house, if that's what is important, and young writers have to understand this.

In her short-story "Her Head a Village," Makeda Silvera raises the issue of those topics Black audiences want to see foregrounded in some cases, or relegated to silence in others, as opposed to the personal issues the writer might want to explore. In your piece on silence, you refer to Makeda's story. Would you like to expand on this?

I was exploring the notion that we must not allow the community to dictate what we write. I remember my own struggle with a piece of writing because I was censoring myself in order to please the community. Finally it came down to saying what I want said, not what the community wants me to say.

My problem is the label "Black writer." Blackness is elevated over my individuality as a person. No one refers to Margaret Atwood as a White writer. I oppose the tendency to lump non-White writers into ethnic categories like South Asian, First Nations, African Canadian, etc.

Publishers and reviewers tag us in order to affirm that there is authenticity to what we've written. But that might take us back to the once very hotly debated issue of voice appropriation.

I write out of my own being so the issue of voice appropriation is a moot point for me.

Just last night someone was objecting to my latest book: Behind the Face of Winter, *on the basis that it depicts the Black immigrant experience, with which he is familiar. He thinks I should be showing people how to overcome the difficulties they face in this society.*

When I sit down to write I don't say, I'm going to write a Black poem or a feminist poem. What I write I write. It may relate to race and it may not. What I'm writing at the moment has nothing to do with race. It's about interacting with people and landscapes. But even so, I still have to watch self-censoring. I want to be truthful about what I'm writing. At the same time I don't want to travesty anyone's reality.

You've edited three anthologies of African Canadian writing. Given the travails inherent in putting together an anthology, why were you motivated to proceed with the work nevertheless?

I never intended to do it. I had arranged a reading at the Art Gallery of Ontario in 1989 with fifteen writers, and Ed Carson from HarperCollins called and said that they would like me to put together a book of these authors. It wasn't my idea, it just happened that way. I had no idea how much hard work was involved, but I knew the authors, thus *Voices* was born. The second anthology, *Fiery Spirits*, followed. It was a larger project, and I knew the writers less. Some of them were well established. In some cases the lesser-known writers' expectations were unrealistic, and they resisted any editing of their submissions. This project required a lot more editing and dialoguing with the contributors. But HarperCollins was incredible to work with. The third volume was the reissue of the two anthologies, *Fiery Spirits* (1994) and *Voices* (1992), in a single volume with a new introduction. In spite of the hard work I'm very pleased that I did it.

You have been very active in founding CAN:BAIA (Canadian Artists Network: Black Artists in Action). In fact that's how I first met you. What were your objectives, and how successful have you—the organization—been in attaining them?

Our objectives in creating CAN:BAIA were to facilitate the development, promotion and appreciation for the works of Black artists and to develop a national multidisciplinary art organization. In my view, the organization came into being at a pivotal time. It has been very instrumental since its inception in 1989 in advocating on behalf of Black artists. CAN:BAIA promoted Black artists' work in Canada and abroad and increased the audience for our work. People began travelling across Canada to promote their work, and Black artists began to receive funding and to participate in ways that made a difference. The two festivals that we undertook were a tremendous success in this regard.

One of them was CELAFI, which I interpreted as a celebration of what had been accomplished and as an invitation to the broader community to take stock of what had been done. Would you care to comment?

CELAFI 1997 was a celebration of the African Canadian arts. From the beginning, our plan was to reach a broad audience. We worked in conjunction with many other organizations: Harbourfront Centre, Canadian Stage Company and Passe Muraille for the theatre, the Royal Ontario Museum and the Art Gallery of Ontario—the first time in fact that the AGO had an African Canadian exhibition curated by someone of African origin: Nkiri Nzegwu. I believe CAN:BAIA was a catalyst for the creation of other organizations. It helped especially to infuse new energy in the area of Black theatre. There is now an annual African Canadian Theatre Festival. We worked in partnership with the Paris-based art publication *Revue Noire* to obtain a number exclusively on Black artists in Canada.

I'm very proud of what we accomplished. For ten years, I gave my services as a volunteer to CAN:BAIA. In retrospect, I can see that it was beneficial and necessary. It gave me insights into many, many things.

Do you think that power in the political and economic sphere affects power in the cultural sphere?

Political power very much affects the cultural milieu. Look at how many of us—a million or so Blacks—work and pay taxes but have nothing cultural to show for it! No museum. Nothing in the cultural institutions. We don't have a permanent collection in the AGO or any other national or provincial art gallery or museum. We need bigger, permanent representations of our culture, more than these mini exhibitions that we have from time to time. We need a strategy, something like a five-year plan, to achieve something more meaningful. We have few employees in these venues.

Getting back to the economics of this, the Chinese and Japanese have their own permanent collections, their museums, etc., and their money goes into it. Most of the pieces are privately donated. We have to find the money to make it possible for a Black collection at the ROM; otherwise we will continue to be invisible in these places. How many visible minority artists are in the Canada Council Collection? There's not much art by Blacks in institutions or in corporations.

One of your pieces in FUSE *deals with the 54th International PEN Conference in 1989 in which non-White writers, termed next-generation writers, were a last-minute addition to the programme and were given marginal publicity and treated as Other. Would you like to comment?*

I believe that you are referring to "The Next Generation." Although it was part of the official programme it was given marginal treatment, because the focus was on the established writers. David McIntosh saw the problem, and he took on the development of it, and applied for funding. That part of the programme didn't get any publicity, but the participating writers found a way to make their voices heard. The initial exclusion reflected the fact that non-White writers were not considered to be a force in Canadian literary culture. Now I believe that things have changed somewhat. The problem still facing us is the lack of publicity in our community regarding these programs.

PEN Canada's behaviour was a de facto demonstration of how they perceived non-White writers.

It was around the time that the Canadian Writers Union was on the verge of changing its policies and practices to become a more inclusive organization.

The fallout from this resulted in PEN Canada becoming a more inclusive institution. We too have to understand that the organizations are there and that we have to join them and be active in them and learn how things happen. Like many nonprofit organizations, PEN Canada is operated by volunteers. Anyone that's interested in the work they do can join the organization. That's one way of bringing about change. If we remain uninvolved, we risk not having a voice.

How do you feel about the state of African Canadian literary creations today? This question references an observation you made in 1992. In a discussion with Roberta Morris, you state the following: "I don't think the dominant culture is really committed to dealing with the nitty-gritty issues of comprehensive accessibility . . ." (Ayanna Black and Roberta Morris, "More Back Talk: Race, Sex,

Differences and Literal Methods," FUSE *XV: 5 (1992), 18).*

I was right! I still feel that way. Check out the arts councils, the museums, art galleries, Can Stage, Stratford, etc., to see how many Black people they employ. The funds for the arts organizations are being cut every year, and the first to be cut are the funds for visible-minority and women's projects.

Your book of poems No Contingencies *was published by Williams-Wallace, as were the early works of some of Canada's stellar writers—Claire Harris, Dionne Brand, NourbeSe Philip—and many who aren't so stellar. In fact, emerging Anglophone Black Canadian writers—Austin Clarke was the exception—had nowhere else to go. Sister Vision took over in part when Williams-Wallace went out of business, but today Sister Vision is silent. What are your views on this state of affairs?*

It was sad when Williams-Wallace went out of business. Mrs Wallace's husband's poor health played a role. She struggled to carry on for a long time. Makeda Silvera (Sister Vision) carried on for a long time and published a large number of titles. She moved the business into her home to cut costs, but eventually she too burned out and had to give up. Where does that leave us? The larger houses have taken some of us on: Dionne Brand, André Alexis, Makeda Silvera, Afua Cooper, and Lawrence Hill. The larger publishing houses concentrate on prose fiction and prose nonfiction because these are the profitable parts of the writing market. Poetry, which is what many of us write, is not considered profitable.

But most of the prose writers are overlooked as well and have to rely on smaller houses: Mercury, Beach Holme, Goose Lane, TSAR, Insomniac, AFO, etc.

Maybe many of the emerging writers will have to resort to self-publishing. Many are already doing so. But distributing self-published books is a problem. I do agree that we need a press, and I am not sure who is going to do it. It's a lot of work.

Since you are a cultural critic, as your articles in FUSE *and other magazines attest, I wonder if you would comment on the need for cultural critics who are familiar with the milieu out of which the art emerges.*

I don't see myself as a cultural critic. I'm aware of the systemic problems. I'll say that we need critics who understand our work: the aesthetics, the form, and the culture. They needn't be Black, only sensitive, objective, and certainly knowledgeable.

How do you feel about the critical response your work has elicited?

I have received some very good reviews, and even when they've been negative, I was able to learn something from them. It disturbs me when the critics claim to understand what they've read but fail to express it.

But there's the fact that on the whole works by Blacks are not widely reviewed.

It depends on how aggressively the publisher promotes the book. I don't depend on publishers alone to promote my work. I do quite a bit of promotion of my own works. If it's with a small house I hire my own publicist.

Thanks for allowing me to interview you.

You are welcome, Nigel.

Austin Clarke

Austin, congratulations on the critical acclaim The Polished Hoe *is receiving. Why did you become a writer as opposed to a lawyer, let's say, which at one time you seriously considered?*

I am going to try to answer that question without taking into consideration the context, because I am obviously a writer. I thought I would like to be a lawyer, a good one, because I was surrounded by lawyers. Sir Frederick Smith, who taught me Latin at Combermere School, became a lawyer; Errol Barrow, who became prime minister, was a lawyer. There were some others from the other islands who became lawyers. I thought I would duplicate the grandeur and prestige. So I wanted to be a lawyer for the wrong reasons. I was always impressed by the culture of talk that surrounded me: sermons by the pastors of the denominational churches—not so much the Anglican Church, where the sermon was more of a lecture; the talk of the popular heroes of the village at night by the standpipe; talk by the chaps who could get the most women because of talk; and especially the talk by the politicians, some of whom could talk for five hours and not lose their audiences.

I almost became a lawyer. When I was at school in sixth form, there was one place left for a boy to article in a distinguished firm of solicitors. The headmaster—I have never forgiven him—a man called Hammond, chose a boy who was my junior, and who was from what was then known in Barbados as the better class. Had I got the position, it would have been a sure case of being paid a little bit of money, and being able to wear a suit, and carry around a leather briefcase, and posing around Bridgetown, and everybody would know that Tom Clarke was learning law. I did not allow that setback to colour my view of the profession or even to alter the friendship I had with the chap who'd been chosen over me.

This desire to become a barrister remained with me, to the point where I'd registered for training at Middle Temple Inn, in England, for a year. For years, every time I watched British movies I had the feeling that I had failed. It's in some way similar to how I felt about my performance as an athlete. I used to be an athlete. The last race I ran at Harrison College at Interschools Athletics was a disaster. Thereafter I could not watch most sports without feeling guilty. That stayed with me for many years.

According to your biographer, you are peeved by any activity that keeps you from writing. What is the allure that writing has for you?

It's an escape from facing reality, and I'm not being flippant. In a very serious way, I had the responsibility of providing for a family, something which, in those days, I couldn't do very well. But there was always this one area: my writing, that provided a respite, a cocoon, in which I could live out this life, the life of the imagination. That ability to withdraw and create a life, or a culture that could not be touched by the most imminent financial crisis. And I was able to populate that area in such a way that it could not be invaded.

How do you envisage your role as a writer?

That's a question that I always avoid answering, because it presumes a certain arrogance. I have never considered my work to be teaching anybody anything. Of course, the older I become, I realize that it's not so clear cut. If I were inclined to see my work as having any function, I would have to admit that it's the joy that the reader might get from the variety, from the way I write, from the way I use language, etc.

So in a sense you are saying that the focus of your writing is to entertain.

Yes. But I don't want to stress entertainment because I don't want to give the impression of entertainment in the sense of relaxation or being smart-alecky, but more so entertainment in the best sense, in the sense of enriching the understanding.

Do you see writing as having a function?

I would say that if there is any era where I can locate my work, it would be the 1960s. Then we were bombarded by the ideas of LeRoi Jones—Amiri Baraka—his ideas about the Black Arts Movement. Black writers were asked to project a positive image of the race, even if it wandered into the realm of fairy tale. In other words, Baraka did not think that Black writers should create derogatory Black characters. I don't think he approved of Wright's Bigger

Thomas; his leanings were more towards the character one might squeeze out of the nonfiction writing of Eldridge Cleaver's *Soul on Ice*. I never felt that that was my responsibility; partly, I suppose, because I am not a Black American, even though I have spent a lot of time in the United States. I always felt, even though I was not declaring war against the English model of the novel—I didn't think at the time that I had enough mental equipment to do that—I always did think that their works did not reflect my reality. I was fortunate to come upon the works of two writers one would not consider similar—one was Ralph Ellison and the other was V. S. Naipaul.

How do you feel about the reviews your books have received?

I have always found that reviewers asked and answered their own questions. When I began writing, the reviewers at the time, all White, could not separate my work from their own views of Blackness. There was nothing in their seeing me—or rather seeing my characters—that they would link to their own experience. The other thing I'll say about that is that the questions asked are often related to how the novel or book of short stories is faring—the PR surrounding it. Their questions, for example, are focused on the market success of the book, and they themselves don't seem to know why they are asking such questions. But there is a certain decency—a certain acknowledgement—that something important is happening. I do not know of a single reviewer who has seen the significance of music in my work. I used to wonder whether this was an artistic failing on my part. I no longer feel insecure to the point of saying that I did not succeed in solving the writing challenges. If reviewers missed something as fundamental as the role of music in the structure of my work, how many other points did they miss? But this comes down to something that I'm sure you are aware of: whenever our works are discussed by White reviewers—I won't call them critics—what they don't understand they dismiss. That is criminal as far as I am concerned. It's like the other chapter on civil rights. At this point we should not have to wait for acceptance from the White community. Nobody in this country can say now—will never be able to say ever again—that writing by Blacks is of inferior quality or whatever dismissive term they choose to use.

Your biographer Stella Algoo-Baksh claims that much of your fiction is autobiographical. And if one compares, for example, Growing Up Stupid Under the Union Jack *and* Proud Empires *one sees that the latter is in part a fictionalization of the former. Comment?*

I would grant Stella her freedom as a critic to make that declaration, but I do not think this is true. I would grant that sometimes the autobiographical is a starting point, but by the time the author has reworked the material, very little of the autobiographical remains. However, I can see where a critic could look at both books and then look at me: the third book, and see some sort of confluence. I understand, but I must say that when I was writing those two books, I was not aware that the autobiographical aspect was significant insofar as the narrative was concerned.

But Growing Up Stupid Under the Union Jack *is called a memoir.*

I did not call it a memoir. The publishers did. And I am not now saying that it is not a memoir. But I would like to say that if you were to draw up two columns and put in one the facts from the memoir and in the other, facts about my own life—both attending Combermere School, etc.—I feel that, even if there's a certain convergence, that that still does not make the work autobiographical. If I were pinned against the wall to dispute Stella's position, I would have to say that even though there are those similarities, what I was interested in was depicting the way my life fit the general pattern in the Barbados of my childhood. Let me say that I'm not chastizing Stella.

Here's something I haven't mentioned to anyone. I was visiting my mother five years ago in New Jersey. My mother said to me: "You think I can't read. You stand up there in Canada telling the White people I was a maid." I can't remember if I said that. Some reviewer did. She was not vindictive about it. She wondered why someone could fracture the facts.

As you know, class is something relative. If you look at how class is measured in Canada—the middle class, let's say; they look at things like income, the number of children, the size of the mortgage, and then add all of that up to make their pronouncements. You and I know that that's not how class is measured in the Caribbean. This comes back to a point I was making earlier: that the critics, meaning the sociologists, the politicians, the journalists—they ask and answer their own questions according to what they already believe.

This reminds me of a situation I had in 1993, when Spirits in the Dark *was published. A CBC researcher insisted that the novel had to be autobiographical. As far as I know, there isn't a scrap of information in it that corresponds to my own life, and I told her so. She went on to say that it had to be autobiographical, otherwise it couldn't be so authentic. I felt like saying, "Woman, credit me with some imagination."*

With some notable exceptions, your fiction seems to me to fall into two very broad categories: works preoccupied with the plight of folk or peasant characters in Barbados or in Toronto, and educated characters in Toronto and Barbados. Is this the result of accident or is it your following the dictum to write about what we know?

When I began writing, I was very much aware of what George Lamming had written, and I was intrigued by the violence in James Baldwin. I could not do what Lamming had done. Anything I'd have written along the same line would have seemed imitative. I turned to the culture of violence that comes through in Baldwin's *Go Tell it on the Mountain.* So, if you look at *Survivors of the Crossing,* you will see, among other things, that the violent atmosphere in which the novel is set is, to some extent, forced. I have to agree with you that those two distinct strains are there in the early writing. Later on I moved from what I would call the agricultural syndrome to what I would call the urban syndrome. The immigrants who people my urban fiction were not defined strictly by financial standing. When I was writing the first of *The Toronto Trilogy: The Meeting Point,* I tried—I hope I succeeded—to present realistic immigrants who were not defined by their skin colour or their employment possibilities. I haven't seen this done by anyone yet, but it would be interesting to compare an immigrant character done by a White writer with one of my own. It would be interesting to see what the differences are: how both writers depict the same reality.

One thing that struck me about the characters in The Toronto Trilogy *is the extent to which they are unaware of the wider world outside them. In 1976, I was student teaching at a Montreal high school, and your novel* The Bigger Light *came up for discussion by the head of the English department. He picked up on the point that your characters seemed disconnected from the wider Canadian reality. But he went on to say that such people shouldn't come to Canada, that they couldn't fit in. I think too that around that time there was extensive discussion of a "green paper" on Canadian immigration; it was generating a lot of heat.*

Immigrants are always lost when they arrive in the host society. I would aver that West Indians are less lost because as colonized people we have had to deal with people from several cultures. As Diasporic people we don't really need White people to tell us how to order our lives.

I was thinking of this a week ago at the Annual Picnic of Vincentians living in Toronto, Ottawa, and Montreal. This year (2006), for the first time, we were joined by Grenadians. There we were some ten thousand of us, and the White world of Canada—its stereotypes and suspicions—for that moment did not exist. In miniature, Dots, Boysie, and Bernice create those spaces in your work; they form a community even with those few numbers. But even so, as I said earlier on, one still feels that they are unsure of where they are going. So much of their time is spent on earning a living, finding entertainment, helping one another—they remain united even when they tear one another down and say horrible things about one another.

Well, first of all, they had no large supportive community to speak of. In the fifties their situation was one of isolation. In spite of what you say regarding that picnic, I feel there is no such thing as a cohesive Black community in Toronto, in the sense of people organized around a set of broadly defined goals. There is a small amount of difference nowadays, in terms of numbers, but I don't have a sense of any organized community. But I won't go so far as to say that we can't form a community.

A major thematic preoccupation of your work is the degree of control a character has over his or her life. Why is this so?

Yes. This is one example where some autobiography enters. I have always felt that a person should achieve control over his or her life. I suppose I extended that to my characters. It's probably a reflection of my puritanical upbringing, the belief that we are morally responsible for our acts. I've never thought of my characters in this way, but now that you mention it, I have to admit that this belief, which was inculcated in me while I was growing up in Barbados, has seeped into my characters. Of course, this makes us think about what is fiction. Characters are fictional only in the sense that what's on the page cannot be pinned in totality to living individuals.

I am not sure if such a characteristic is a strength or a weakness. I am probably thinking that for the immigrant, it is a determining feature. It might even be a caution. The immigrant who loses the sense of responsibility for his or her life is in trouble.

Would it be fair to say that your novels set chiefly in Saint Matthias and Flagstaff are in some measure your way, albeit fictionalized, of documenting the lives of the people who lived in these and similar villages in Barbados?

Yes. Certainly.

So it was your way of trying to make sense of their lives via the imagination . . .

I was in Barbados recently and I went to some of the places where I used to live. And the feeling I had—I am looking at the standpipe which now exists as a hole in the wall, changed from how it used to be . . . I remember who used to live in some of those houses, and not much material progress has been made on this stretch of the road. The house where the politician used to live is now boarded up—derelict. I felt as if I had gone back into history, looking at the ruins of Flagstaff Road, hoping to associate the ruins with the time before the ruins. But my great disappointment was that this area had not moved forward.

Each of these novels expands our understanding of these communities, as if you were a painter presenting the different but interlocking features of the same landscape. Each novel is, as it were, an enlargement, another addition to the montage. This includes, The Polished Hoe, *which comes out decades after these earlier novels. In it, for example, we get our fullest portrait of Sarge.*

Yes. I see your point. Last year I did a thorough rereading of *Pig Tails 'n Breadfruit* in preparation for republication, and I was shocked to see that I must have been preparing to write *The Polished Hoe*, because, as you said, there are characters in it that are enlarged in *The Polished Hoe.* I did not initially think this was the case with *The Polished Hoe.* But now that it is written and that I've reread it, I find this fact uncanny. But, then, I've always felt that the artist cannot describe the whole in one attempt, and it might be that he didn't grasp the entirety of his character at the time. That brings me back to something I used to contend years ago. If you could only write what you know, then, certainly, you must revisit certain, fixed tombstones and skeletons. I feel that as you continue writing, you will tend to revisit some of those situations. And even though the careful eye would say that this is an addition or a thickening, the artist might feel that this is a new character, even though there may be surface resemblances to characters of the same name. Of course all this must be linked to the artist's ability to conceive and create. I don't think I could have written the character Mary-Mathilda in 1990, certainly not in 1980. These might have been questions going around in my head at those times but which I did not then have answers for. So I agree with you that there are already intimations in the earlier work of what I did not yet know was to come.

Survivors of the Crossing *and* Among Thistles and Thorns *were published just before Barbados became independent in 1966. The images of squalor, physical and verbal brutality, and class oppression in Barbadian society that these novels present are faces of Barbados that the Barbadian bourgeoisie and ruling class of the day would have preferred to see hidden. What was the Barbadian response to these works?*

Wonder. Amazement. Rejection. And the conclusion that the images were wrong, were distorting. The Barbadian middle class would read those books and laugh, laugh at the characters, and laugh because the characters were not reflections of their own reality. So the Barbadians of that class would look at those characters more or less in the same way that White Canadians made fun of Blacks.

Your most unflattering portrait of Barbados is in The Prime Minister, *a novel which, for fictional convenience, you set just before independence. This novel eviscerates every major Barbadian myth. I'm using myth here in the sense of national structuring beliefs. For the reader who knows Barbadian society, John Moore's personal experiences strip bare the official discourse on independence, democracy, freedom of expression, press freedom, etc., and show them to be mere rhetoric. This seems to me to represent the artist stripping away the masks of custom and complacency to show reality in its utter grimness. Comment?*

Absolutely! You've said it all.

Your latest novel, published in fall 2002, revisits the same settings as Survivors of the Crossing, Among Thistles and Thorns, Proud Empires, *and* Growing Up Stupid Under the Union Jack. *But most important, it focuses, through the character of Mary-Mathilda, on an issue West Indian writers have been loathe to deal with: the rights powerful men gave themselves over the bodies of powerless women. It's a subject Caribbean writers have avoided.*

I go to a bookstore at the Reference Library that sells books that have been pulled from circulation. Two Thursdays ago, I was there and saw a book *Father, Daughters Incest.* I bought the book because a friend of mine told me that the author is the authority on the subject of incest; and I felt it would be useful for the novel I am working on. This book answers the question of why incest is generally hidden in the family. Her argument is that the structure of the family is such that the man in the family has absolute power over his wife and his children; probably for the same reason that it is generally kept quiet in this country. Returning to *The Polished Hoe*, I decided that if I was going to depict oppression in the society, it would be better to present it from the point of view of a mature woman. It would have been easy to reject it, presented from a man's point of view. When I think of Mary-Mathilda now, I feel that I should have shown her more in situations where she was exposed to violence.

I am not sure I agree with you. I think you have enough of those situations to make your point. I think, for example, of the occasion when Mr Bellfeels knocks Mary-Mathilda's mother down to prevent her from telling him that Mary-Mathilda is his daughter, not to mention the scenes of command sex. There are also the horrible acts at the card games. Those are powerful scenes depicting excruciating violence and humiliation.

In the Barbadian novels, you create many characters who seem euphoric with their power to abuse others. Moreover, these characters are often Black, some are politicians, and even Sarge (in The Polished Hoe*) gets into the act. What's worse is the philosophy on the part of the victims that the powerful will have their way; therefore, it's best to succumb to them. Am I misreading you here?*

Not at all. You are right on. Here's a story that I think illustrates the sort of class reality that's fictionalized in my books. When I was at Harrison College I was friendly with a student whose father was a merchant on Roebuck Street. By the time I got to sixth form my mother had gained sufficient status where she could credit groceries from this merchant. At the time I was courting a girl in my area. She was in high school. She had a bigger sister who worked in town. They lived in the middle of a cane field. I would visit her, and it got to the point where I was able to go inside the house, and they would offer me tea, souse or black pudding. But after a while I began to see a car parked outside the house. In those days cars were so few in Barbados that we knew who owned them. It turned out that the older sister was having an affair with the merchant, my schoolfriend's father. My sense of preservation told me that I could not visit the house when he was there. But one night I was there when the car pulled up. The mother told me I would have to leave. She didn't have to explain anything to me. He wouldn't tolerate meeting me there. I was angry, but with maturity I got to understand that he was the sort of man who'd have sent a mule-cart of groceries that could last her a month, and she couldn't jeopardize that. That's the sort of lesson that Mary-Mathilda's mother would have learnt and passed on to her.

What's the role of Wilberforce in The Polished Hoe*?*

Wilberforce is the remnants of a colonial education system. The more education he has the less he learns. Wilberforce comes back and wishes to enforce his views, and his mother is less of a woman in that situation. He expects that she would accept all his thinking. I know that his name has historical connotations, but I did not wish to make much of that. He is called Wilberforce in much the same way that Black American mothers name their children after historical figures, American presidents usually. But Wilberforce is harmless; he is decent and kind in the way he supports his mother.

You told me in an earlier conversation that The Polished Hoe *was being serialized in the Barbados newspaper* The Nation. *Quite clearly this indicates that the society is now sufficiently confident to face the more sordid aspects of its past.*

I am still not sure how or why this happened. I can only give you a story that illustrates the change. My Jamaican publishers arranged for a signing of *The Polished Hoe* at Cave Shepherd, the same store that's mentioned in the novel. I was there all day signing books. Around two o'clock, this man comes to me and says, "Man, you here all day signing books; you ain want something to eat? Man, I proud o' you." He was the owner of Cave Shepherd.

Another incident would illustrate the change. I was in Australia to give a lecture and a reading after *The Polished Hoe* had been launched at the residence of the Canadian High Commissioner. When I was finished I saw this phalanx of Australian women waiting for me. When they opened their mouths I realized they were all Barbadian. These were people who'd left when Barbados became independent; they'd left rather than be governed by Blacks, and they'd left at a time when Australia did not accept non-White immigrants. They told me I should go to Perth because that's where most of the Barbadians live. Now here they were to celebrate one of their own. It didn't matter that I was a Black Bajan, just that I was Bajan. Emigration was a disaster for many of them. They did not get the jobs that their colour would have ensured them had they remained in Barbados.

In Proud Empires *and* The Prime Minister *politicians fare very badly. Oddly it is political science that Boy studies at Trinity College. And one isn't sure whether he is returning to Barbados to become an attorney or to become a politician. I suppose the best separation one can make between fiction and reality is present in your own devastating representation of politics and your actual political involvement to the point of being a candidate for the Progressive Conservatives in Ontario. Would you comment on both?*

If I were going to write another book about politics I would tend to be more balanced. In these books I was looking at only one aspect of the politician. I don't think I was making any other point other than to show the corruption and the unpreparedness of the politician for his role. In any event, the politician's role was circumscribed. One of the things that disillusioned me in my role as advisor to the prime minister was how few people knew what was going on, and just how limited the power of the prime minister was.

Wilberforce is the sort of character that shows who these politicians are. He shows the futility of serious thought. He has a head full of facts and can do nothing worthwhile with them. Of course, he can't. The system doesn't permit him.

The bulk of your fiction, especially your short fiction, is set in Toronto. Let's talk for a moment about The Toronto Trilogy. *In the* Trilogy, *Toronto comes across as a prison. Is that how you saw it when you were studying at Trinity College?*

Yes. It was a prison in many ways. When I look at my life at Trinity College, it was like a prison: a class prison. We dressed formally to go to the dining hall. There were numerous class prejudices that came into play in almost everything we did, and most especially in our attitudes to the girls we dated. Everything about our behaviour showed the ways in which we had been colonized. A certain young woman we knew, who worked as a domestic servant, told us her father was a substantial landholder in Jamaica, and we didn't believe her. Years later I met her, and she told me she was married to an Italian whom she'd helped put through University. But the point that I wish to make is that we couldn't see how she could be from a wealthy family in Jamaica and be a domestic here.

It was also something of a physical prison for us. We stayed within a few blocks of the University. College, Yonge, and Charles streets marked the limits beyond which we didn't go, because it was recognized that if you were in that radius you were a student at the university. Outside of that area we ran the risk of being misidentified as railroad porters.

You have two interracial relationships in the Trilogy. *The one between Henry and Agatha is a standard relationship. But Estelle and Burrman's is not. It can be argued that Estelle's attraction to Burrman is because of his power to procure her landed immigrant status, that she is preconditioned to respond in this way.*

First of all, Estelle went into that relationship without understanding what was at stake. I think Bernice could not imagine that her sister would become attracted to her employer. Mr Burrman too is naïve. He never takes into account the possible consequences of his relationship with Estelle. In some ways he does accept, after the fact, the consequences of his relations with Estelle—that is, after getting her pregnant, he assumes the financial responsibilities for the child, and, to some extent, the moral responsibilities for his act. The Jewish community was mad at me for this episode in the *Trilogy*. When I wrote this there were relationships between Black women who were house maids and their male Jewish and non-Jewish employers. I'd heard numerous stories of this sort. The other thing too is that those of us who came here never told the truth to others back home about the conditions that we found here. Estelle is a victim of such lack of knowledge.

I'm interested in your opinion of why this was so. I myself was certainly guilty of that. And it was a deliberate decision. I did not want to tell people who thought Canada was some sort of Promised Land that it was not so; and I certainly did not want to recount the painful experiences I was having here.

Yes. People did not want to shatter the dreams of others. So in the case of domestics, they never mentioned in their letters back home to Barbados and the other islands details of the racial and sexual difficulties they were having here.

While you were writing the Trilogy *you were also intimately involved with African American literature, studying it and teaching it, as well as the Civil Rights Movement in the US. How did each of these impact on the fiction you were writing then?*

I have to say I cannot gauge the impact African American literature had on my writing. I should say that in those years, 1968–1972, I wrote one book. The others of this period had been written before. Regarding the Black civil rights movement and African American literature, I approached both as a freelance broadcaster for CBC Radio in Toronto. My approach to them was intellectual-academic; it wasn't in the sense of seeking a basis for my own creative work. But there was some impact. In the years I was dealing with them I wasn't aware of how to use them in my own work. But now, looking back, it's obvious that I've used them: in short stories, certainly, and in nonfiction, particularly in two books I've written on LeRoi Jones (Amiri Baraka). One of them is called "An American Dutchman"; I've forgotten the title of the other. Both books examine his work within the context of the Black civil rights campaign. I'd like to say that I interviewed every leader of the civil rights movement at that time. The only person I did not interview was Martin Luther King.

An important event at this time was my meeting Malcolm X. It changed my life radically. I had gone to New York City, not to interview Malcolm X, but rather James Baldwin; but Baldwin proved elusive, and I was urged to remain in Harlem and track down Malcolm, which I did. At the time Malcolm was minister of Mosque Number 7 in New York, and Farrakhan was his assistant or ministering at a subordinate mosque. Malcolm changed my life. He got me to fast at least twice per week, and he certainly exposed me to the righteousness of the oppressed. He put some order in life. At the time the Muslims in the US were very keen to recruit Black intellectuals. I found Malcolm's speeches informative and exciting. I would see him preaching on Friday nights on the corner of Seventh Avenue and 125th Street in Harlem. I remember that on one occasion when the police arrested a Black man, Malcolm was able to get the members of all the Black mosques in Manhattan to demonstrate peacefully outside the police station. The police felt that it was unhealthy for a single Black to hold so much power.

My biggest joy of this period was the music. Miles Davis, John Coltrane, Art Blakey, Thelonius Monk, Sarah Vaughn, Nina Simone. To be able to go to Harlem on a Friday evening and sit in a room and listen and watch these musical giants play! I always felt that this was essential to the civil rights movement, that there could not be a successful civil rights movement that excluded culture. I deeply appreciated what was taking place culturally in Harlem—and I say Harlem because, for me, it exemplified the best and worst of what existed in Black American society at the time. There was where one was likely to find the best African American artists, including comedians like Dick Gregory and Richard Pryor. To be able to go to the Apollo Theater on a Friday or Saturday night and be exposed to such wonderful dynamic beauty was exhilarating. The ecstatic reactions of the audience! I found myself in an incredibly enriching and exciting milieu. One other thing about being in Harlem was that I could go to the Red Rooster, a bar where James Baldwin, Abbie Lincoln, Max Roach, Count Basie, Duke Ellington, Ralph Ellison drank and socialized. I remember we all drank Cutty Sark scotch and soda water and smoked Kent mentholated cigarettes. To me the best juke box jazz in the world was played at the Red Rooster. I have fantastic memories of this. So even though life for Blacks was brutally, explicitly racist, our souls were enriched; we were warmed by the expression of beauty by our artists. This enabled us to face the billy clubs and the water hoses the next day or the next week. In a nutshell, this is what this period means to me.

But I must say that my position at Yale University gave an intellectual basis to my fiction. I was put in a position of great trust and power. It made me aware that we in the West Indies had followed the right course in the priority we gave to education. But it also created problems and tension, because when I look at Yale—from the time I got there in 1968 to 1972, when I left—there were six Black professors, four of whom were West Indians. The Black American students undergoing identity problems made the point of saying their great great-grandmother was West Indian. I am sure that Yale was playing some sort of game in hiring West Indians over Black Americans. It was one way of dividing and ruling, of creating a clique, an aristocracy. Even so these years were an exciting time. And I am very fortunate to have lived through this. Now, how has that affected my work? It affected my work in many ways. It taught me not to imitate the Black American novelists, except for the best of what was in Baldwin, Wright and Ellison. I must say that I am disappointed that since *Native Son, Invisible Man, Go Tell It on the Mountain, Dutchman,* some plays by Ed Bullins, we in America—America in the Diasporic sense—have not done much.

I disagree with you. There are many writers who've equalled them. Toni Morrison, certainly.

Sorry, I forgot Toni Morrison. And there's the Barbadian American, Paule Marshall.

Toni Morrison has expanded the domain of the African American novel. And there are some writers who haven't become household names: Leon Forrest, Clarence Major, Charles Johnson, and quite a few more.

I would add Wideman as well. I want to say too that when you look at the books produced by West Indians in England from 1954 up to Naipaul's last books, they are, per capita, books of a higher quality than the African Americans produced over a much longer period. And this is so even though Heinemann sacrificed the West Indian canon in order to embrace Africa in its African Writers Series. I am not arguing superiority or any such thing. I'm just puzzled that we in America didn't perform as well in the literary domain. Is it because we've devoted so much of our energy to jazz production? To humour? To comedy? To make my point sharper, I hope, I would like to say that I cannot understand how it has come to be that in this city of Toronto, we have eight brilliant Jamaican poets: Honor Ford Smith, Louise Bennett Coverley[1], Ayanna Black, Lillian Allen, Olive Senior, Lorna Goodison, Pamela Mordecai,

Afua Cooper. Is it because of the snow? Is it because of the water? Is it because of jerk pork?

It's a confluence of many factors, some of them accidental. It is true that Toronto is an especially active centre for literary artistic creation by Blacks, most of whom are from the Caribbean. But Toronto is also the literary capital of Canada, and that helps to feed the creative urge of the many artists of every conceivable ethnic group who live there. However, on the subject of African American literary production I don't know if I agree with your assessment; but it may well be that the book industry in the US hinders writers from producing more profound works. Government assistance to publishing in Canada makes it possible for many small presses to bring out artistic work that would never be published in the US.

I should say though, in spite of these musings, that it so happens that we came here for reasons other than writing and that we happened to be on the scene, and our contribution is a magnificent one that cannot be gainsaid.

I am deeply ambivalent about the colonial education I received; but that said, I am reminded of Derek Walcott's statement that the library in Castries—and the same could be said of the library in Kingstown—was quite small, and for that reason there was no room for trash. There's no question that many of us brought a high level of literacy when we came to Canada, and have been able to use it to explore the reality of life in Canada, and the life we've left behind or brought with us, and whatever else that struck us about the human condition.

We came literate, and we came informed. And it's Derek himself who said this: we met Europe in the West Indies. So when we came to this city or country, there wasn't a great deal that surprised us. We bandy around the term culture shock. What culture shock! I knew Canadians who taught at my school. As a matter of fact, it was a Canadian who planted the idea in my head that I could come to Canada to study. He explained to me that I could go to school in the day and work at night. In Barbados I knew no one who worked while he or she went to school.

A comment made by some reviewers of your work is your disregard for political correctness. I will admit that the male gaze at the female body in your books is an intense one.

I was brought up at a time when it was considered healthy for a man to acknowledge the beauty of a body, in the case of my writing, a woman's body. In the novel I'm currently revising there's a woman, a domestic, who has to

[1]Louise Bennett Coverley died shortly after this interview was recorded.

walk by a group of Italian men on a building site, and they would make references to her body. At the beginning she is offended, but she eventually comes to understand that they are harmless, to the point where she'd pose for them and even flirt with them.

When I arrived in Canada it was the fall season. The following year, when the weather turned warm, I was surprised to see, as we used to say in Barbados, "the pulchritudiness" of the female body.

You see, I belong to a time when a man could say, "I like women," and it meant just that. I am well aware that one has to be very careful nowadays about what one says to women and about the way one looks at women. But, I'll say that I am still, in spite of my experience, quite naïve about much of this. I live on a street where there are the homeless, the indigent, the drug dealer, the prostitute—every kind of person, you'd read about in the newspapers and who are not considered model citizens of this society. It took the explanation of a woman for me to understand why women coming toward me do not look me in the eye. They avoid doing so to prevent the encounter from becoming confrontational. I found this absurd. It's anathema to the way I was brought up in Barbados. We were accustomed to looking directly into a woman's eye, and wink, and tell her she was looking good, or just simply smile or say, "Good morning, Ma'am."

I suppose this raises the issue of self-censorship when one writes. I guess you are saying you aren't prepared to do any of this.

I understand the importance of that. I suffer from it sometimes when I am in the company of women. I'll open the car door and they'll spurn the gesture; or it might be a situation where I offer to pay and they refuse. Another example: two days ago when the temperature in Toronto was thirty-six with a humidex of forty-eight, I would stand outside my door which is protected by a wrought iron fence and ladies-of-the-night would pass; some asked, "Do you want a date?"; others, "Do you have a cigarette?" I replied that "I don't smoke but if you wait, I'll go inside and get you one." Now, I do that the way I would give a loony to a man who's begging. My position is that I cannot live in a neighbourhood without having a lighthearted, friendly relationship with the people who live in or frequent the neighbourhood. It is my way of claiming my freedom, of reminding myself, that I have to function in whatever neighbourhood I happen to be in.

Your social criticism, especially in your nonfiction—I'm thinking particularly about your essay "Police Violence and Black Youth"—reveals an activist side to you.

I used to write more of this years ago, when I was active organizing demonstrations against racial discrimination, against racist comments by powerful Whites—comments like the one made by Garfield Weston that the Black mammies of South Africa like white bread. He owned Loblaws in those days. I organized a boycott of Loblaws. I used to live on Asquith Avenue in those days, and there was a Loblaws directly across from me. My only ally was Rabbi Feinberg. I got very little support from Blacks. Overall, most of my support came from the Jewish community. In those days I wrote for *The Star*, *The Globe*, and *The Telegram*. But whenever something of mine was reviewed, the reporter would begin something like this: "Austin Clarke, who has interviewed Malcolm X, said . . ." I resented the association, because I knew enough about journalism to know that . . .

This was being used to taint whatever you wrote.

Precisely. But I came along at a time when Blacks weren't doing any of this. I got my determination from an unlikely source: Pierre Berton. He was then writing for *The Toronto Star*. He was the first non-Jewish person I knew of who wrote about discrimination against Jews, who were prevented from renting cottages in the cottage districts of Muskoka, Thousand Islands, and Collingwood. My undertaking was quite serious. There was little support from Blacks, especially Black people who'd been here for centuries. They saw West Indians who protested these situations as muddying up the waters and disturbing the tranquil life of accommodation they had made with the White world.

When I came to the University of Toronto in 1955—and this lasted until about 1957—and I looked around the campus, I saw no Black Canadians attending university. I couldn't understand this. Here was a university in a city where there were Black people and they weren't going to university! This struck me as being all the more anomalous, because I was coming from the West Indies where the University College of the West Indies had just opened, and almost all the students attending were Black.

Coming back to the article you mentioned—and it surprises me that it is still being read today—I wrote that one night while my blood boiled to see how the press misunderstood—and the press has always misunderstood—the reality of Black people living here. And the politicians have always distorted our reality. I have no confidence that politicians would ever solve this problem. For the mayor of Toronto to say that the root of the Black problem is the absence of the Black father—I'm pretty sure that's what he said; if I am misquoting him, I apologize—is absurd. I come from Barbados, where the father for all sorts of reasons was conspicuously absent, but it did not militate against the stability of the Black family. In our case, our mothers were our mothers and our fathers . . .

And we did have surrogate fathers.

Of course, of course!

In the remaining time, I would like us to talk about the artistry of your writing. I am struck particularly by the way in which you use setting as signifiers. A critic of The Toronto Trilogy *comments on the slight plot in these books and it is true: they are about how these characters survive and deal with challenges. But it is clear to me that the backward and forward movement and repetition of key details are core aspects of your composition. I thought of music and particularly jazz. You've already confirmed the vital role of music and jazz in the structure of your writing. Would you like to elaborate on this further.*

Whereas I would be the first to admit that I was never schooled in plot, I, however, schooled myself in narrative. In narrative one could find all the elements of plot. And if the narrative is related to music: blues, jazz-variation, variation on variation, call and response—I feel that these are more vital and dynamic elements in the construction of the novel and of narrative than simplistic notions about plot. I have reached the point that I would not object to someone saying that the plot or plots are slight. It might be the opinion of the particular critic or reviewer. As I said earlier, I was quite aware that I was using music as a theme on which to structure the narrative of *The Meeting Point*, *Storm of Fortune*, and *The Bigger Light*. To that extent, a reviewer who is sharp would have seen that my approach was in lieu of the more conventional use of plot. What is the plot of life? What could be the plot in the lives of these dislocated, frightened, religious, insecure men and women who'd come to a country where the first obstacle is the severity of winter?

You told Stella Baksch about the difficulties you initially had with the Barbadian vernacular. But you are one of the few Caribbean writers of an earlier period whose "schooled" characters speak in the vernacular. Through its use you impart a Caribbean ethos to your work.

You mean what Kamau [Brathwaite] calls nation language? Well in Barbados, the language of the village is not standard English. And even though you've been in school functioning in English from eight to four, the moment you reentered the village you spoke your language. My mother reacted quite strongly to people speaking to her in a language she could not understand. I remember once my mother asking me if I wanted cocoa or tea or chocolate. I said I wanted a cup of "toy." (Laughter) She exploded, "Boy, what the ass is wrong with you? You gone crazy! You can't talk proper English!" Of course, growing up in a calypso culture had its impact. Once I began writing, it was clear to me that I would use the popular language. It gave authority; it made the work authentic. But even in a Barbadian context, it made the work difficult to read; it's one thing to hear it spoken, it's another to see it written and to presume that those reading it would grasp its many nuances. For, as I was discussing with someone in Barbados two weeks ago, even though Barbados is a small place, there are various ways of speaking Barbadian in various parishes of Barbados.

I was fortunate to have had as a master of English someone who was a poet: Frank Collymore.

The founder of Bim.

Right. I sent my manuscripts to him. About the use of Barbadian, he said, "You have to think seriously about how you do this. You don't have to write, 'I gine home, man.' If you understand what your language is—the rhythm, the nuances, the musicality—then you should focus on capturing that." This was excellent advice. There's a woman in Barbados, Jeanette Layne-Clarke, who contributes a weekly column written in Barbadian to the *Barbados Nation.*

"Lick-Mout' Lou."

"Lick-Mout' Lou." It takes me a long while to understand what she's saying. And she's authentic. I borrow some of her things, but I won't use the apostrophe as often as she does and spell the words using exact onomatopoeia, etc. Of course, there are certain words that can't be anglicized or translated into the English.

You have written several short stories that often turn on obsessions: gambling and philandering, for example; economic downfall; failed expectations, etc. What do you find are the salient challenges in using the short-story form? For example, having to condense situations, compress meanings?

I have never had that challenge. I've never thought I was doing that. I haven't said this before, but I have always wanted to be a poet. The first poem I ever wrote was in the style of Oscar Wilde's "Ballad of Reading Gaol." I'd studied it in school. I loved the rhythm.

I had fallen in love with a neighbourhood girl. Today she's a retired headmistress of a Barbadian college. And I knew I had to be on good terms with her brother to have access to her. So I wrote a poem, "The Ballad of Bandy-Legged James." Everyday I would add two stanzas until it became quite long. After that I focused on writing serious poetry. Regarding the short-story, I always felt that my short stories should be based on the telling of a story.

That it should borrow from the oral form?

Yes. There was the BBC's Caribbean Voices programme that I listened to. But more important, I was steeped in oral culture. There was my mother, who would gather the women in the house, and they would talk. Of course, there were the fellows under the street light talking. Of course the hero of those were the guys who, as we would say, told the biggest lies.

As I said before, I was never overly concerned with what the critics call plot. For example, a character spills a drink, and the consequences of the spilling, etc. I would be more interested in how he holds the glass and what's visible in the glass. I'd want the reader to see the house the character came from in Barbados. I am more concerned with holding the readers' hands and guiding them over the terrain of the story. Another thing I should say about this is that when I started out—that was in 1963—I knew that writing a novel would take me about two years. In those days, publishers offered me three hundred dollars. That was my first contract—three hundred dollars. I knew I could sell a story to CBC Anthology (produced by Robert Weaver) and get five hundred dollars. So when I got to page fifty, I would reexamine what I'd written to see how I could reshape the material into a story that I could sell. I got much more money from the short stories than from the novels. When I taught creative writing, I always told my students that no one writer is excellent at everything, at every component in the short-story. You find out what your strengths are and build on them.

Most Black writers in Canada are quite anxious about the audience for their works. It is difficult not to see that books that challenge the dominant Canadian myths get short shrift. Publishers and literary agents tell me and others that the audience for writing by Blacks is small and fickle, and so they are afraid to publish books by Blacks. How do you feel about this?

That's racist.

But it's a reality that we face.

You've only mentioned part of it. The other part of it is that they tell us not to use dialect in our books, not to set our books in the West Indies because no one is interested in books about the West Indies. I never accepted any of this. My personal experience told me otherwise. One of my favourite stories is "A Child's Christmas in Wales," which I used to play religiously every Christmas. I asked myself why this story resonated with me. Although I grew up in Barbados and did not know the physical experience of snow, I could relate to everything in the story. I use the first sentence of that story in every creative writing course I give, in order to point out why it's such good writing.

That attitude from publishers is racist, and I will say this anytime to anybody. Something that turned me off Canadian books written by Whites was this: in the Sixties when you walked down Yonge Street, from Bloor to King, you saw Black people, you saw them on the university campus, you saw Black people in the hospitals as janitors, cleaners, nurses, and the occasional doctor, but when you read scene descriptions in Canadian books—scenes on Yonge or the workplace—Blacks are absent. I said to myself, Be-Jesus-Christ! How come they can't describe a Black person as part of the background, not as a character, just being there? Next publishers started with their quota. They were very proud to say that they were publishing Austin Clarke. So when Cecil Foster and fellows like yourself approach them, they say, "We already have Austin Clarke."

Which is to say that Black writers are treated by Canadian publishers the way Black writers were treated in the US in the 1960s.

My American publisher asked my agent to get me to write a book that excludes West Indian reality. I am supposed to write a book that is appealing to her and her readers, so I don't know what the ass to write about. I doubt they tell [White] Canadians writers what topics they should or shouldn't write about.

To what extent do you feel power in the political and economic sphere affects power in the cultural sphere? Those who belong to the dominant culture are the ones in power. They control the institutions, and they determine what gets out there as culture, what gets promoted and what doesn't get promoted.

How do I feel about this? If you'd lived in Toronto for as long as I've lived here you'd understand what I am about to say. I remember saying to Rinaldo

[Walcott] two years ago that the time will come when the gay parade would be bigger than Caribana. Caribana started with a small group of us; people like Charles Roach; Howard Matthews, who owned The First World Club and later The Underground Railroad; his wife Salome Bey; Judge Romio Pitt; a couple of others; and myself. At the time *The Star* was running a series of articles about Black people. We got together and asked the city to give us some money so we could rent space to show the [expletive] we had culture. We went over to the island. Howard Matthews made some "baad" curry chicken, because there was no place selling that kind of food here. Derek Walcott came and put on an act or two of his plays, Salome Bey sang and played, and I read poetry. That was the start of Caribana. It was cultural. It grew and grew. We used to walk down University Avenue. I know the papers spoke about the benefit it had on those who were ill; they were brought to sit outside on the lawns and watch the parade go by. Enter the merchants, who claimed they were losing money because of this congregation of Black people parading through the streets of the city. White businesses have always been scared of throngs of Black people in the downtown area. You probably know the story of the radio host, Phil McKeller, on CFRB, who uttered those racist comments about it. This hotel [The Grand Hotel where the interview was being conducted] is already booked up [July 20], and all the other hotels, for Caribana. It is the only festival that brings so much money into Toronto in a weekend. We have long ceased to be the primary beneficiaries of Caribana. That's the long way of answering your question about how power works.

Austin, thanks for giving me the opportunity to interview you.

George Elliott Clarke

George, in your introduction to Fire on the Water, *you state, "For Africadian writers, being is body and soul. Their literature shouts and sings their being, their personhood." To what extent is writing an essential part of your being?*

I write because I can't sing, and I'm not a musician, which is what I would have preferred to be, and I've elected not to be a preacher. Writing is the poor sister. I mean the other act, the only other way I can attempt to articulate my community, my sense of things, and who I am. So, in that sense, writing is fundamental to me.

I always thought that you had a profound knowledge of music. Your poetry and your plays seem shaped by music.

I studied trombone for two years when I was a boy. I didn't like the trombone; I wanted to play the trumpet. But it was in a public program offered by the city of Halifax, and there weren't enough trumpets. I was told I had perfect pitch and a real ear for music. That's all the music I've ever studied.

One of your poems in Blue *deals with the Conservative Party's defeat of Pierre Trudeau, in 1979, when you were nineteen. At what age did you begin writing poetry?*

Age fifteen. I wrote a few things when I was thirteen, and before that I wrote something up when I was five. They were songs rather than poems. Again, it was the frustration of not being able to sing or play an instrument. The day I graduated from Bloomfield Junior High School, end of June 1975, I started writing four songs a day. I read books on how to be a good songwriter—books about Bob Dylan, blues musicians, Blind Lemon Johnson, Leonard Cohen, and Joni Mitchell. I listened to their lyrics and tried to copy their styles. Somewhere around fifteen, going on sixteen, I started to write poetry, but only so that I could become a better songwriter.

The speakers in many of your poems express ambivalence about writing. How autobiographical is this?

I think it had something to do with growing up with a literary/oral clash: growing up, on the one hand, in a house with lots of books and magazines and lots of discussions about world events. My father loved classical music, Broadway show tunes, Harry Belafonte, and CBC news; that was the kind of stuff he was always listening to. My mom listened to the Supremes, James Brown, the Temptations. Economically, we were probably one step above working poor. My dad worked initially as a baggage handler; my mom had a teaching certificate, and she did run a daycare for a while when I was still a boy. But she stayed at home for most of my upbringing. My dad did rise in the railway. What I am trying to get at here is that even though my family was probably, relatively speaking, not well off, I always felt rich when I was a child. But that richness came not from income, but from the fact that we had a house full of art, music, books, and magazines.

My father was self-taught. He left school in Grade Ten. He had, still has, a huge vocabulary, much bigger than mine. He was a stickler for proper enunciation; you had to use standard English at home. I grew up loving print in part because of his influence. I loved reading and I still do. I used to go to the library with my mom from the time I was eight years old, and I'd just load up on books every weekend. I read every day almost and I loved it. And we travelled. We got railway passes. We went to Winnipeg, Toronto, Ottawa, Montreal, and into the country. I always felt very rich.

On the other hand, we—I have two brothers—had to negotiate the streets outside our home, and for that we had to be serious, articulate speakers of Black English. School and home were print, the streets were orality. My mom was more closely associated with orality. Although she was a teacher, she was the one to break into Black English. She was the one who'd do country talk. So in order to feel closer to my maternal side and the street side, I had to eschew print; but to be close to my paternal family, I had to embrace the literary, hence the root of my ambivalence.

I understand now why you insist so much on the roots of Africadian literature being orality, and why you accord the church such a central place in your work.

At nineteen, I went away to the University of Waterloo to study English. At Waterloo I basically read British poets. I studied a total of three Black poets while I was there: all Black Americans: Langston Hughes, Amiri Baraka, and

Gwendolyn Brooks. My entire undergraduate education at the University of Waterloo was about British poets, with Dickinson and Whitman thrown in. I got an honours BA in English. Cool. I published my first book of poetry when I was twenty-three and still an undergraduate. Fine. Came home to Nova Scotia and got this job working as a social worker in the Black community. Terrific. Invited to do a fundraiser for the Black Cultural Centre. April 1986, Halifax. I stand up in front of an audience of two hundred people, mainly Black, mainly from my community, lots of them my relatives, my school-friends . . . And I start reading in a dull, uninflected way. People yell at me: "Get off the stage, you're boring! Go home!" I had to quit that nonsense—immediately. So I read a poem I had just written, which is in *Whylah Falls*: "Love Letter for an African Woman." I started reading that, and the people quieted, and the yelling became: "Testify! Preach it! Amen! Hallelujah! All right! You're home now!" At the end, Nigel, the applause was the richest applause, so far as I'm concerned, I have ever received in my life. It reminded me of a basic fact: in our community—and I think this is true for most Diasporic Black communities—you can stick to print literature—that's ok—but when you stand up before a Black audience, you must perform.

That story reminds me that I come from a culture where there's a clearly defined aesthetic. I like telling the story to White audiences and White writers. A White audience is usually quiet. Even when something is funny, they feel it's impolite to react. But in the Black community, the audience participates in what you're doing and saying.

I experienced this first hand when I lived in Durham, North Carolina. Geeta and I sometimes saw African American films where the audience was almost all Black and the audience was half the show. People would yell back at the screen; they would talk about the characters. Here, in Toronto, too. We went to see a movie here at the Eaton Centre—one of those two-dollar Tuesday night deals—a Black movie, majority Black audience, and the same thing happened: everybody was talking back to the screen and commenting on what the characters were doing. It's a full engagement.

In your introductory essay to Odysseys Home, *you call yourself an essentialist. Given the trouncing the term constantly receives why do you feel justified in using it?*

Because even though I feel that we are individual human beings—with separate births and deaths, responsible for our lives in a pseudoreligious sense, etc.—I also know that we live in a society that generally follows along the lines of somebody's state, somebody's nation, whether we are a majority or minority in that place. That influences who we are: so we're French, Armenian, Jamaican, Vincentian . . . on top of our individuality. Then, there's religion or faith, there's gender, there's sexual orientation, there's class. These things combined make us who we are. So on the one hand, we are independent, but on the other, we are also parts of groups—many kinds of groups, some more influential than others. I am an essentialist insofar as I can say that who I am is partly something that might be called Africadian, something related to the African Diaspora. I could still be Africadian without belonging to the African Diaspora. I could say that I am not Africadian, just a plain Nova Scotian, or plain human being, and nothing else, and that would be fine too.

People berate you for saying you are proud of being this or that. I say, hey! Come off it! We all take pride in who we are. It's one thing to be proud of your roots, your history, but it's another thing to use that to attack somebody else's. There's nothing wrong with saying who you think you are.

One of your signature statements is: "All art is a cry for identity." You imply as well that the Africadian artist subserves the Africadian community. One might say, comparing the two anthologies you've put together on Black Nova Scotian writing with your own writing, that Africadian history and mores are the bedrock of your poetry.

Yeah. Look, the history of Black people in Canada is one of erasure. And it continues to this day. We don't have the institutions that Blacks in the US have, that disseminate knowledge of ourselves, and so we're beholden to the majority-group institutions that have historically not been interested in recording the legacies of Black achievement, of the Black presence, and so on. So we're constantly running up against this massive ignorance: a constant chorus of "I didn't know." So those who know must fill in the blanks, because, even if Canadians in general might think that this history is irrelevant, it isn't. Even now it is shaping the racial and multicultural attitudes of this country. It's important that we know, for instance, that we did have a death penalty. We readily executed; we were happy to execute anybody who was from a non-British, WASP background. We executed WASPS, too, but we were really happy to execute Aboriginal people, Francophones in droves, and people of colour. Being White didn't save you from the noose; you had to be a particular kind of White person. We need to understand that because it continues to have an impact on how we organize ourselves now and on who gets sanctioned most severely.

In several articles and reviews, and in Odysseys Home, *you articulate and critique some of the directions African Canadian literature and its critics have taken.*

There's a tendency to treat African Canadian literature as a subset of Caribbean literature or as a subset of African American literature. The temptation is there because our people tend to come from one of those two locations. But it leads to, in my mind, some false reasoning around how writing gets done. For instance, Marlene NourbeSe Philip, because she comes from Trinidad, shouldn't necessarily have the same worldview as Michelle Cliff. Granted, there's a certain parallel in terms of their both writing from a location outside the Caribbean. But Michelle Cliff and Marlene NourbeSe Philip are writing out of different locations which shape their perceptions. This fundamental fact ought not to be overlooked.

Yes, Austin Clarke is a Barbadian writer. In a lecture at Duke University in 1997, he said, "I don't think of myself as a Canadian writer, I think of myself as a Bajan writer." Cool. But Austin Clarke has lived in Canada since 1955—since he was twenty; most of his books have been published here, out of Toronto, and not out of New York or London; and much of his fiction is set here. His vision of Blackness emerged in large part within a Canadian setting.

And he did something here that he couldn't easily have done in the United States: be a Conservative. In the US, he would have had to be a Black Republican. How many Black Republican writers are there in the United States? Perhaps George Schuyler, who's a very minor figure in African American literature. Of course, there's much more to Clarke than his politics. The essay I wrote on his work highlights its Tory qualities. But I want to emphasize that for the most part I admire his oeuvre. And I don't think that his work has received the kind of really searching and thorough critique that it deserves. It's been forty years since he published his first novel. Forty years! There's a body of work there that has to be engaged in a very serious way.

I have also a grudging admiration for his ideological stance. I think it's legitimate and cogently expressed. Think about it: here's a guy who comes out of the same generation as Baraka. Baldwin, Baraka, and Wright are the models he had—Wright especially. But look at what a different writer he is! Basically their writing can be described as Black Nationalist. Austin's is Black conscious, but not in any way Black Nationalist; and also so deep! So dedicated to understanding people's economic dilemmas! Wright's works, though grounded in Marxism, reflects little of the economic awareness present in Austin's writings.

What pleases and displeases you about the direction African Canadian literature has taken?

I hope it is becoming more understanding of the cosmopolitan, multicultural nature of Canada's Black communities. We ourselves are never going to have the kind of consensus, where 95 percent of all African Americans think this or think that. Our backgrounds are too disparate. For instance, it's bogus to say that André Alexis' work is not Black enough. People who make such statements have to be able to say what Blackness is, before they excommunicate André.

The fundamental point for me about African Canadian literature is that it put forward different visions of Blackness, all of which can be legitimately held. The broader understanding of Blacks in Canada should include people who look White, people who identify themselves as Canadians, and people who hate Black music. I don't mean we shouldn't tussle with those folks about these and other issues—even if they don't like it! (laughs)

You once edited The Rap *(and before that a student journal). Would you comment on how such ventures help to bring new voices into print?*

I think that when we have a possibility to do an anthology we should, or a journal, or what have you, just so that we can allow for better discourse, better debate and so on. And I will venture this private opinion, which I don't mind making public at this point: I am disturbed that so few Black Canadian writers have bothered to try to put together anthologies. I think it's an act of charity and an act of humility to try to expand public knowledge of who is out there, and to encourage other, usually younger, Black voices to get into print. It's all well and good for somebody to buy my books. On the other hand, it's also important that they pick up *Fire on the Water* or *Eyeing the North Star* or the special issue that deals with Africadian literature. So that they can see there are others: Frederick Ward! Gérard Etienne! . . . Give everybody a different idea about what these authors are doing and at the same instant create a community. Every anthology is a canon and a community—every single one of them; so the more of them we have, the more of a debate, a democratic debate, we can have.

How has the cultural space altered since 1983, the roughly two decades since you have become a published writer? I'm thinking of, for example, the Portia White Award that you received.

Well, that's a really terrific question too. I think, in my mind the nineties was a terrific decade for African Canadian writing. And just for Nova Scotia, 1990 was a crucial year. We had three Black poets all in print in that year—at the same time: David Woods, Maxine Tynes, and my second book *Whylah Falls* came out. It was quite significant. That same year Dionne Brand was nominated for the Governor General's Award for her book *No Language Is Neutral*, and my *Whylah Falls* won the Archibald Lampman Award the following year, 1991.

Claire Harris got a Governor General nomination . . .

In 1992. I've lost track of all the awards. Stanley Péan, of course, has done very well in Québec. Dany Laferrière won the Prix Caräibe back in '93 for *L'odeur du café*, and of course there's the success he's had with *Comment faire l'amour à un nègre sans se fatiguer*, which was made into a film in the 1990s. In 1995 Nalo Hopkinson won the competition for the best first novel in science fiction, which is a major accomplishment for a first-time writer. She beat out everybody in North America. The work had been rejected by several Canadian publishers.

But 1997 was the big year: Austin Clarke's *Origin of Waves* came out and got some fairly good reviews; *Eyeing the North Star* came out and got mostly good reviews; Dionne Brand published *Land to Light On* and won the Governor General Award for poetry that year. Rachel Manley won the Governor General for nonfiction for *Drumblair*; and there was a third African Canadian winner for his children's book illustrations; Cecil Foster published his article "Black Stars Rising" about what he perceived as the rise in public consciousness about Black Canadian writers. The article was picked up by the Southam newspaper chain across Canada, and it really opened up public acknowledgement about Black Canadian literary creativity; in 1997, the second CELAFI conference took place; and *Whylah Falls* was done as a play that year.

In 1998 Dionne Brand won the Trillium Award for *Land to Light On*; Djanet Sears won the GG in the category for drama; André Alexis' *Childhood* did very well in '98. In 1999, George Boyd was nominated for the GG for *Consecrated Ground*, his play about Africville.

Which has since been made into a film, giving him even greater visibility. In a sense, then, you are actually saying that Black writing made it into the foreground.

Yes. But, there is a "but!" And the "but" still has to do with access to publishing. This has a lot to do with the general contraction in the publishing industry in Canada. But you know, I happened to have read through a lot of contemporary Canadian poetry in the last couple of years and the numbers of books by Black authors has certainly not gone up.

I think it has gone down.

That's a real problem. I mean the quality of the material is excellent, but who is getting into print and who is able to get into print? Who is reviewing the books? Are the reviewers understanding the materiel they're reviewing? What we lack still are critical institutions of reception and propagation of the material. And so, basically, the successes we've had are just thin ice. The visibility we had can very easily disappear again.

George, you write in many genres. Would you like to comment on the challenges inherent in the different forms you employ?

This arises from the fact that I thought that there was a need to make our history available in other forms. Writing *Whylah Falls* I knew I would have to do it as a play. And one of the happiest moments for me as a writer was sitting in the audience in Halifax when it was first done and seeing all those faces around me—the audience: Black and White, laughing, smiling, and the singing is brilliant, and the music is great, and the acting is phenomenal and just engagé. People were singing along with the spirituals at the end. It confirmed for me that people who might never buy a book or want to read the poetry could still access the information via the theatre. Take *Beatrice Chancy.* When I did that as an opera in Halifax-Dartmouth, again Black people came out who would never normally go to see an opera, but they came out and saw this one. They stood up and gave a standing ovation that lasted four minutes, and they beat their feet on the floorboards in the theatre, and it was like a crescendo. Thundering.

A salient feature of Beatrice Chancy *is the agency you accord your slave characters.*

That's because historically slaves had agency. To believe otherwise would be to accept the propaganda that people are happy to be slaves. The truth is most of the time slaves created spaces where they could still live out their lives as best they could under this overwhelming oppressive system. So I could see them having their debates and their arguments about "massa," and this constitutes a form of resistance.

You dedicate the book to Marie-Josèphe Angélique and Lydia Jackson.

Lydia Jackson was a Black woman who came to Nova Scotia to escape slavery in the US and was basically tricked into signing herself into slavery again in Nova Scotia. She was abused physically and sexually by her master and became pregnant. Her master forced her into a spontaneous abortion by beating her very badly, and then she ran off. She ran away to join the colonists who went to Sierra Leone. For me, her story is a heroic one. Slavery was horrible for everybody, but was particularly horrible for Black women because of the fact that they were open to this kind of sexual abuse, deliberate sexual abuse, that had to be part of the process of slavery because it was one way for the slave master to increase his holdings.

If my observation is correct, it seems to me that you have decided to hold on to pretty well all the techniques poets have bequeathed us. I am curious about this because there is the general opinion among poets and critics that one has to set oneself apart from all that has been done.

This is the fat issue of modernism, and postmodernism, for that matter. I've heard NourbeSe Philip talk about this. She argues that people must work against the conventions of poetry, and that the Caribbean has always been postmodern. And that's true. I believe that what White poets call the constraints of the past—the so-called constraints of rhyme and meter—were never perceived as such in the Black writing community. I love the fact that at the same time that T.S. Eliot and Ezra Pound were smashing up meter and saying do away with rhyme, the blues emerged in their fullness, which is the greatest advance in the use of rhyme. Rhyme and meter were being renovated and put to new uses in a modern, vernacular way. This is Houston Baker's argument. There was a Black modernity that had room for rhyme and meter, so how can I say that that stuff is passé? I can listen to rap and hip-hop and calypso and see that rhyme is brilliantly used. And I can see its dexterous use by a poet like Derek Walcott. For that matter, in terms of the interest in public performance that Black writers often, and Black poets especially, need to do, it's a crucial asset.

So you're saying then that these are sound resources with a communal resonance. Am I missing anything there that fits into this particular choice?

No, no. In some ways, the White Euro-Anglo-American modernist is important for the work they did in advancing the standard for writing English poetry and experimenting with form. One of the problems inherent in Euro-Anglo modernism was that it was very elitist; and, as we know, a lot of those guys were fascist or pro-fascist, making statements like, "We don't trust the common reader anymore, we don't trust them to understand what we're doing or to respect the long and glorious history of English poetry. So we are deliberately creating poetry that's hard to access, poetry for the educated reader who'll get the references, understand everything." But while all this was going on, there were Black poets like Melvin B. Tolson. Think of *Harlem Gallery*. He's far more sophisticated and harder to understand and inaccessible—way more inaccessible—than Eliot or Pound. At the same time he's also very much steeped in vernacular forms.

There's a critic by the name of Kevin McNeilly who describes my writing as vernacular formalism—and I happen to like this. Another critic, a music critic, actually describes *Whylah Falls* as oral-based visionary writing. I think that, yeah, that's sums up what I'm trying to do. I still respect formal structure. I think they have some power behind them. At the same time, I also respect the vernacular and want to use its power so that my lines don't just sit there on the page, but erupt from the page. And that's how I try to bring modernism and postmodernism into play in my work.

The first twelve poems in Saltwater Spirituals and Deeper Blues, *which you call "soul songs," are titled after actual churches in Nova Scotia, and are followed by photographs of some of these churches and of the people who attended them and led them. Yet the poems are built on signifiers drawn from the land and sea, signifiers that communicate the travails of the congregations but hardly mention religion. Why?*

I guess I was trying to do a number of things in these poems. I wrote them for a competition, a provincial contest in Nova Scotia, which I won. Yeah! 1981. And, I wrote them here in Toronto. If you really think about it now, it's weird—wrote them here in Toronto. But the whole purpose of writing them was to announce that this community existed. I mean the churches are representative for me; they were signifiers of the community of Black Nova Scotian culture, and the cultural experience is really what I was trying to get at as opposed to the religious experience. I would argue too that at the time I was writing those poems, every single line was imbued with some memory of these churches. I am not a member of the church in any formal sense, but when I wrote these poems, I considered myself to be a member, so I didn't perceive any sharp separation between the church and myself.

The church is the only thing that connects us right back to those first colonists who came to Nova Scotia. The spirit of what they put together. I respect their achievement and the fact that it's still real. There are lots of other institutions around, but it's still the only institution reminiscent of the original postcolonial organization.

I would like you to comment on "Beech Hill African Baptist Church": its stoic tone and Sisyphean determination, and anything else.

In my mind, "Beech Hill African Baptist Church" is about struggle—struggle in the sense that in the African Diaspora it has been about struggle everywhere. Everywhere! In some places less harsh than in others for reasons of climate. It was particularly harsh in Nova Scotia because the climate was inclement and numbers were few, and so the only thing people had to hold on to was their faith. Those churches were built by the people themselves. Not with money sent from England by the Baptist Church. They were destitute and illiterate, but still they did it. That's why, for me, it is an epic story, a heroic story. They had to survive on subsistence wages and take a lot of abuse from their White employers and the police and all the rest of them. What the churches did was to soften the pain of that endurance.

It's as though the physical structure of the church put there by Father Preston and his followers against all odds encompasses the speaker's faith that if they could accomplish this, he too would find the faith that will take him through his adversity. I'm trying to translate here what is perhaps untranslatable.

I like that. One more thing about this, Nigel, I love the idea of African Baptist. I love the fact that in the nineteenth century when there were not a lot of Africans around in Nova Scotia, they called themselves African Baptist.

In another poem "Childhood," you imply your own views about the poetry, the wisdom, the signifying, the force inherent in the vernacular.

To come back to my experience when I came home to Nova Scotia as a social worker—I ended up being a social worker in all these little Black communities in the Annapolis Valley, which is where *Whylah Falls* was engendered. It was a shock in some ways, which preceded the shock I received at the Black Cultural Centre in '86. So I come home in '85 and I have all this British poetry in my head: I've read *Paradise Lost* three times; I love iambic pentameter; I love Wordsworth and Keats, and, suddenly, I'm put right back into this community that I proudly came out of as a boy. But for the first time in my life, for the very first time, I realized that the way that the people are speaking is poetry: unadulterated, pure, shocking, fresh, colourful poetry. People were talking to me, I would come and sit down at somebody's kitchen table, and someone would come in, knock on the door and come in with a case full of beer, I mean full of beer, come with eight full beers. Tuck themselves down beside the table, uncork the beer, and start talking. And then there would be this old woman, this old woman sitting in one corner of the kitchen, and she would do a commentary on what this other person was saying. And it would be funny, it would be insightful, and full of wisdom, tact; salty at times, at times subjective. And I'd be sitting there and this stuff was just like a stereo coming all over me, and I'm saying wow, wowwwww, mighty, mighty, mighty speech. And they were not self-conscious, because this is the way they spoke, this is the way they communicated.

So that would be in many respects the genesis of Whylah Falls.

Exactly, exactly, that's what it was. *Whylah Falls* in a nutshell, for me, was the wedding of their speech and iambic pentameter. It's not strict rhythm most of the time, but that was the ghost rhythm that was underlying what I was trying to do in that book.

Well, language itself is a preoccupation in Whylah Falls.

Well, that's because language has to be challenged too. I mean you know, I was talking earlier about how in my mind there was always debate in the slave quarters. There was always talk and negotiation about how we handle this problem. Well, same thing with *Whylah Falls. Whylah Falls* came while listening to conversation, debates ongoing, which I recognize now as being a very Black-community thing. There's no privacy, forget about that.

In fact, there are many styles of language here: the language of the blues in their dual aspect of lament and celebration. And there are the languages of the demotic and the standard. What was your goal in experimenting with these different languages? How conscious were you of this while you were preparing Whylah Falls?

This is a difficult topic, I think, for all of us Afro-Diasporic intellectuals and writers: our relationship to the vernacular. That's the one question we cannot escape answering. I mean actually our audience is demanding because it does expect us to be able to handle standard English too; Black audiences expect us to be able to do that because we're writers. On the other hand, we also have to give back the voices of the community in the community's own terms. We have to be able to do both, and it's a challenge. It's a huge challenge.

Part of what interests me here is how you convey the nonverbal, a whole nonverbal language where, for example, you talk about the language of white rum. There is so much subsumed into, condensed into that statement.

As a social worker I didn't help anybody really. I would give people advice. I gave them their welfare, their unemployment cheque; I would contact the principal for somebody, a schoolteacher for somebody, talk to them on behalf of the student, whatever; that was really the extent of my intervention in people's personal lives. But I was really an observer. People were nice enough to invite me into their homes and feed me. I would hang around for the parties, the dances, the drinking fests, and I would just hear these stories that were sometimes pretty horrible. But I would also hear memories. I would see courtships take place. I was being a big sponge. I just sat there and sometimes that's how I would put the words together.

But we see your distillation, your craftsmanship, in a line like "this gospel, this sermon of a man delivered by liquor."

But I heard that story. I heard that story of a man who came in puking blood after a three-day wine binge, and his wife or his girlfriend delivers him to the hospital. And then the part about Jesus coming through the rooftop. I was at the funeral and the minister said that. The man had puked up everything, and suffered a massive heart attack as he tried to raise himself out of bed in the middle of the night. Now the minister translates that into "Did he see Christ coming into the room through the ceiling?" And I'm, like damn, of course he did! He saw it, and he tried to reach up to Him…I had to use that.

So you're saying that you found that in the community.

I found that, and it's, like, just listening to people talk. I mean part of it is my own invention too, but I tried to link up what I was hearing vernacularly with my training...It depends. I mean some poems get written like that and other poems I work on them for years before I'm ready to publish them.

Well, yeah, I mean, it's obvious too in the importance you attach to sense, your sense of words. You quite clearly have to go through them: you taste, you measure, you calibrate.

It's essential. I mean they're, like, organic. I play with phrases and word combinations all the time.

A few of your poems in Blue *evoke paintings you've seen. I suppose that your bringing the painter's art to poetry is a conscious endeavour?*

Well, I can say that I'm frustrated about that too. My dad used to stay home during the day and work at nights, so he would be there to take care of my brothers and me, and he would paint, oil paint on glass. In fact the picture on the cover of *Fire on the Water* is his. He painted until I was about eight, nine, and then stopped. He'd been a signpainter's assistant in Halifax at one point. That's how he learned to paint. Later he went to art school—my mother told me this—and he was subjected to criticism, which apparently he didn't like, and so he stopped. I've tried to get him to do different things at different times, but he hasn't gone back to it. But that was really important for me as a child to see him as an artist.

He may well have passed on the gift to you. You've transmuted it into language.

Oh no, I don't think so.

And talking about that, it's obvious that, for you, the poem must be visible and must engage as many of the senses as possible. This is obviously the cardinal requirement for you. I know this from the reviews you wrote of Maxine Tynes' and David Woods' books. You abhor abstractions.

Abstractions have their place. I'm a reactionary Romantic poet. I mean reactionary in the positive sense of the term. I think there was a lot of good Romanticism. I love what I perceived as being the openness of it, the liberality of it to a certain extent. I also think that there's a kind of African Romanticism or Black Romanticism, which I call Black Modernism. Someone like Claude McKay, for instance, I really love his stuff, some of Jean Toomer's too. It's very rich in imagery of food and drink and bodies. Frankly, we haven't had enough of that in the Diaspora.

Do you like Shelley?

My relationship with Shelley has to do with another Shelley, an actual person, whose name I use in *Whylah Falls*. But the Shelley who wrote *The Cenci*, I do love. I don't know Shelley's work that well. What I know is that he's a poet of statement and abstraction; but in *The Cenci*, he is so down to earth. It's an atypical Shelley product: it talks about blood, it talks about rape, it talks about murder, and it's all very concrete. The language itself is not pitched to the sort of height you find in some of his other work. I have a hunch that Shelley's writing of *The Cenci* was influenced by his reading of slave narratives because the same kinds of motifs that are present in slave narratives show up in *The Cenci*: detailed description of the food, the clothing, the water, the cruel master—in this case Francesco Cenci is the villain who rapes his daughter. So there are clear parallels between *The Cenci* and the slave narratives that people were reading at the time. And this might have been his one way of intervening in the whole abolitionist debate, which was raging at the time.

There's a certain genre indefiniteness about Whylah Falls *which leads some people to call it a postmodern work. How do you respond to that?*

I'm happy. I wrote it as a reaction to postmodernist ideas in some ways. I wrote it deliberately to try to recapture a Romantic epoch, but I was writing this work in the mid-nineteen eighties. I was writing it after I'd read postmodern writers; I was writing it in the wake of Rita Dove, and Michael Ondaatje, and many other writers whose work I admire. Someone like Ondaatje could be very easily tagged postmodernist. I was also drawn to magic realism, which can be seen as Romanticism for the poor, since magic-realist writers are often from relatively poor countries. I had a meeting with somebody recently who sees *Whylah Falls* as an avant-garde work.

Somewhere I think somebody said that you call it a novel-in-verse.

Yes, because there are seventeen characters. And there are all these different voices, and there is a plot. I saw it as the easiest way to describe what I was trying to read to people when I was doing public readings. It was simpler to say that it's a novel in poetry. I did want to play with genre. I envisaged *Whylah Falls* as a community; but, in all of its various schools of verse, it is a kind of community too, so why can't they all be reflected in one work? Why can't we have a Miltonic poem rubbing up against the Romantic Shelley in tone?

Because a community is not just one thing; it's a whole bunch of discourses that are taking place. And, as I was saying before, I saw that, I witnessed that: heard the metaphors, the digressions, the asides, with explications of things. And so community isn't just one way of communicating.

Execution Poems *won the Governor General Award for poetry. What motivated you to write these poems? "Rufus and George too must have their song?" The relationship between poverty and violence?*

My writing has always been at least semiautobiographical, and I have touched on family from time to time. Some of the portraits I draw in *Whylah Falls* come from family members: my blood relatives. And you know, I got away with it; nobody said, you can't come home, or don't talk to us anymore. I said ok, so long as I change names and try to be decorous, no one is going to come after me with an axe. But the story of George and Rufus had to be told because it had been buried as a family secret. But it's one of those things that as soon as one person mentioned it, then everybody wanted to talk about it. My mom mentioned it to me out of the blue. May '94. I was getting ready to head off to Duke University. I was living in Ottawa and I'd come home, newly Mr PhD, to take part in a conference. But while there I stopped by my aunt, my mom's sister, and my mother started talking about these two guys, saying oh it was terrible what those two boys did. I said, what? And she told me about it.

How did your relatives feel about your making the subject so public—now internationally so, because it won the Governor General's Award?

I can't say anybody celebrated, nor did anybody say, how dare you? I mean, basically, enough time had gone by that all the principals who could have been affected by my story were gone. Well, most are gone. The two brothers have a sister who is still living in Montreal. I actually had one phone conversation with her about this, and I'd like to go interview her, but I haven't had a chance. One brother, George, had children who survived him, but one was only a year old and another just born when he died. His widow remarried and moved out West. In any event, for my own immediate family, the idea was we now have to clear the decks; we have to reclaim these bodies. We have to take these skeletons out of the closet and repossess them as ours, because they are ours. What they did was wrong. Absolutely! But they paid the price. You know, the man they murdered, he had family, he had children. They are all still living. In fact, they elected one of the siblings to write to me. She said, "Don't write the story, we don't think it's right. You shouldn't be profiting from this." I replied that it was not about profit. It's about revisiting an event that had repercussions for, of course, your family. But it's a tragedy for my family too, and I have a right to talk about it. And justice was done. One man life's was taken; two other men's lives were taken in compensation for that by the state. Yes, most directly, your family suffered, but my family suffered too. They suffered the humiliation, brought upon us by these two guys.

At the time, fifty years ago, disgrace was a huge thing. Here's something I wish I did not have to mention, but George and Rufus' grandfather was my great-grandfather, and their grandfather was George Johnson, my mom's grandfather. He was so shaken up by the deaths of his grandsons that he stopped going to downtown Windsor, Nova Scotia to pick up his mail. He could not endure anyone pointing him out as the man whose grandsons had been hanged. Back in those days, everybody would know; they would know family, connections, in small towns. There was a curse on the entire family, and the disgrace was worsened by the fact that George Johnson was a very, very proud man. Now his daughter married and became a Hamilton, and she produced his grandson George Hamilton. But when George Hamilton was executed, there was nobody left to carry on the name of a man who was a very proud man, who was in fact involved in the Baptist Church. He was a deacon, George Johnson. So it was a big calamity for him that he lost this male heir who should have carried on his name. I was the next one. I was the next one! My mom was ten when these cousins of hers died. And I don't know if there was ever any conversation—I never got a chance to ask her about this—between them to the effect that I, another male, was to carry on his name; but I'm pretty sure that something like that happened.

At the same time, their fate encapsulated in many ways the situation of the Black community in the Maritimes at the time: the particular predicament of Black men, without a whole lot of education, and no jobs open to them except being labourers, which was extremely seasonal, just no security at all, and they probably could not get on the railways because all the railways jobs were spoken for. So, anyway, what were they going to do? What on earth were they going to do?

Which is my next question. As far as you are concerned, they too must have their song, to paraphrase Countee Cullen. And their song shows the relationship between poverty and violence.

This is not a true-to-life depiction at all. I deliberately decided to give Rufus more of an intellectual background, which is false because if he'd had that sort of background, he would not have ended up trying to rob a taxi driver with a hammer. His English was actually commented on in the courtroom. He only had a grade-three education. The crown prosecutor, attacking him, said, "Your English is pretty good for a Negro," or something like that. And he said, "Yeah, yes it is." And I thought, yeah, bravo.

The real way for me into Rufus' character was through Shakespeare's Aaron, his other Black character that nobody talks about. I'll say he's the smartest character in the entire play. He's way smarter than Titus; he's way smarter than the Queen, Tamora. He outsmarts the Roman emperor. He's way smarter than Queen Tamora's sons. He should be emperor, but, of course, he can't be because he's Black, because he's a Moor. And I think—Shakespeare does not spell it out—my understanding of Aaron's character is that he has been fed up for a long time with the racism of imperial Rome and with the Goths. He's not only sleeping with Queen Tamora; he's having some revenge, big time. He's like Nat Turner; he's got that kind of attitude.

It's interesting, though, because if this play were presented to an audience of southern White supremacists, segregationists, they would probably see it as reinforcement for their argument that Blacks should he kept down.

Yes, they would, and they should see it as that kind of confirmation. Shakespeare does not spell it out, but in my opinion, he gives us a character who is culturally alienated. And this is the point about alienation: if you want to alienate somebody, you better be prepared to do some heavy-duty oppression, so they can't get back at you, because if they can, they won't be turning the other cheek.

Any indebtedness to Wright's protagonist, Bigger Thomas?

Oh he stirs in the background, but I was really struck by my rereading of *Titus Andronicus*, particularly Aaron. He was the Black man seeking vengeance. But there are other people I could link him with: OJ Simpson, for instance. You know, this kind of thing about Black man-White woman, having some kind of vengeance through sexual means, which should not be. I mean, morally speaking, it's wrong. But, in terms of racial politics and people's psychology, it's there.

Another thing that I thought interesting was the dialogue that you had going on between both of them in which they are able to express their situation. There is this knack that you seem to have to know when drama is the appropriate medium to get the poetry across.

I just couldn't literally think of doing it any other way. But the book came to be published in an unusual way. I was asked by Andrew Steeves, the editor of what is now *The Gaspereau Review*, for some poems. I sent him a bunch of things I had been working on about this case. And I said, choose whatever you want: one, five, how many you want, or none, for that matter. He just said, "Look I want to bring out a chapbook." I thought a chapbook: 20, 30 pages, fine—I was planning to write a novel about this story; park these poems in a chapbook and they will never be seen or heard of again. But he surprised me and shocked the Canadian literary establishment by bringing out this specially produced book that is two feet long and one foot wide. It sold for fifty bucks a copy, which is way under priced, but everything about it was done by hand. But to return to your observation, I decided to write a series of poems where the speakers are talking to each other. A kind of linked suite of poems.

Your preface to Beatrice Chancy *informs or reminds, as the case maybe, your readers that slavery existed in Nova Scotia. I imagine this preface would be read in a performance.*

When the opera was performed, it was used as part of the program to clarify things for the audience. Too many people think that slavery never existed here. I point this out to some scholars from time to time. The play is heavily influenced by slave narratives. I took the plot from Shelley, but the reality of slavery came from slave narratives. One, in particular, about a woman who ended up murdering her master, who'd bought her for sexual purposes. She fell in love with another slave, was having a relationship with him, and told her master not to 'bother' her anymore. She told his children, who were adult women and men themselves, "I don't want your daddy bothering me anymore." And for whatever reason, the children decided that it was their father's right, so they didn't interfere. So, in his last attempt, she killed him.

Which is exactly what Beatrice does to her master, who is also her father.

Following a reading I did from *Beatrice Chancy* in fall 2000, a man in the audience told me a story he'd heard about an incident that took place in the eighteenth century in Annapolis Royal. The legend goes that this woman's master used to put apples on the children's heads and shoot arrows at the apples. So she fixed him: put some poison in his food and that was that. No more problems with master shooting apples off her children's heads!

Chancy, Beatrice's father and owner, tells the Anglican minister Peacock, who wishes to buy Beatrice to make her his mistress that "She's too expensive to waste. I'll graft her/ On some slavery-endorsing Tory/ To fat my interests in the assembly"—your way of letting your audience know that the practices of slave masters in Nova Scotia and in Upper and Lower Canada were in many instances as vicious as those elsewhere in the Americas.

Look, we know that slavery was this one huge exploitation thing and a big bonanza for basically the White men who were carrying it on and of huge economic benefit to the empires of Western Europe, and crucial to the founding of most of the New World nations. Who'd want to give that up! Slavery was a shortcut for a lot of people to get fabulously rich and to have all the illicit sex they could ever imagine wanting, even if they had to be brutal with nonconsenting women, and men, for that matter. So they could do whatever the hell they wanted—and they did.

That's what New Orleans was for. To be "sold down river" from Mississippi to New Orleans meant being sold for sexual purposes. It was well organized. And everybody knew it. There was a market for it, and it wasn't about somebody's morality; it was about evading the hypocritical puritanical Protestant and Catholic morality people supposedly paid lip service to. Sort of a large red-light district in a sense.

Canada was hardly different. Look at Robin Winks' history of Blacks in Canada. He states that when the Jamaican Maroons got to Halifax, 1796, Thomas Wentworth, who was governor, got himself some of the finest Maroon women. And one of the richest merchants in Nova Scotia—his name is still on a street in Nova Scotia: Ochterloney—he supposedly got himself a "seraglio"; that's the word used. We know that the Colley family, a Black family in Nova Scotia, descended from a union between Thomas Wentworth, the governor, and one of the Maroon women.

And even when "consensual," it would have been nonconsensual given the power-economic imperative.

Your essay assessing the criticism of the work of Dionne Brand, NourbeSe Philip, and Claire Harris has, among other things, a list of criteria for evaluating the poetry of African Canadians. I felt uncomfortable with your criteria. To me, critics seize upon what interests them in a work or body of work; and what interests them is always anchored in their ideology. If one applies, for argument's sake, a Marxist approach, or a humanist approach, isn't it on the basis of such an approach that one's findings should be judged?

First of all, Nigel, I appreciate the reservations you put forward. I was really trying to say that the criticism, generally speaking, of these three writers tends to always follow the same pattern and produce the same results.

So you're saying that there is a certain critical laziness when it comes to dealing with the works of these writers.

Yes, that's the word: laziness. Speaking about these three particular writers, I was saying that there has to be some room for other kinds of critiques. I make the point that most of the critics discuss these writers as "bridge builders." I can understand particularly liberal-minded critics thinking, yeah, ok, Dionne helps Black women and White women understand each other better, NourbeSe Philip is doing that, or Claire Harris is bringing together women from various ethnicities, helping them to unite.

Yeah, but that's not poetry necessarily.

Exactly. To me that's laziness. It does not engage the work seriously. Instead it pushes these writers into basically a kind of sociological service camp. It also implies that only works that make somebody feel good are vital, and important, and engaging, and interesting.

I want to say too that I just think that a lot of this criticism has been racially and gender coded. The vast majority of the critics of Black Canadian writing are White women. They have every right to be our critics, and they do a good job, generally speaking. At the same time, there is a kind of liberal feminist agenda at play, which while useful and helpful and good, is also limiting, obstructionist, and vague about what particular writers are trying to do.

Don't you think though that it is part of the heritage of humanism that goes all the way back to . . . Horace, Pope, Matthew Arnold . . .?

I really want to have a whole lot of discussion and voices in context—in perspective—taking on the literature from different vantage points.

I, for example, have a penchant for Marxist theory.

I don't mind Marxist. What good Marxist criticism is there on the work of Dionne Brand—somebody who is a Marxist—and NourbeSe Philip? NourbeSe has a lot of Marxist thought behind her work too.

Well, their attempt to subvert the language is beautifully Marxist in the sense that they work against the whole commodification edifice—the superstructure that attempts to appropriate, eviscerate, and neutralize. Their work resists that.

But you know, I get your point. I was trying to shift the terms of the debate so that other perspectives would come out. I mean I did go into that whole

Marxist thing by pointing out that Grenada has been important to Dionne Brand's development as a writer. So why not talk about what the death of that dream meant for her work?

There is also an audience factor. I wrote one essay on Dionne Brand, and my essay was intended to introduce Dionne Brand to people who are not scholarly.

I think that it's the kind of writing that needs to be done, and other kinds of writing as well. Some of their arguments aren't even arguments. Carole Morell writes in her introduction to the anthology she compiled of Brand's, Philip's and Harris' work that these women are teaching us about racism. I read that and I said, well, ok, but Black women and men in Canada historically have been saying a lot of stuff about racism for a very, very long time.

So, really, what I was asking for is an end to this lazy critique. The end of the kind of lazy critiques that Austin Clarke used to always get.

An amalgam of clichés.

That's exactly what the criticism has been: "an amalgam of clichés."

You acknowledge your debt to various poets overtly and covertly: TS Eliot, Ezra Pound, Langston Hughes, Robinson Jeffers, Wallace Stevens (I think). Which other poets have I missed?

You can't be a Black poet in America and ignore Langston Hughes, because he had the gift to put complex issues in down-to-earth vernacular and capture people's realities in clear metaphors. He's an unacknowledged modernist master in many ways. Pound I come back to often. Eliot was there in *Saltwater Spirituals and Deeper Blues.* He is the poet I don't want to come back to.

Well, you do a Hugh Selwyn Mauberly thing at the very end of Blue, *where your narrator talks about writing being his coffin. I didn't mention William Carlos Williams.*

William Carlos Williams. Ok, that makes three: William Carlos Williams, Ezra Pound and Yeats. These are the trinity of that particular group. I love the density that Yeats gets in his lines. But the poet I come back to, that I tussle and wrestle and identify with—at least the good part—is Pound. It's got to do with how he uses the American voice. His prosody. His rambunctiousness! I want my poetry to be rambunctious.

He's a huge contradiction in terms. On the one hand, he's steeped in world poetry in many different languages, and he's very much a classicist. At the same time, he is willing to use everyday language and voice, and to combine the two. Classical references in one line might be followed with something like, "these fucking assholes"; and that could come right after a line in Latin.

You can probably say, if you're looking at Langston Hughes, the blues.

Oh the blues, definitely.

Though you could probably group the blues and the spirituals.

Yeah. Hughes is coming after and pulling from the spirituals as much as he is pulling from the blues, which is the same impulse as the spiritual, but in a more secular sense, of course, as James Cone has argued. For me, Pound is the poet who goes further in trying to work with classical structure and vernacular voice, and to really get the tension between the two. In the African American tradition Melvin Tolson and Robert Hayden do something similar.

Your saying that makes me think of Sterling Brown.

He was a major influence while I was writing *Whylah Falls.* What a fusion of Blues and spirituals and folktales, and vernacular and life!

You have been a mentor to many writers. You have pointed out weaknesses in my own work. David Odhiambo speaks of your mentoring in glowing terms. How do you see your role as a mentor?

I think that it's something that we have to do, that we're called to do, and it's all part too of expanding the number of voices available, nurturing talents, and so forth. Let's just say that if I'm in a position where I could help others, as long as they ask me, I'll do what I can.

Nigel, this has been such a great conversation. This is such a swell idea and I feel so happy to have a chance to talk and to answer such really terrific, probing and insightful questions. Your project reminds me—I have to go back thirty years—of *Interviews With Black Writers.* That work brought together Ishmael Reed, Amiri Baraka, James Baldwin and everybody who was publishing. I read that book when I was a teenager, when I was starting as a writer. It was very, very important: you could be a Black writer, i.e., an American Black writer, and be taken seriously and have somebody listen to your ideas and transcribe them.

It is I who must thank you for generously giving me so much of your time.

Wayde Compton

Wayde, you use the term Halfrican in the poem "49th Parallel Psalm;" one reviewer states that it's how you describe yourself; you employ the term in Bluesprint *as well. What's the advantage of such a term as opposed to, say, Eurafrican or Afro-European for that matter?*

Halfrican is just a pun. It's a wordplay that I came up with. I have been trying to find a good term. I guess I grew up having to explain who I am, and it's a good explanation. I envy people who can use one word and everyone knows exactly where they are from. I do not use these terms in daily life.

In your introduction to Bluesprint, *you state the following: "in [...] 'On being a Black Woman in Canada (and Indian and English Too)' we see entirely new social configurations of the topic of miscegenation. Avoiding the autoexoticist 'tragic mulatto' narratives, these writers seek to dismantle binary and standardizing racialized epistemologies." (35) In this I read a certain discomfort on your part with narratives in which miscegenation is figured as traumatic.*

That hasn't been my experience. I have not been trapped between two worlds. Maybe that's the case in some communities and in certain places. I know that in terms of African American culture, which is my roots, people of mixed race get thrown into a larger Black category.

This has a long historical lineage—this fear of ambiguity. It was once part of the definition for sin. And racial ambiguity got conflated with sin and subserved racism, and a bizarre mythology sprang up around it. Popular culture fed off it. I can think of films like Imitation of Life.

I read a book about the 1881 or 1891 census in the US. They were trying to categorize exactly what percentage of the Black population was mixed. They realized they couldn't do it because everybody was mixed in so many different ways. People didn't know or couldn't explain their racial composition. They'd say I'm part Indian or part White. And there was an actual study that was undertaken to see if it would be viable to create a caste of light-skinned Blacks. But they never did.

There's a book by Danzy Senna called *Caucasia*. The author is from Boston, and is mixed-race, and her protagonist is mixed-race. The novel does a really good job at getting at all the problems that mixed-race people encounter, but avoids the metaphors mixed-race people get reduced to.

If one were writing a realistic novel set in the 1950s and '60s Caribbean about Black women working on White-owned plantations, it would be difficult not to address the issue. When you get around to reading Austin Clarke's latest novel, The Polished Hoe, *you'll see it explored there. Clarke pointed out in an interview in* The Globe and Mail *that it's an issue Caribbean writers have avoided—something we've been terribly ashamed of.*

Some of your poems interrogate the way Western languages have sullied Blackness. I wonder whether you would like to comment on this.

For me, the way that I have been playing with languages reflects the way that I received Black English. At home my father spoke a kind of Black English. He has lived in Canada longer than he lived in the States, but he still has the accent; but my knowledge of it comes also from records and mass media. I speak standard English and most of the people that I knew growing up in Vancouver—other than my friends' fathers who were from somewhere else—would speak as their neighbours do, which is a kind of standard English. I think I address that in the book through certain characters that are dealing with a second wave of Black English through hip-hop. In a certain way, it's an ironic position to be in: your father speaks a certain language, you lose it, and then try to readopt it in your twenties. There's that. But looking at the literary aspect, and taking into account all the stuff that I've read, probably my biggest influence in this has been Kamau Brathwaite: his way of using rhythm and breaking words on syllables. I would read half of his poem and stop and go back and read it out loud. *The Arrivants* was a book I was reading over and over again.

There's someone in Rinaldo Walcott's *Rude* who talks about continental Africans immigrating to Canada, and in high school finding hip-hop culture and not assimilating into Canadian mainstream culture, and speaking what the author calls Black English-as-a-second-language. I love that term. I think that's what I am employing as a political and conscious strategy. It's not only me, but the kids on the street—even White kids on the street—are using this Black English-as-a-second-language.

My father says this is nothing new. In the sixties, much of the language that the Hippies used had originated in the jazz communities. The word groovy, which we think of as a hippy word, is actually a jazz word. Later there were words like cool. It seems that the process has accelerated now. It's coming through hip-hop primarily. There's a language explosion—of Black English. I am using it straight and also with some irony as I try to figure out what my role is.

It seems to me that a Caribbean demotic underlies "TO"; it emerges as a hybrid of Canadian-Caribbean, which is itself quite interesting, since Caribbean nation languages are a blend of African syntax, rhetoric, tone, tense, and pronunciation with mostly European vocabulary. Comment.

It's titled that way as a sort of tip of the hat to Toronto. It's the one poem that actually tries to use language that is completely alien to my cultural background. Again, I think that it's a media representation. I have been thinking about this a lot lately: the fact that culture more than ever—it's postmodernism, right—for my generation is influenced by television and radio and video representation, and that applies not only to the general society, but to all the subcultures.

While reading your poems, I said to myself that I could never write poems like this—I am from a book culture; the electronic media never played any significant role in my education. As I examined the different tones and vocabulary, I thought: this guy is steeped in the popular culture of his generation; but you are also highly literary, and your poetry reflects both.

Yeah, that's what I'm aiming for.

Coming back to your Brathwaite influence, I find it interesting the way you deal with the poetic line, oftentimes splitting words so that they pun (... sync/ opate ... "Sam" 14 ; the ful/ crum), or introduce a syntactic singularity the reader is forced to assess, or create unusual anaphora and rhyme as well as humour. For example—

> *from the rock. like the word*
> *made flesh. like A*
> *dam and Eve peopling. multiplying.*
> *calling one down. and if she carrying*

low, a girl. names over
flowing, like a walking
song.

What does such versifying contribute to your poetry?

Well, there is also a dual problematic. When you read it—it's the same with Brathwaite—you read a line through once, and you have to read it again. I like that splitting, that continual splitting, those forks in the road. It's disruptive. It forces a slower reading, and suggests multiple meanings, and asks for full reader participation.

Your arrangement on the page of "The Commodore" is similar to Claire Harris' in those poems where, I think, she wishes the reader to understand that she intends two (or three) voices to be simultaneous and or contrapuntal as the case may be. Comment.

I was thinking of the flip side of records; you have the A-side and the B-side. That is why one column is A and the other B. The two characters are in the same room, and they are both talking about the same event: the suicide of the blues singer Johnny Ace, and offering different readings of it; that was a real event. Both are talking to their friends, and then they both see each other and are about to get together. It was in a real place, in the Commodore, even though the characters are fictional.

The racial dynamic is in some way related to my parents' origins. My father is Black and my mother's White. My dad was born in the thirties and grew up in Texas. I am amazed sometimes, when I look at his life—from the thirties in Texas to the twenty-first century in Canada—how much he has seen in terms of vast sweeping change. Young Black men of my generation are fetishized. There's this superficial interest in Black people now, like it's a cool thing to be. My niece and nephew are subjected to that. My father is witness to that, but he also came from the worst phase of segregation. He has said to me in the past that where he came from a Black man could get killed for looking at a White woman in the wrong way. I know the history, and I have heard it first hand, and it is still so abstract in a certain way.

A practice seen in some of Claire Harris' work, NourbeSe Philip's, and your own is to frame or extend the literary product by including the material that inspired it (a metafiction of sorts). What are your reasons for doing this?

One of the influences on my writing is postmodernism. Metafictional writing suits this era or social climate, because you are dealing with conditions beyond modernism. In terms of metafiction, definitely. I know it's sometimes cheaply used, but there are aspects of it that are useful.

There are instances too when the choices you make are superbly enriching. I think of the altercation rendered in drama in "Evening at the Colonial." Your use of the plus and minus signs that evoke positive and negative electrical charges to symbolize the Black and White interlocutors enhances the signifying power of the poem. Comment?

I was thinking in terms of numbers. What you always hear when anyone talks about the Black population in British Columbia is that there are few Blacks. In the past, there were more Black people here per capita. At one time a tenth of the population of Victoria was Black, and now we couldn't imagine that. In the poem it's like a game of numbers: the plus is the Black and the minus is White. If you look at segregation and issues of institutionalized racism in the larger community, it was most intense when the Black population was largest. When the numbers dropped, the Black population was considered not much of a threat, so most of the racialized hostility was diverted to Asians.

It is unusual for beginning poets to have voices that are distinctly theirs. This leads me to ask which poets/writers have influenced you. You mentioned Brathwaite earlier. I know you wrote an essay on George Elliott Clarke's Saltwater Spirituals and Deeper Blues.

George Elliott Clarke, Amiri Baraka, also the writing community in Vancouver, and people that are closer to me, and friends that I have had here for the last six to seven years—since I have been taking my writing seriously; Roy Miki, bp Nichol, and George Bowering; Bowering turned me on to writers like Ishmael Reed and Toni Morrison—my B.A. and an M.A. are from Simon Fraser.

A search for identity in its numerous variants is a strong preoccupation of your poetry and prose—to the point where you at one point caricature one manifestation of the identity quest. At times, too, your personae adopt a Caliban mask; in "Diamond," for example.

What do you mean by a Caliban mask?

Prospero claims that he gave Caliban language and Caliban's only profit from it is to curse.

I definitely work through *The Tempest.* This is more evident in the writing that I am doing now: those old scripts and poems which are not the original thing anymore but only representations of themselves; sort of like the Djanet Sears play *Harlem Duet* with allusions to the O.J. Simpson case but also to *Othello.* They do not signify anything real anymore; they signify to the representation itself.

The allusion has gone through all sorts of permutations and has been stripped down to an essence. That's probably not a bad thing. People know who Caliban is even though they haven't read The Tempest.

That's what is interesting when these scripts become myths, and popular myths when people have not even read the original source. It is sort of fitting for BC, since it was one of the last places colonized in the west. C.S. Giscome writes about that in terms of African Americans—he parodies *Heart of Darkness,* turning it into the heart of whiteness—like white is part of North America—and tries to follow a Black lineage into this place. I am not sure if I answered your question.

You haven't answered the part about the identity quest.

Black identity in British Columbia has never really gelled in any way. I write about this in *Bluesprint.* There's never been any consensus among the people that live here. We are at a stage now where the population is getting large enough, especially in terms of art—we have a greater number of artists than we've ever had: writers—and spokespeople. There is no centralized Black community or commercial area, so there is no centre for the Black community. I'm thinking of Vancouver.

In that case, can you call it a community?

Well, that's the thing. It comes together in February, for Black History Month, and pulls apart again. But there is a desire to keep some kind of connection; it is not a cultural nationalism; it's a loose desire. The experience I am having is a first-generation experience in terms of the Black lineage in my family: child of an immigrant—my mother born here, my father born in the US So, there's that. Being mixed-race, being mixed-race Black in Western Canada in a very small population—is this identity a Western Canadian one? Is it a BC identity? So I decided to focus just on BC, but I think these things apply from Manitoba on over. People I have spoken to in Calgary seem to have a parallel experience.

There's probably more of an entrenched Black culture in Winnipeg because of the city's connection to the Black railway porters. Lawrence Hill makes great use of this in his novel Some Great Thing.

But in terms of identity it has become regional. The more I think about it the more I realize that I am shaped by the region I am in. I don't think I saw that in my early twenties, but now, at thirty, it's all I think about.

If you were to leave BC and go elsewhere, perhaps to the Prairies, you would probably realize the impact that landscape has had on the shaping of your psyche.

This is another of the things that fascinate me about Brathwaite. His essay "History of the Voice" talks about the sonnet and the pentameter in English as the result of European landscapes and influences. Caribbean writers, he argues, have to find a fitting form to express things Caribbean, to write a hurricane, for example.

When I started thinking about these regional issues, and after reading Brathwaite, I wanted to know what my "local" is, the ethnic experience of my "local," and that was part of the motivation for Bluesprint. I wanted to know what writing had gone on here already. I didn't expect to find as much as I did find.

In many of your poems, history is trope—of oppression, of silence, etc. Comment?

There is a strange dialogue between past and present in the book. Across the board in the Black community there seems to be a hunger for history. Like the character in the "Blue Road" whose idea of a past is an empty space. My motivation is the same as everyone else's. There's some irony, too; in "Diamond," for example, with the character DJ Osirus, who brings up these ridiculous facts that are popular. I read one the other day—it was great—on a Black history site that gives a fact every day; and these are designed to empower you, to make you feel good. Somebody, S. R. Scratton, African American, patented the curtain rod in 1889!

You certainly do a good job parodying that sort of thing.

But it's serious and it's kitsch at the same time.

I suppose there's a difference in saying it was a Black man who invented the cotton gin, and not Eli Whitney. To which one might counter, it's a pity he did, because without it slavery would have been abolished sooner.

The character occasionally screws up and gets it wrong. He says that Garrett Augustus Morgan invented the traffic light, which is not true; he patented a type of traffic sign!

Your poems remove some of that silence as it applies to BC: Blacks on Salt Spring Island, the betrayal of Blacks by Douglas, Black miners, segregation in public places, etc. Moreover, in your introduction to Bluesprint, *you state, I "seek self-awareness through an examination of the ancestors and the Black author's relationship to them . . ."; and in* 49th Parallel Psalm *you state, "I try simultaneously to write a history of Black B. C., place myself within it, and yet keep the myth-making process transparent enough that the arbitrariness of identity and place is shown." Comment?*

In a lot of ways, I'm not sure if I am thinking of the audience or not. Histories have already been written, and I am glad about that. But there are things that poetry can do that you won't find in history. Poetry brings emotion and intuitiveness. Take Douglas and that betrayal—if you read the histories, it would probably come across as mild. None of the historians seems to talk about Douglas' betrayal of the Black community. I don't think they have focused on him in the same way that I have. I have sort of a personal identification with this. He personally invited the Black population to BC and changed the racial composition of the colony. Before this nobody questioned his ancestry. It was then that people started figuring out his background—even if they'd known already—and they started using it against him politically. So he was in a very strange position, depending on how you read what he was doing. Some historians praise him for being antiracist. His wife was not White; she was Métis. But he was a colonizer.

According to your poetry he could not deliver the freedom that he promised Blacks.

But then it comes down to how much of that was him and how much of it were the policies of the colonial office. He was almost an autocrat. My feeling about him is that he wavered; he danced between these two things. The first nine years of his life he grew up with his mother, who was classified as coloured, and knew he had a Black lineage. His father was a Scottish planter, and it seemed that his father was waiting to see what he would look like as he got older, and went and got him when he was nine—and it was clear he looked White—and brought him to Scotland and raised him as an outside child, and educated him.

A handful of White planters did that, even in the US I think one of the presidents of Georgetown University came through a similar system. Perhaps you'd like to comment on your place within this history.

That is one of the things that I could do with a book of poetry, because it's playful and emotional; it's totally subjective, and I can run away with the character and let history give the outlines. Even the need for the book is individual. It's a project that a lot of people are working on out here in the province, people like Peter Hudson, and I could name several others. In my own case, it has been about my personal questions.

So you are saying that there was a dearth of cultural nourishment for Black people living in BC, and so Black people have had to actively seek such sustenance.

Yeah, I think so.

NourbeSe Philip speaks about inserting silence in her poetry—letting silence speak in its own voice. To this end, there are the spaces that she leaves between phrases and individual words. You, too, on occasion leave similar spaces. What's your rationale?

I hadn't been thinking of silence in that way but more in terms of interstitial writing; for example, in the poem "Jump Rope Rhyme of the 49er Daughters." So instead of standard history—what wars happened and what governments there were, etc.—I wanted to look at the things that are sidelined, cultural references that wouldn't be highlighted. For sure, "Jump Rope Rhyme" is made up; it's imaginary; but I am imagining the children of this community belonging to that part of the population that is silenced by history and left out of fictional accounts. The ones who are not the power brokers of society. So my intention was the exact opposite of silence.

Poems arranged like this are quite difficult to read. Do you skip over them when you read/ perform your poems? On the other hand, some of your poems seem to have been written with performance in mind; their rhetoric facilitates recital: "Babylon Slim's Song," for example. Am I right?

Many of the poems in the book got revised after I'd read them; that was part of the process. Even the feedback and the feeling I got from reading them made me go back and rewrite. I have never been able to figure why reading to a live audience makes such a huge difference. I read my poems at home, and read them off the computer, and out loud, and it is never the same as reading them in front of an audience. For some hidden reason, reading them to an audience I hear myself differently, and that makes for better revising.

There's the problem of onomatopoeia, which, depending on how it's expressed, makes for very difficult reading.

There are some poems, like that poem "DJ," where the alliteration and fragmentation in the short lines are imitative of scratching.

What are your views on performance poetry, read poetry, and page-bound poetry? I am grateful to NourbeSe Philip for the third term. She refers to her poetry and the poetry of Dionne Brand and Claire Harris as page-bound.

On this subject I've made an interesting observation: I read poems at different venues before the book came out, and some people were calling me a spoken-word poet. When the book came out that fell away; people were less inclined to call me a spoken-word poet. I've never called myself that. I am not sure what that means in my case.

Very often it means that there's a huge reliance on rhyme and meter, imagery and metaphor, and diction that glides off the tongue; so, if one were writing strictly for a performance, one has to be prepared to make those sorts of compromises. None of this is to say that a good poem couldn't be useful for both. Many of George's [George Elliott Clarke] poems work well at both levels.

But no one would call him a spoken-word poet.

Many of his blues poems in Whylah Falls *could be spoken-word poems.*

I guess I'm thinking more in terms of the identity—the label.

I am wondering if your reason for saying so, as regards George, isn't because of the abundance of erudite allusions in his poetry, allusions that aren't accessible to most audiences.

Dub poets and rappers, I wonder how they compose. Do they sit down with pen and paper and write it down—or on the computer? Or does half of the work get composed in performance? Musicians do so by ear first. I always write it first and then read it back to see if it's doing what it's doing in my head.

The Legba figure fascinates you. It reappears in your work in various guises. One of your best uses of it is in "The Blue Road: A Fairy Tale." Would you comment on the tale's allegorical qualities as well as the trickster tradition among Blacks?

It's not a hard allegory. It's a dreamlike allegory. It's not a one-for-one equation; rather more of an overall feeling of immigration allegory: that movement from South to North.

Which makes us sort of identify the ethnicity of the character, given the semiotic figuration of North and South.

My first encounter with Legba was through Ishmael Reed, via his novel *Mumbo Jumbo.* After reading that I started reading works like Henry Louis Gates' *Signifying Monkey*—works that draw on Legba to formulate critical theory. I have used Legba for my literary purposes. Ishmael Reed uses the figure effectively. I don't share Reed's right wing politics. He seems to get in trouble with his fetishization of Voodoo, his praising of the Duvalier regime in Haiti—that sort of thing. I like the way you can use Legba to undercut; he's a sort of satirical figure; I also like the existential qualities of Legba. The trickster gives you good and bad things: things you ask for you may not get and you get things you didn't ask for. It's never how you'd intended it.

Yes, the trickster figure is always amoral.

One of the seductions one could fall into in doing this kind of book is to create upliftment, that sort of feel-good thing, but that's not what I think I wanted.

There's a lot of angst that comes through . . .

That's not necessarily empowering. In the "The Blue Road," the trickster-protagonist does things to get himself out of a trap but always falls into another one. One eye can look in the mirror and the other outside.

And perhaps that is only as far as one can get, unless one has the power to change prevailing values and attitudes, and pass edicts to consolidate and promote such changes. A tall order. Even so, by thinking differently, by not accepting what is—by not falling into line, one might improve one's situation.

Yes. He moves forward. He's better off at the end than at the beginning. The people who've journeyed from elsewhere to the land of the North are better off because Lacuna has given them a tool with which to see at least half of what's going on.

You are interested in other figures of the Voodoo pantheon. You evoke the figure of Baron Samedi, for example; in fact, you seem to have a certain fondness for him.

I think it is the existential qualities in these figures that attract me. Because I come from a Christian background, I like the contrasting openness and materiality of these spirits. They come into the material world and they are really here.

They have a way of dressing and identifying themselves that's almost carnivalesque.

Yes. Yes. I like that. If anything, if I could make comparisons, they are more like the classical Greek and Roman Gods; they lust after mortals, etc.

They're more real in an anthropomorphic sense. How do you feel about the critical response your work has received?

It has been pretty good. There was nothing said that was outrageously wrong. It's gotten some mixed reviews. There was one reviewer that said that the book was too much about Blacks relating to Whites and I thought: come to BC, and take a look around, and you will see why! All things considered, it did well.

There's a feeling among many Whites and some Blacks that when Blacks write, it should be about themselves; they should avoid White people's reality and should treat topics like racial inequality satirically.

Some White people who have read *49th Parallel Psalm* accuse me of being angry. I don't think the book is angry.

Do you think that it might be a problem of reading skills?

Yes! It must be. It's also a defensive response.

I think it is difficult to say that your work is angry because there is so much playfulness in it. Though they might have been thinking of "Evening at the Colonial" . . .

The lines: "Hell Freezes Over / White People Discover Empathy."

That would make me laugh if I were White!
In the introduction to his latest book, Odysseys Home: Mapping African Canadian Literature, *George Elliott Clarke laments what he observes as a tendency by some critics to subsume African Canadian literature under the rubric of African American literature or to elide it altogether. Do you concern yourself with the issue of defining literatures?*

Yes. Absolutely! Especially in regard to the poetry project that I am working on now. It's a turntable poem that deals with issues we've mentioned earlier: literacy, morality—and also hip-hop. I am mixing my voice—it's recorded onto dub plates—with instrumental hip-hop; sort of live, semi-live performance. The subject matter of the poem is hip-hop in Vancouver. I have been working on it for about a year and a half now, including the writing and the performing, and I've come to the conclusion that this is an anti- hip-hop poem in certain ways, and most of what has come out of it are my criticisms of hip-hop and of the passive reception of hip-hop in Canada. It has forced me to think more and more about American culture.

Hip-hop's not altogether American; there's also a Jamaican component, directly from Jamaica and from the Jamaican Diaspora.

Yeah. Jamaicans invented hip-hop. But, in terms of the way it shapes identity here, it is American. You get young White kids, or Black kids, or Asian kids here in the city speaking and thinking of themselves and their society in a paradigm that was created in the United States. Hip-hop is this beautiful theory that works down there, and is given as a response to situations that don't exist here. It's incredibly influential.

I think that when something else comes to supplant it, it will go. But look at the demographic that supports it: it's the young; they have a dress code that goes with it; you see them with their head wraps and their earphones, and you know what they're listening to. It's a temporary identity phenomenon that goes with this age group. Within five–ten years, most of these young people would have outgrown that identity and developed a surer sense of themselves.

Maybe. But whether they do or not, I am looking at these things in the long term. The music I like—the music I keep returning to—is the music of the sixties and seventies: soul and R and B. I place hip-hop within this long tradition, so if something comes next that is fine. Quincy Jones says that if you want to learn the history of Black America, you'll find much of it in the music. I think that's true. But, in relation to Canada, hip-hop is irrelevant. The tone, the violent emotions, the gun talk, all of that bravado, they are American responses to an American situation.

But, Wayde, that scatological stuff has always existed. In the past, it couldn't get into mass culture or even print, given the censorship that existed. Today, you can find it in texts that are called toasts. Richard Wright's character Bigger Thomas is straight out of the toasts. Now it's possible to riff on that stuff, versify it, and get rich off it—if the rapper lives long enough.

In the Black youth culture it is dominant and is the only tone. The thing that frustrates me about hip-hop is that every rapper has the same emotional tone.

There is a range of about that big [gestures one half of an inch]. Soul and reggae range from sadness to joy. In hip-hop it is only anger: one emotion.

But if you talk to those guys—and I am sure some of them are sociopaths—they'll say, "Look, man, go take a valium. It's what sells. It's what the record companies want." Pretty soon, when you start writing fiction and get an agent, he or she will tell you the same thing: Put your people down, mock them. Readers will snap it up.

Nevertheless, it is inadequate. What bothers me is the inappropriateness of it all. You get Black groups from Victoria rapping about guns; kids who've never touched a gun. Rap about your reality; that's what I would rather see.

Taking the form and pouring their own content into it, so to speak.

I'm all for hybridization of forms. I worry that we are victims of a certain type of American imperialism, and this time the face of it is Black.

You are a young writer. I suspect that you are hoping for the day when you'll be able to make a living from your writing. To what extent do you feel that power in the political and economic sphere affects power in the cultural sphere?

Lately the most important issue to me is saving universal health care. My politics are somewhere between anarchism and social democracy.

And in terms of how politics affects the arts—the Black presence in the arts?

It's always a worry that minorities would get overlooked. Some of the excerpts in *Bluesprint* are from the Black writers of the seventies who self-published, and there was no readership and no reviews. These are talented writers that were ignored, writers that might have continued on. That's very frustrating. It's probably easier to get published today as a Black writer in Canada.

It is somewhat easier; but, according to one literary agent, only if you are a Black woman. The agents say that it's mostly Black women who read the books written by Blacks, and they prefer to read books by Black women, about the realities of Black women.

One of the biggest frustrations is Chapters. It's disastrous for small presses, especially for books of poetry. You couldn't get my book there one year after publication. People went there looking for it and got told that it was out of print when it wasn't. It is frustrating. They won't even special-order it. And they claim that they support Canadian culture!

Other aspects of your writing you would like to comment on?

No, nothing that I can think of.

Thanks for discussing your writing with me.

Afua Cooper

Afua, since your work is set in both Canada and Jamaica, would you, for the benefit of our readers, provide a brief biography regarding your years in Jamaica and in Toronto and how your experiences in both places have influenced your writing?

I spent the first twenty-two years of my life in Jamaica. I pretty much grew up there. I went to both elementary and high school there. Jamaica formed me. My sensibility was shaped there. I got my sense of who I am as a person from living and growing up there. I came of age in the 1970s, a time when Jamaicans—I should say Jamaicans of African descendant, in fact, West Indians of African descendants—were rediscovering Africa. We were discovering who we were as Africans and making it central to our identity. Popular music—reggae music especially, dub poetry with drums in the background—and theatre with a focus on African style and issues of African identity were all ways we used to reclaim that heritage.

I was exposed to all this, because, although I was born in a rural area, I grew up in Kingston, which was the major centre where these arts flowered, where all this cultural ferment was going on.

Nevertheless many of your poems have a rural setting.

Yes. I lived in the rural areas, specifically in Westmoreland, until I was eight. However, every summer I went back to Westmoreland or to St. Thomas, where I also had relatives whom I visited on weekends throughout the year. Christmas and major holidays were spent with these relatives in the country. On the face of it, I do have a rural sensibility. I must say also that much of the cultural expression in the urban centre is drawn from rural life. Take Bob Marley, for example. Shows about him tend to feature scenes of Trenchtown, but Bob Marley was born in Nine Miles, St. Ann. Like me, he returned to the country on weekends and holidays. He often referred to himself as a country boy. He never gave up his country roots. You probably know he's buried in the rural area.

How do you envisage your role as a writer?

In the past I never did see myself as a writer. Now, I suppose that I see myself as a kind of healer, not the laying-on-of-hands healing, but rather healing through words, through revisioning our understanding of the world from a holistic and compassionate perspective. Poetry helps effect my own healing and the healing of those who hear the words of the poems. That's the best I can say.

In 1993 or 1994 you referred to yourself as a shamaness? Do you still use that title?

I still like that label (laughs). When I examine my work—that is after I've written something and left it for a while—when I go back to it, I find myself asking: what's this? Why did I write this? And these questions arise because I find that such poems seem to want to engage with the other world. And that's what shamans do. They explore both worlds—many worlds.

This is a follow-up to the last question. In some of your poems you assume the persona of the bard—I can think of your poems on aging, and Western society's fear of fatness. Do you see this as one of your roles?

Yes, that's how the poetry has been coming to me over the past twelve years. It's not that I specifically set out to right a wrong or correct a wrong. It's about applying my particular vision to a situation and recognizing the fact that we human beings are damaged people that relate to the world in a damaged way. We Westerners—and I'm referring here to Caribbean people as well, although some would say we are at the fringe of such Westerness—have absorbed such damaging concepts. Fatness, for example. We fear we might not get the right job because of it, that we miss all sorts of opportunities because of it.

In regard to aging, our fear of it astonishes me. We must age. Aging is a natural, beautiful process. We spend billions of dollars masking it. We look at the anti-aging ads and allow ourselves to be programmed by their message. I read somewhere that only 13 percent of the women on television are over forty-five. We fear the aged. We ostracize our old people, not so much in senior citizens' homes as in the sense that we don't see them as useful. No doubt, this is a consequence of capitalism, the belief that we are only useful when we are productive. Companies shy away from hiring workers in their fifties on the rationale that they can only get a few years out of them before they retire. The quest for eternal youth, which I see as damaging, in part springs from this. Our fear of aging is symptomatic of the superficial way in which we lead our lives. Because of it we are afraid to look inside.

In "Poetry in You," a poem addressed to your son Akil, you imply what some of the qualities of the poet are. You specifically focus on the observations he makes as he hears the drumming. Quite clearly you are pointing to some of the qualities the poet must possess intuitively?

Yes. Yes the ability to imagine. Does the drum talk? Does the drum sing? Nowadays professional drummers and drum makers from diverse cultures tell us that the drum has a spirit. For a little child to intuit that the drum is more than just a piece of wood and animal skin shows a poetic imagination, the sort of imagination that we hope everyone could develop.

That might very well be a tall order. Do you have a definition of poetry?

No, not different from what's in the dictionary: literature in metrical form, in verse form. Poetry is aural—oral literature, it's scribal literature. Poetry must have been our first language. I sometimes think that when humans began to speak, to form words, it was in poetic form.

Some people say dance and music, but I guess music isn't divorced from poetry. In fact music was integral to poetry. Perhaps that's one reason why you're interested in dub poetry, which is often accompanied by music.

When I think of poetry I go far back into time. I think of ancient poets like the Celtic Bards who sang their poetry accompanied by musicians; or the West African poets: the griots, who are accompanied by musicians—ballaphon players, cora players, and sometimes drummers. In such performances the poetry emerges from the interplay between the bard and the cora players. I've seen videotaped performances of them. The bard recites in elevated language, then leaves, and the cora player plays, then returns and they both perform in unison. It's poetry that relies on music, whose very soul is music.

It seems to me as well that the poet is like the dancer in your poem "She Dance," who is able to effect a oneness with the universe, to melt into its divine essence.

That poem came out of a dream. I had a dream in the early morning of a very black woman dancing. It seems to me that the music was in her head because there were no musicians. I thought of the Voudun dance. I am not a dancer, so the only way I could express what I saw in the dream was to translate it into words.

It's interesting that all the arts try to communicate things that are ineffable in human existence.

I concur. Sometimes when I write I long for another medium to express what I want to convey. Language alone doesn't do it. I cannot paint.

You choose to write in the diction of everyday language and to make the quotidian and ordinary the subject of poetry; in these respects you're like the American poet Walt Whitman—and others, of course. How deliberate is this choice? Is it out of consideration for your audience that you do this?

It wasn't deliberate. A friend said that when she read my poetry it reminded her of Walt Whitman. So of course I got hold of Walt Whitman's poetry and read some of it. Any resemblance is accidental. That was the language that came to me. The first poems that I wrote when I was a child were on epic topics, national heroes, etc.

So you actually wrote poetry when you were still a child?

Yes, when I was around nine or ten. I would publish them in the children's own newspaper. Poems about our national heroes, the deeds of Nanny of the Maroons, Paul Bogle. That was good for then, but as I grew older I became interested in making poetry out of everyday things.

Your mother walking down the slope, going to the market, people ploughing the soil.

Yeah. This might sound ambitious, but let me say it. It's giving back to the people who gave me the language. I want everyone who reads my poetry to understand that.

Would you say then that your diction is chosen because of your audience?

Yes, the people whom I started reading early wrote that way. People like Nikki Giovanni. I found that very attractive.

You employ the fable sometimes, in "Sheep," for example. Is this too audience-related or is it because it's a form that you find common to Black reality?

Both, I think. It's acknowledging that you are part of the tribe and therefore live according to the dictates of the tribe. Living like this is necessary for our collective survival. When we become wholly individualized, trouble begins.

This is not to say that we don't need both types of consciousness.

It seems to me that the tension between the two could be very creative. Trouble begins when the tribe stones those who disagree with it.

You employ metaphors sparingly, but of the few you employ, some are quite intriguing: a closed windowless room to depict the situation of the lover of a married man in the poem "Six o'Clock"; sunset to embody the end of a relationship; as well as the various metaphors that point to repressed truth in your poem "I Don't Care if Your Nanny Was Black?" Would you like to discuss the pros and cons of using metaphor?

I remember one of my teachers saying that metaphors are good and we must use them. Sometimes they are the most effective way to say what you need to say.

You do know that poststructuralists in literature—in history as well, since history is narrative—insist on examining metaphors before we use them because they come freighted with the meanings of past usage. I'm thinking of Bakhtin's observations on this, but even more closely to us Afro-West Indians, of NourbeSe Philip's and Dionne Brand's views on the subject; they address this phenomenon frontally. Have you yourself seen any political and cultural baggage in metaphorical language—metaphors that you shy away from or feel the need to challenge?

Not particularly. Metaphors are useful because sometimes I think what they do is allow one to speak in a mythic way, and sometimes that's useful. But as you've just said they need to be examined. I don't think I use metaphors a lot. My language is ordinary.

Some of your poems owe their strength to the fact that they are written from the stance of the quiet observer, and in a deceptively quiet tone. I'm thinking of a poem like "The Rich Have Colonized the Trees". How useful is the stance of detached observer for writing poetry?

This brings me to the point of seeing myself as a social activist. There are some very concrete things that one can do in social activism. There are other things one cannot do, but can do as a poet. Walking through a neighbourhood and seeing a superabundance of trees and just a short distance away there are none, the sun blasting away at you because there is no shade—you begin to reflect on the disparities that cause this. So it's from that vantage that this poem was written.

Ancestry in the broadest sense—from Nanny of the Maroons to your biological and community parents—is an indispensable source for much of your poetry. Would you like to elaborate?

Oh yes, Oh yes, definitely. My family is important. Without it I probably won't be a poet, because I wouldn't have much to write about. That's a bit of an exaggeration. Storytelling was very important in my family. My paternal grandmother was a great storyteller. I'm not sure how aware she was of this. She constantly told stories about her life: as a young girl, a woman, single, married, widowed. There were many stories about finding herself widowed at thirty without an income and with two children and an unborn to fend for because her husband had been the breadwinner. It resulted in my father having to become a worker at the age of fifteen. She told interlinking stories, stories within stories, about the struggle to bring up her children and about the times in which all this was happening. They were told with great energy and in graphic detail. When I became an adult, I saw those stories as gifts from my grandmother, and I felt that I too should be a storyteller albeit in a different medium.

On the maternal side of the family I had a grandfather who went away and started another family. When I got to know that family, many stories emerged from that encounter: that my grandfather had to run away because he had been caught with another man's wife; that he could drink a bottle of rum without getting drunk; he was taller than other men, more handsome than other men, his yams bore better than other people's—he had taken on for them and for me epic proportions. These stories were a treasure trove for me.

Of course, there are the ancestral figures like Nanny of the Maroons who live on in our collective psyche. They've become legendary figures in our history.

Do you in any way subscribe to the Akan concept of Sankofa, i.e., making ancestral wisdom axial to our understanding and negotiation of reality?

You mean the symbol of the rooster gazing back at its tail?

Yes. One of the Adinka symbols.

I think there's a movie about it. Somehow the Akan managed to exert a sort of cultural dominance among Jamaica's Black population, although they were never numerically superior.

They seemed to have been the culturally dominant Blacks in St. Vincent as well.

I remember one of their detractors—Edward Long, I think—calling them natural-born heroes. To return to your question, one of the things we're always saying, in our roles as cultural workers, social activists, and poets, is that we have to know where we're coming from before we know where we're going. Using the past is therefore vital, not just as a springboard, but also as a canvas that we can take instruction from. Yes, although I have not thought of my work within the framework of Sankofa, I can see that the ancestral links are a fundamental aspect of my work.

Your poem "At the Centre" is a poetic rendition of your manifesto to hone your tropes from and find your themes in "brown women / who turn the soil with their hands/ making vegetable gardens and tending fruit trees." The portrait depicted in stanza three of the poem becomes a metaphor of the new, reborn poet who intends her creations to come out of her being. Yet in an earlier poem you identify yourself as a Rasta woman battling against constraints imposed by men. I wonder how you reconcile these seemingly antagonistic tendencies.

Remember my earlier statement that I see myself as a healer. There is certainly an evolution that's ongoing. To attain self-knowledge one has to go through several stages. Feminism is definitely part of who I am, how I define myself. But for me, today, feminism needs to become more of a holistic movement, one in which everyone is empowered—both men and women. We all have to share this world. This is not to say that we women are not going to challenge practices like misogyny. But coming back to "At the Centre"—what I am saying in that poem is that every act of creation must come out of the self, even though one can certainly be influenced by the external. We are part of the natural world, and the natural world is a part of us—I don't mean this in a dialectical sense, but more in the sense of an interconnectedness of all that's in the universe, whether it be stones, trees, human beings, etc. That poem is about developing a new vision, one that both embraces and challenges external reality. In literature, at least in North America, we find certain writers receiving lavish praise. Sylvia Plath is an example that comes to mind. Feminists lavish honours on her. But how much of a role model is she? If I want to live the life of an empowered woman, how much of a role model is she? She committed suicide—and that is unfortunate. But somebody like Sonia Sanchez is a better role model, somebody like NourbeSe Philip is a better role model, because they've been through shit and survived, and with a strong determination to write.

Which is what the narrator in "At the Centre" says: "No longer shall I speak of electrocuted poets /or the ones who inhale gas until/ they danced in the dizziness of death/ but of brown women/ who turn the soil with their hands/ making vegetable gardens and tending fruit trees." And the last stanza: "today the craftsman has come/ to make a design for me/of a woman sitting in deep repose/ with doves flying from her head." The doves flying from her hair is a contrasting, corrective to Medusa. The doves evoke peace and spirituality as opposed to death and petrification.

Definitely. And wisdom born of tremendous cost, which is probably the only way wisdom comes.

To quote another poet [Theodore Roethke]—"I break my bones their marrow to bestow/ upon that god who knows what I would know."

Perhaps this would be a good point to ask you about your poem "A True Revolution" which debates Kamau Brathwaite's poem "Spring Blade." In the final two stanzas of the poem you state the prerequisites for a revolution:

> *We need, yes/ for the people to cleanse themselves/ to respect themselves/ to respect the female part of themselves/ and to know/ that woman degradation/ Black woman degradation must stop.*
>
> *We need for the people to realize love/ for themselves and their neighbours/ and to know that love indeed is divine/ then Kamau when all these and more tasks/ are completed/ we will have a true revolution.*

Would you like to comment?

I still feel the same way about the conditions listed in the poem. The Russians effected their revolution in 1917, and now they've adopted capitalism. External changes are one thing, revolution quite another. It is primarily achieved from within and involves a total transformation in the way we see the world, and must involve the understanding that what I want for myself I must also want for my neighbour.

Referring to the concept of love mentioned in the poem, I'll say that love involves respect and compassion and mercy for others. Without this—we could change our political systems from one -ism to another—without love, compassion and mercy for others, we're still mired in the behaviours that keep us greedy and exploitative of one another. This is not to say we haven't had changes. We've had them in the cultural field, in politics as well. Look, for example, at how the rigidity that used to exist among the social classes in Jamaica has broken down. But I'm wondering by way of the poem about where do we go next. What's the next step? There's definitely the feeling that the revolution has not only stalled; it has been turned back.

The US certainly didn't like the direction it was taking.

That's certainly true. We have exchanged one set of colonizers for another. What does this mean for our [Jamaica's] independence?

Certainly if one reflects on the destruction of the Jamaican economy to punish Michael Manley for his attempted rapprochement with Cuba, the prognosis is grim. Guyana has suffered a similar fate because Forbes Burnham had opted for socialism.

The impact has been dire on Jamaicans. Now every Jamaican wants to be American.

In your artistic creation, you opt sometimes for a bilingual approach, English and Jamaican. Louise Bennett's (Miss Lou's) poems that you include in Utterances and Incantations *are all in Jamaican, and one of them, "Bans a Killin," is a satire on those who wish to suppress the use of Jamaican in favour of what they term standard English.*

Prior to the English Caribbean islands gaining their independence, 3 percent of the population determined what was valuable as regards culture and learning—education in the broadest sense. This 3 percent ridiculed those who spoke nation language. Even those who spoke it felt that it wasn't a worthy language. And when they went to places they identified with power and "high culture" they felt obliged to use their best English. It created something of a split personality in the overwhelming majority of British Caribbean folk, and when artists like Louise Bennett addressed this in her poetry, she was mocked and caricatured, but she persisted—talk about role models, she's certainly one. By the sixties she got support from prominent writers like Roger Mais, who said this is how people talk, we must create a bilingual literature—in English for the wider market, and in Caribbean languages for those at home. Today several writers choose to write in nation language. We mustn't ignore the DJs; I'm not sure we can talk about poetry without giving credit to the DJs, people like Big Youth, Beenie Man, Buju Banton and others. They sing in that language, and it's taken for granted; it's no longer a debate.

Having been a beneficiary of the struggle to legitimize the people's language, I took to using it quite naturally. And why shouldn't I? It was the language I spoke at home, it was the language I used in the schoolyard with my friends. English was restricted to the classroom.

And for that reason it is the language that expresses our deepest emotions. Not to use it would be to function permanently in an artificial world.

Definitely. For me, therefore, there are these two languages. As you know, in the Caribbean, there is what can be called extreme English-language speech, extreme patois-speech, and various registers in the centre.

Although the battle to respect nation languages has largely been won, there is still a residue of suspicion, a notion that it is less than English. There are still people who express the view that newspaper columnists such as Carolyn Cooper should not be writing in nation language.

How pure is the vernacular that you employ? Trinidadian writer Earl Lovelace, for example, told me that his use of the vernacular in, for example, The Wine of Astonishment *and* A Brief Conversion and Other Stories, *is an invention, a literary version, so to speak of the vernacular. Do you reproduce the language as you hear it, or edit it for literary purposes?*

I do both. In some cases I reproduce it as I hear it. But oftentimes I edit it. There are audience considerations too, for even though we say we write for ourselves, we want to be read. I ask myself whether the readers will understand it. The ultimate objective is for the reader to comprehend the idea or essence of what I'm trying to say. I couldn't say in the end how pure it is.

When the word is transferred to the page, one tries to make it work as written language, as literature. I think that's where the tension enters. It's one reason why I love to perform my poetry. In performance you can conjoin both. Near purity can be achieved if the writing happens first. Oftentimes a poem will create itself in my head after which I'll write it down. And sometimes while I'm performing, it changes to suit itself better to an oral form.

Even so I would argue that in Canada to write in a Caribbean language is to make an implicit political and cultural statement. Moreover, mainstream publishers find this a convenient reason not to publish the works of Black writers here and in the US.

That's certainly true, but I can't get away from using nation language. As Caribbean people struggling to establish our cultures, it's one of the inconveniences we have to learn to live with. We may write in English, but nation language is an essential part of who we are.

It's our being.

Publishers would have to go out on a limb. It has to be a leap of faith. Louise

Bennett mentioned performing in Chicago to an all-American audience, and they laughed in all the right places. People have to be willing to engage the language. Why is it that on television or in the movies we make an effort to understand someone speaking a mangled form of English or with a heavy accent? This is part of what I meant earlier on by being compassionate. I don't mean compassionate in the sense of being sorry for people. I mean, for example, taking the extra time required to understand a work. We Caribbean people have already done that. I remember Julie Dash, the filmmaker, saying that when she sought mainstream distribution for her movie *Daughters of the Dust*, Hollywood told her they could not understand the language. She told them to use subtitles. It's a mentality that refuses to engage seriously with people of colour.

If we look at this from the perspective of Marxist theory what really Hollywood and those who refuse to publish our works are saying is that they possess the power to withhold or attribute value on their terms. To the extent that they can commodify this thing or appropriate it, make it serve their purposes, they would stamp it with their approval; if not they'll exclude it.

Exactly. When hip-hop began, it was marginalized, mainstream culture ignored it. Now the mainstream embraces it.

Now mainstream culture even shapes it. You hold a PhD in history and much of the content of your poems comes from the history that was for a long time erased. To what extent do you see your writing as a de facto writing into history the African and African Diasporic experience?

I think that's something that happened unconsciously. It still happens unconsciously. I never sit down and say I'm going to write a poem about this or that aspect of history. I look at my work and see that the preoccupation with history is there.

Perhaps that's why you've studied history in the first place.

Yes. Yes. I suppose I wanted to emulate Walter Rodney. He was one of my heroes. He had been to Africa, had taught there, and had written about Africa. As you know, he was expelled from Jamaica, and there were riots to protest his expulsion. I was growing up during those heady times. I grew up trying to understand what was happening to Black people. When I was nine I heard about some people about to be hanged in Africa. I wondered why Africans were hanging Africans. The domino and Ludo players at my uncle's rum shop told me what apartheid was. That was my introduction to apartheid and its impact on Blacks in South Africa and internationally. At some level I felt that if I wanted to know these things fully I would have to study history

The distortion of history is the subject of your long poem "Founding Peoples." Would you like to comment?

This poem emerged from my study of Canadian history at the University of Toronto. It was settler history from top to bottom, in which Natives made cameo appearances. I felt I couldn't take this anymore. And of course there's the ongoing debate about Quebec independence and the argument that Canada is comprised of two founding peoples. I kept thinking: what a falsehood! Natives have been written out of it, Blacks, Asians, and other Europeans have been written out of it.

In fact, many French Canadians will tell you that they hate Trudeau for introducing multiculturalism, because its intent, they claim, was to reduce their culture to one of many, as opposed to being one of two. As your narrator asks: "Did they not see the Huron/ Iroquois/ Mississaugas/ Micmac/ Ojibway/ and Cree/ did they not find people living on this land/ living with it in harmony?"

And this is supposed to be the history of our origin! So the poem came out of that. They say it's the conquerors that write history.

Or, as Chinua Achebe says, "When the lions write history, the antelopes fare badly."

There is a huge challenge ongoing but the resistance from the academy has been strong.

So one of your goals as a historian is to challenge some of these concepts?

Yes. I want to get other voices, other figures, into the narrative. It's a conscious effort. And there is a price to be paid for doing it. I'm often told that Black history, which is my field of specialization, is not at the cutting edge of history, that Blacks are unimportant because they comprise only 2 percent of the population. They recommend that I do Quebec history, something more mainstream. If we don't challenge what's there we would continue to read the same old lies.

We spoke earlier about nation languages, specifically publishers' claim that if you write in it they won't be able to market it. But some publishers are more blunt than that: they've told Black writers this work is too hard on Canada, we won't publish it.

It's censorship, regardless of how it's masked.

You are so right! I have been verbally assaulted for reading "Founding Peoples." Audiences seem to enjoy hearing poems about my grandmother, etc., but are hostile to the poems that deal with historical and political subjects.

You mentioned Walter Rodney as a seminal influence for your pursuit of historical studies. Are there similar figures for literature?

In the seventies I read books like *Soul on Ice*, Angela Davis' autobiography *If They Come in the Morning*, and *The Autobiography of Malcolm X*. All those books were banned during the sixties. They were unbanned in the seventies when Michael Manley became prime minister. Prior to that if you were caught reading *The Autobiography of Malcolm X*, you could have been imprisoned.

The African American poets influenced me a lot: Sonia Sanchez, Nikki Giovanni, Jayne Cortez. Ellison's *Invisible Man* was an eye-opener. In general, we were interested in African Americans, because, even though they were marginalized at home, they still had a lot of cultural capital and were the de facto leaders of the Black world. In high school the literature we studied was Caribbean.

You had a choice that I didn't.

Yes, my older sister did all British and American.

In 1968, when I left St. Vincent, I could not buy Caribbean books there. They weren't available. I discovered Lamming's In the Castle of My Skin *and quite a few other books, Fanon's works in particular, when I came to Montreal.*

I studied Caribbean literature: authors like Roger Mais; V. S. Naipaul; E. K. Brathwaite: his plays as well as his poetry (I had the pleasure of having him come to my class to talk about his work); George Lamming; Samuel Selvon. I studied Caribbean history and Caribbean geography. Oddly enough, Canada was what we studied for external geography.

Are authors who write in nation language now included in the curriculum?

Yes. It's the people of my generation who are writing the textbooks (laughs).

Most of the books by Black Canadian writers challenge the various national and racial myths and are therefore unpopular with White readers. What implications does this state of affairs hold for Black voices in Canadian literature?

Well, we have no Black publishers. Sister Vision no longer exists. Do we have any Black editors?

Althea Prince.

Critics? Donna Nurse.

George Elliott Clarke. Larry Hill does some reviewing, too.

You are talking about cultural capital in the Black community. Major publishers take on one or two Black writers and push them. And it's really never more than one or two. In Canada there is a widespread feeling among publishers that books by Blacks don't sell. Canadian publishers would probably tell you that for them a bestseller is five thousand copies, but they are not willing to do the promotion to get there.

When African Americans began publishing in large numbers in the sixties and seventies, it was in part because they founded their own presses and journals: Broadside, Third World, Thunder's Mouth, Black Scholar, Obsidian, Black American Literature Forum. Blackarts *(which became* Calalloo*). Today most major US publishers have Black imprints and Black editors. And now there are Black literary agents.*

What we really need is a good Black publisher. Black writers might have to come together and form a collective, that is, if they can put aside their egos for the greater good.

Are there other aspects of your writing you'd like to talk about?

I think we covered a lot.

Thanks for discussing your writing with me.

Bernadette Dyer

Bernadette, why do you write?

Writing is a passion. I guess that one of the reasons I write is that since I also paint, it was not a giant leap to be creative in another artistic field. My writing comes from an inborn awareness that form, even life itself, is comprised of textures, both subtle and deliberate, and that colour and experiences can run the full gamut from darkness to light. It is reassuring to find that writing has taken me beyond where painting left off. I have been rewarded, for, with my determination to stick with the craft, my writing has not only reached, but moved many more people than even I had originally thought possible.

Wordsworth refers to painting as poetry's sister art. Both forms can be complementary. Derek Walcott is also a painter. You were born and raised in Jamaica and you have been living in Toronto for . . .

Thirty-one years.

How has living in both places influenced your writing?

Living in both countries has affected my work in significant ways. It has truly defined the past and the present. My writing draws a line between the dynamics of having lived among palms to ending up living among pines. One remembers the reality of living in households where servants and gardeners did everything. That life, such as it was, is now mere fodder for my fiction. It's more difficult to write stories about Canada; it is almost as though even the climate here resists my imagination. However, both worlds, Kingston and Toronto, are bustling with diversity; and, as readers will see, *Villa Fair*, my short-story collection, addresses, among other issues, ethnicity. That is what Jamaica is: a mixture of different peoples. Toronto is something of a complement: it too is a melange of the world's peoples, and it informs my writing.

So in that sense Toronto reflects Jamaica.

Yes.

Do you see writing as having a function?

In my case it would be to reach out to the world. Hopefully, it will give a better understanding of where I came from, and where I am now.

My impression is that the Black community expects the work of literature to be temple, community fair, and academy. Have you had people telling you what they expect your work to be?

Fortunately or unfortunately, I have not had a lot of exposure to those members of the Black community who make those demands of their writers, so, in a sense, I have been able to be myself without undue influence.

Fortunate indeed. That hasn't been my experience.

Well, perhaps it is a good thing that they don't even seem to know that I exist.

My impression is that you are experimenting with different ways of storytelling in both the realist and magic-realist modes.

That's true. Storytelling is so intricate, compelling, and absorbing that, for me, it's like attempting to create a perfect painting. And as the painter varies his techniques, carefully laying things down, so does the storyteller. There are some stories that, as I am writing them, I find that they take on a life of their own, and lead me from realism into the realm of the mystical and magical. I cannot resist such stories. However, there are many approaches to addressing this art form; one can only strive to master some of them.

I see. I'm thinking of your story "Close the Blue Door." It seems to begin in the magic-realist mode but later the magic-realist mode is deflated.

"Close the Blue Door" has proved to be one of my most successful stories. Rather than say the magic-realist mode becomes deflated, I would say that the story builds itself on trust in the magical, and gently tugs us back into the world of reality.

This story—all your stories for that matter—is told in a very clear, distinctive voice. Would you like to comment?

I am pleased that you found the voice clear and distinctive, for that is indeed how the story came to me in a flash of revelation. I would say that the techniques used in oral storytelling served me well in writing this story and in my longer fiction.

When you write, do you imagine yourself as an oral storyteller, talking to an audience?

Yes, I do imagine an audience, since most of my stories have a narrator who relates events, much the same as oral stories.

Your immigrant stories are set in different places and different epochs: Portugal in 1548, Jamaica of forty-five years ago, present-day Toronto. Any specific reasons?

To begin with, I am from a very ethnically mixed background, and it affects the way I view the world. I have always been fascinated with history, and I tend to enjoy researching the past, whether it concerns the family or otherwise.

So you are interested in immigration as a continuum, from way back when.

You've mentioned the story "Leaving Faro" that begins in Portugal. Perhaps you've already suspected that it is a family legend. I don't know how often my father Edmund Gabay would tell us as children about the Jews who were driven out of Portugal during the time of the Inquisition. He said that four Gabay brothers were among those Jews that ended up in Jamaica at that time, and that they were his ancestors. My story is a fictionalized version of the brothers' journey to Jamaica.

Your stories are graphic depictions of multiculturalism in Canada and Jamaica. The Jamaican stories seem to embody the Jamaican motto: pluribus uni (out of many one).

You've hit the nail on the head.

Anything further?

I think that every story I write is a testament to that motto.

Your depiction of life on a Jamaica plantation contrasts with the depictions of other Caribbean writers who explore similar themes. I am thinking specifically of your story "Remembering Serge." It depicts an idyllic life. You probably know from reading other Caribbean writers that they focus strongly on the exploitation of the workers.

You must remember that that story is written from the perspective of what a child saw. The story is actually about my brothers and sisters and myself growing up, seeing reality through our childish eyes. We were not judgemental or realizing the possibility of exploitation. We were only concerned with being children and seeking out the small pleasures children find in eating sugarcane and drinking coconut water. We roamed the countryside freely, relishing the fruits such as mangoes, bananas, and citrus that were available. We rode on donkeys, waded in rivers and streams while enjoying Daddy's farm. It was never a question of wondering how and why such privilege was given to us. But you must also remember that the story ends with none of us returning to Serge as adults. Serge lives in all of us only as memory.

It's an interesting story for me. I have cousins who could have written a similar story up to a certain point in their lives. That point ended when the plantation sugar factory closed, and they were thrown into the world of basic survival.

That didn't happen to my family and hence the story I've written.

A few of your stories deal with themes of interracial, interclass, and intergenerational sex in Canada and in Jamaica.

That goes back to my previous answer about my own multiethnic origin. The theme of multiethnicity fascinates me most likely because of that. I am intrigued by the dynamics of different cultures coming together.

Your novella "Roberta on the Beach" combines several of the themes you explore in the other stories, but it adds to them the theme of philandering and naïve love. And I am wondering why.

"Roberta on the Beach" was first written under the title "Roberta of Jamaica" and published by the *Toronto South Asian Review*. Some of my readers felt that the story was incomplete. They wanted to know more about Roberta. "Roberta of Jamaica" ends at the point where Chester arrives from England. Readers said they loved the family and wanted to know more. So I decided that rather than continue in the same vein, it might be interesting to present the story not from Roberta's point of view, or her sister's, but rather from a male perspective. I suppose it had in part to do with the fact that I grew up with brothers who expected my sisters and me to think like they did. This was an experiment on my part to dissolve into Caleb's male persona. Thus the extension was called "Caleb's Story." I knew readers would want his character to be fully fleshed out, so I brought in Sheila and the others.

Sheila brings an added dimension to the story because up to that point, apart from Roberta, the family seems to be too perfect.

I agree.

"Roberta on the Beach" and "Johns Lane" depict among other themes the sense of responsibility that the more fortunate feel for the less fortunate in the Caribbean. Would you like to comment further?

Just to say that this is widespread in the Caribbean. It's not limited to just family. It extends across the population. The characters in "John's Lane" are mostly all Chinese, but I wanted to show that despite racial differences they basically share the same concerns as the mixed-race family in "Roberta on the Beach."

This is one instance where your work is functioning as temple and community fair because these are stories where West Indians feel themselves reflected in the best possible light, idealized. Anything you'd like to add?

Just that as an author—and you know this because you yourself are a writer—you surprise yourself. The family in "John's Lane," as well as those in my other stories surprised me. They spoke for themselves, and demanded to be heard. It didn't feel as if I was creating them, and I did not feel that I had to idealize anyone.

"Roberta on the Beach" reflects how some choices are made, in this case as regards those who would be allowed to continue their education and those who would not. The less gifted are sacrificed, passed over, so that the most gifted would realize their potential. This is a Caribbean fact. How do you feel about that?

I saw that happen in my own family. I have a sister who lives in England. We were both in high school in Jamaica when our parents announced that she was going to be sent to England. To me, going to England was almost like going to live on another planet. My sister was chosen, because she had always said that she wanted to be a nurse, and there were excellent training programs in England. I was considered too young to be sent away, but, nonetheless, it was a devastating blow to lose my best friend and companion. I do not think I ever got over that loss.

This is how you have Sheila responding.

I think the pain of having "lost" my sister that way—I say lost because it is a loss despite our remaining in touch by letters that took far too long to arrive—is in part the genesis of "Roberta on the Beach."

In the story you show that such giving, such sacrificing, is not disinterested, that it imposes obligations on the beneficiary. This is a true reflection of the

Caribbean. What are your views about this?

It wasn't something that I consciously thought about while writing. But now that you point it out, I realize that it's there. Perhaps it is my sister who at some point must have realized that such gifts come with obligations, like it or not. Yes, it is reflective of our Caribbean culture, for many families were only in a financial position to send off one child for further studies. Being the last child in a family of six, it almost felt that my turn would never come.

Did you see Roberta's betrayal of her family as sacrilege?

Ummmm! I saw it as her betrayal of her potential.

She does betray them.

Yes, she does betray them. I wouldn't call it sacrilege, but rather a horrific act. How isolated she must have felt, and how unbearable her life must have seemed despite her love for Chester. No one, not even I, can ever say why she resigned herself to such a horrific end.

We all know stories of people who've come abroad and lied about their social circumstances and who're devastated when they're confronted with the truth. Is there any particular reason why you make her commit suicide? Punishment?

No, this was not done to punish Roberta, but, to my way of thinking, Roberta found it difficult to confront her own lies that surely would have come to a head with Chester's arrival—there were explanations she would have had to give, and her lies would have compounded. Realizing the mess she created, she chooses to cop out, by taking her own life. Surely, this is not the route taken by many immigrants who speak about imaginary lives that they supposedly lived elsewhere.

Ironically Chester arrives and accepts the family. He certainly would have felt betrayed by Roberta.

Yes. He would have.

Another of your stories that intrigue me is "Driving through Red Lights." This story deals, it seems to me, with the possibility that immigration offers to break from the tyranny of tradition.

I didn't think about any of this before undertaking to write this story. The story originated in a friendship I made with a South Asian woman. She was so bound to tradition that she could not envisage the possibility of saying no to an arranged marriage. When it came to marrying her own daughter, she couldn't even imagine her daughter going against tradition. "Driving through Red Lights" is my fictionalized concept of just such a situation. I chose to create someone who is Canadian-born perhaps as a way of showing that this could happen.

In this sense, you are using your fiction to educate. You also use your imagination to explore possibilities other than those we are presented it, which is one of the functions of imaginative literature. Why did you title the story "Driving through Red Lights?"

Do you remember at the end of the story when she says she wants to get to the man she loves? That reckless impulse to get to the person you love, regardless of consequence, is what drove her, even if it meant driving through red lights to get there. It's alluded to at the beginning of the story.

For me the title resonated the taboo topics the story deals with: homosexuality, defiance of an arranged marriage, interracial marriage. You yourself are outside of the South Asian traditions and could be accused of voice appropriation.

I do not feel that I would be accused of voice appropriation. The story was reviewed in a South Asian magazine here in Toronto, and it received an extremely positive review. The reviewer went so far as to compare it with another story he was reviewing by a South Asian author, and stated that Dyer seems to know our community better than this other author.

Also, the fact that I am racially mixed—my mother was part East Indian and part Black, my father was part Jewish and part Black—has given me some insight into these difficulties, and deepened my interest in each of these cultures.

"An African out in the Cold" could be read as portraying the precarious situation that immigration could be for immigrants who speak neither of Canada's official languages and who have no "home" community to sustain them in the new country. I am curious about the genesis of this story.

It is an imagined story. However, whenever I'm on a streetcar, I usually take particular interest in the people aboard, and quite often conjure stories in my mind about them. Once I saw a young African man sitting alone, shivering from the cold. The story immediately played itself out in my mind, title and all.

But cold in the story extends beyond the weather inasmuch as the protagonist has no one to talk to. What begins seemingly as a reward degenerates into something resembling a curse.

I would call it a nightmare. I cannot imagine what I would have done, given the same circumstances.

And yet it's such a graphic reflection of what the immigration experience could be and probably is for some immigrants.

In "Six Little Sparrows" I was intrigued by the intensity with which the mother and her children are subject to the narrator's gaze. Here the narrator is sympathetic. Oftentimes, however, gazers are not. I mean it in the sense in which terms like "those people" are employed. In "Six Little Sparrows" the narrator wants to know, wants to enter their world.

It's fitting that we should talk about "Six Little Sparrows" while we are seated in this room at the very branch of the Toronto Public Library where that story came to me. I used to work at this library, and before it was renovated there was a window from which I could look straight into the park outside. It's where the story was born. It was my mother's favourite of all of my stories. And that is why I included it in my first collection.

Altogether your immigrant stories have something of a built-in dialectic on immigration—its beneficent as well as its maleficent aspects. Would you like to comment?

I felt I had to reflect truthfully what happens to immigrants. Canada is not always the land of milk and honey one is led to expect. There is suffering that many immigrants undergo, suffering that most Canadians don't even know about. I felt the need to portray the immigrant experience from both the negative and positive standpoints.

What has been the critical response to Villa Fair?

Villa Fair never received the exposure that it should have. It was published by a small press located in Vancouver. In spite of *Villa Fair*, I am virtually unknown, though I am hoping that when I publish my next book, things might be different.

You would be able to build on your existing readership.

Most of the books by Black Canadian writers challenge the various national Canadian myths and are therefore unpopular with White readers. This is my own assessment and the assessment of some writers I know. I don't know whether you agree. Would you like to comment on this?

I work in a library and I would say that I don't quite agree with your assessment. Books by Black authors are checked out often by non-Blacks as well as Blacks. But they are usually by authors who have received a great deal of exposure, e.g., George Elliott Clarke, who won the Governor General Award for poetry. This is also true for Austin Clarke, who won the Giller Prize. Exposure is important. Mainstream reviews too, if we can get any.

Part of my point, though, is that few writers win Governor General Awards or the Giller Prize. Worse yet, for the most part our books go unreviewed.

I agree with you on that.

Or receive hostile reviews. One of Canada's national myths is that Canada welcomes and accommodates its immigrants. History shows otherwise. When our books show this, we are challenging such myths and we are punished for it.

I totally agree with you on this.

As you know there are no viable Black publishers in Canada. How do you feel about that?

What I always say to myself is that I want my work to be published. I prefer not to see these issues in racial or ethnic terms. There was a Black publisher in Toronto that didn't publish my work, perhaps because they thought my work wasn't "Black" enough. Who knows? But on the other hand, I am pleased that a publisher in Vancouver did it without considerations of colour.

I probably need to clarify this. I know for a fact that before Williams-Wallace—the Black publisher that came onto the scene in the early eighties—the only Black professionally published writer, was Austin Clarke. For a while, even he too was out in the cold. It was only because of the efforts of Ms Wallace that the situation was corrected. Some of the authors that she published—Dionne Brand and Claire Harris are notable examples—were picked up by other publishers. My point is that these are writers who might have otherwise been ignored by mainstream publishers.

No might about it. They would have been.

For me Black publishers bring to light valuable work that would otherwise be ignored. I remember when Harold Head brought out his anthology of Black Canadian writing because no one else was publishing our stuff. That in part explains what I mean when I say there is a need for Black publishers.

Yes, there certainly is a need. However, insufficient financial support for culture is also a serious problem. I don't understand why more isn't being done.

Any important aspects of your work that I've ignored?

I think you've covered the important aspects of my work: its multiculturalism, the presence of magic realism in stories not primarily magic-realist.

What are you working on now?

I've just finished working on *Abductors*, a fantasy novel for young adults. I've also completed an adult novel set just before World War II titled, *Waltzes I Have Not Forgotten.*

Thanks for discussing your writing with me.

Cecil Foster

Cecil, since your work is set in Barbados, Canada, and to a lesser extent Jamaica, would you, for the benefit of our readers, provide us a with brief biography regarding your years in Barbados, Jamaica and Toronto, more specifically perhaps your using them as settings for your works?

I very much appreciate the chance to talk about some of the things I've been trying to do in my writing. As you indicate, it is Diasporic. I deliberately try to make it Diasporic, because I am playing with the notion that there is a common culture that was produced in the Western Hemisphere, a syncretized sort of culture, one that has brought all the various influences from various parts of the world together. For a very long time, there was an attempt to project the idea that Canada was no such culture. This vision influences my writing. Positioned in Canada, I'm trying to make sense of the world I exist in.

So you're saying that Canada is a space, a meeting point, where many of these already syncretic cultures are further syncretized?

Yes, Canada is a very beautiful country in that regard. I think Canada is a good example of how the body (the ruled) does not respond to the mind (the rulers). I mean the body as having a will of its own. If we look at what we might consider to be Canadian history—I mean the constructions of memory that go down as official history—we would see something of a dialogical struggle between the vision of the rulers and the reality of the ruled. The rulers tried to implement their vision, unsuccessfully, in the way they marginalized First Nations and devalued Blackness. Take, for example, the events of the year 1782, when the Loyalists, fleeing the US, came to the country that would eventually become Canada—a full 10 percent or more of these refugees were either African slaves or free Africans. Even If Canada did at times acknowledge that there was a Black vein in it, there was always the suggestion that it was so altered that it was no longer African.

Regardless of how one looks at it, we see that the Canadian ideal of who was to be Canadian was always aborted. But the paradox is that this resulted in Canada's becoming a very beautiful country. Let me explain: for each epoch that Canada needed immigrants, a certain type of immigrant was envisaged. At the very first, the English were the preferred group. When they became too few, the category was broadened to include anyone from what's now Great Britain and Ireland. When these too proved insufficient, there was a further broadening to include Western Europe. Eventually the category broadened to include southern Europeans, and so on and so forth. The "ideal" immigrants were never to be had, and so the door was opened to the so-called undesirables. If Canada is a success story, it is because of the triumphing of the Other. It is the Other who now dominates demographically at least in Canada. Part of what engages me is the fact that many of the groups that are excluded from the official narrative are germane to what Canada is as a lived reality, regardless of the contours that the rulers seek to impose on Canada's reality.

From the criticism I have received of my own work by people who are generally not university educated, I have inferred that the Black community expects works by Blacks to be temple, community fair, and academy. They come to it expecting to worship. They seem to expect their writers to be prophets and to provide them with a vision for their lives. I am not thinking here necessarily of the expectations of academic critics. Does this reflect your own experience?

I think your assessment is correct, but these expectations also apply to academic critics. Almost invariably when the latter review our work, they often begin with a formulation of what we should have written. If they sense that we've veered away from their expectations, and have been—God forbid!—innovative, desirous of changing the gaze, they use their criticism to bring us back on course—their course. They tell us indirectly that there is a specific form, type of, and approach to, writing that they expect from us.

There are good and bad aspects to such criticism. What's bad about it is that it inadvertently puts restraints on the creative process. For example, for my last novel *Dry Bone Memories*, I wanted to challenge the novel form and the standard forms of storytelling. I wanted to create a novel that would be a faithful representation of life itself, one in which no conversation has a true beginning because there is always something that preceded it; there's no non-referential knowledge; moreover, no conversation ever ends: it continues on out there, and becomes part of the new consciousness. I guess the analogy I might use is an old forty-five record whose sound we already know. It's already in our head; we hum it. We can put the needle on at any point, listen, become distracted, return, start over. There's no clear beginning, middle, or end. Applied to writing, it can be seen as the slices of life we choose to focus on. That was what I was trying to do.

In this respect, I'm reminded of what Northrop Frye said of Canadian literature in the 1960s, at a time when critics were trying to say what it is. Frye said at the time that they were dealing with an immature literature, one closely tied to history, particularly the obstacles that had to be overcome in the creation of Canada. Of necessity, such books had beginnings, middles and ends. As Frye saw it, Canadian literature would only be mature at the moment when anyone reading it would be unable to exhaust the mythology that constitutes it. Every book would be part of an ongoing epic. Much as I suppose Greek tragedians could write about specific parts of the mythology of a continuous epic. I think I was trying to see the creation of literature in a similar way—although I wasn't then familiar with Frye's views on the subject of Canadian literature. I think that I was trying to indicate that there is an experience that is of the Americas. In Barbados, there's one version of it; in Boston another; in Toronto, Halifax, Vancouver: places I deal with in *Dry Bone Memories*—there are manifestations of it; but the fullness of the mythology can never be exhausted.

So, coming back to your question, we writers have to deal often with the conflicting situation of whether we're creating literature that exhausts the mythology—i.e., works rooted strictly in the experiential, historical—or creating literary works that find their place in a wider, global setting. Statements like, "I can't understand such literature; it doesn't speak to me" are vexing. Critics who make them need to broaden their understanding of the vast mythology out of which literature is produced. Therefore, it seems that we are dealing with a double consciousness—in Du Bois' understanding of the term. Because of the very nature of literary production and its marketing, we are forced to deal with these issues. This isn't necessarily bad: the clash between the particular and the universal enhances creativity.

You were a journalist in Barbados and here in Canada. In fact, your coming to Canada was largely because of the fallout from a newspaper article you wrote about a debate in the Barbadian parliament of Tom Adams. Are the media here as unfettered as is generally reported?

It is true that the practice of journalism is different in these places. The difference isn't as great as some might want to believe. Some of these differences might be related to the very notion of "developed" and "underdeveloped" countries. Something I discovered, as I got older and perhaps wiser, is that I did not fully appreciate the fact that journalism is not necessarily in opposition to the dominant ethos. My youthful idealistic position was that media constitute a fifth estate, and play an oppositional role. In fact, the contrary is true: the media play a supportive role; moreover, they are a reflection of the society. What the media do in Barbados, therefore, reflects the essence of Barbadian society and supports the Barbadian social consciousness. The same can be said for the media in Canada.

You have done a stint as an advisor to a minister in the Mike Harris government. Was this your putting into practice your opinion, expressed in A Place Called Heaven, *that West Indians living here must abandon the notion that they are temporary sojourners and become active in the politics and economics of Canada?*

Yes, that was part of my thinking. At the time there was a very right-wing conservative government in power. Many immigrants felt that this government was hostile to them. I felt that the opposition to this government was polarizing, and was relegating Blacks to the periphery. I have argued consistently that if we are going to be a part of this society, and if we are going to assert our freedom here, we have to be present in government. Moreover, Black immigrants—all immigrant communities—embrace a wide spectrum of political beliefs, including the far right. I felt too that when we all park ourselves in opposition, we are doing a disservice to those of us in our own grouping who hold similar views. In addition, I believed, perhaps naively, that if one is in the circle of decision-making, one has the opportunity to influence policy.

Yet Chapter Six of your book A Place Called Heaven *analyzes the experiences of those African Canadians who have made the foray into politics, and the report, as you document it, is not very encouraging. And while most African Canadians are happy to see the faces of Blacks and other non-Whites in government, most wonder whether their presence extends beyond window dressing. It does not alter the fact that the salaries of university-educated Blacks are on par with those of high school educated Whites, and that the unemployment rate for Blacks is twice the rate for Whites. It does not alter the dominant majority's perception of Blacks as cheap labour and even cheaper humanity. How do you reconcile these views—your own as well as others'—with your own political involvement?*

I try to reconcile them by trying to isolate and, sometimes, even removing the question of intention. If we are going to enter into these spaces intent on remaining there as our pure essences—if there is such a thing—to express the Black voice, or the West Indian voice, or the immigrant voice, and we resort to a binary of "us" and "them," and insist that the "them" must listen to "us," then the process becomes for the "us" a frustrating monologue. And the de facto dialectical process that is politics is negated. Yet, if we enter the political space at any cost, our intentions might well turn out to be hollow. These are the extremes that politicians from so-called minority groups are sometimes trapped in. On the one hand, they might fall into the trap of advocating radical overly idealistic change; on the other they might dissolve into the party's fixed agenda.

Cecil, the issues you've explored in your journalistic pieces, in your columns, your essays and your novels do not promote the myths of the dominant majority. This comes with a price. What has it been in your case?

I don't believe there's such a thing here as a dominant majority. I see it as a majority that is fluid, constantly shifting. It is up to those of us, then, who feel that we are at the margins to become part of this majority—but at the place where we want to be, not where that fluid grouping decides our place is. In a sense, that's a central characteristic of democracy: the majority is always shifting. There may even be times when those who have been dominant in that majority themselves become a minority.

Canada represents itself officially as a nonracist welcoming, society. You challenge the nonracist notion, and you challenge the welcoming notion. I know too that in this regard the themes of your fiction aren't separable from the themes of your nonfiction. I am wondering what sort of reception you've had because of the challenges you have mounted to the official mythology.

Challenging a myth always involves paying a price—myth in the sense of a structuring ideology. Those who challenge myths are considered to be sacrilegious, given that myths are almost always deemed to be of divine origin. My challenge to those myths comes in my criticism of the decisions that the founders of Canada took. People take such criticisms personally. In self-defence, they say, "You can't understand our mythology because you are not a part of it. To you, it is a foreign language, a foreign culture." As regards the response to my work that raises these issues, reviewers respond with expressions like, "Here's a journalist trying to write fiction. He's trying to write too fast. He's dealing with too many issues. There are too many things he hasn't thought through, but that's probably because he is a journalist." When it comes to my journalism, they say: "This Foster guy, we can't understand him; sometimes he's a journalist, sometimes a writer of fiction. What is he?" The attitude is one of throwing up their hands. But the real reason, I think, is that they don't want to deal with the issues I raise.

I guess I had in the back of my mind the scurrilous remarks made about NourbeSe Philip when she won the Toronto Arts Award: comments to the effect that she's a writer who defecates on Canada, and therefore does not deserve to be rewarded. In other words, NourbeSe should be punished for her narratives that question the veracity of the dominant Canadian narrative.

The person who made that comment was perhaps less Canadian at that point (in terms of formal citizenship) than NourbeSe was. That person was, so to speak, "just off the boat." But he disembarked feeling that he belonged at the centre of Canadian society. He came from Britain. In his mythology, Canada is an extension of Britain. Leaving Liverpool or London for Toronto was hardly any different from settling in Birmingham or Manchester. Paradoxically, NourbeSe is an immigrant from Trinidad and Tobago, part of the Caribbean colonized by Britain, in Canada, a country colonized by Britain. Yet for him her place is on the margin.

Northrop Frye in his earliest reflections on Canadian literature has noted that it is people with insecure identities—immature cultures—that punish those who examine and question the mythology on which the national identity is founded. If I assert that Canada is not welcoming of immigrants of all races, and I am proven to be wrong, in the process the belief that Canada is a welcoming place for all would be strengthened, not weakened. It is via self-criticism that we get to know ourselves better.

In your novel No Man in the House *and in your memoir* Island Wings, *you transform emigration into a powerful trope with irony at its core. In both works emigration is fuel, shredder, and pathogen. For Howard it is initially fuel and then shredder. For you and your brothers it was similar. Perhaps pathogen is too strong a word. Comment?*

Pathogen is not too strong a word. If there's a reason to my writing, it has been to confront that pathology. Non-immigrants do not know the emotional cost of immigration. I did, from the time I was two, when the immigration process took my parents. They went elsewhere, well-intentioned, in search of a good life, and were devoured by the process. I grew up with the erroneous belief that my parents had gone to a promised land and I would join them. But what it resulted in for me was something of an early metaphorical death, when I realized that my parents were living in what I thought was heaven and had abandoned me (something similar to what your own character Pedro endures living with his grandmother when his mother goes to live in Canada), only to find out later that they were catching hell—that they had died metaphorically. Going to "the promised land" was not life; it was death. What could be more pathological!

I have therefore had to balance two sides of me: the side of me that always wanted to be an immigrant. Ironically, we participate in a mythology that is global, that is inexhaustible as Frye would say—that is bigger than Barbados, or Trinidad, or St. Vincent—and for our greatest actualization, we head farther afield, only to arrive in places like Canada and Britain to be told: "There is no place for you in our vision of who we are." We are pushed to the margins where a death of sorts occurs.

No one leaves a country of friends, family, customs, societal warmth, familiar landscapes—the things we enjoy, the very things tourists come in search of—nobody gives these up without the belief that she or he will attain something more valuable, more worthwhile. Trauma ensues when immigrants discover they've exchanged home for something worse.

No Man in the House *shows us Howard orphaned by the emigration of his parents;* Island Wings *shows us the travails of the character Cecil Foster—I say character because a memoir is constructed from memory and in the process the author turns him or herself into a character—enduring a similar process, with a difference: he provides answers for the questions Howard never answers. Would you like to comment on what accounts for the different configurations and emphases in both works, the differences between the memoir, let's say, and the novel?*

A very important point about the difference between *Island Wings* and *No Man in the House* is that *Island Wings* covers a longer period. *No Man in the House* ends when the character is around eleven. *Island Wings* ends when the character is around age twenty-four, by which time the character had long eaten the fruit of the tree of knowledge and life. To some extent the character in *No Man in the House* is still uncomplicated.

But he has already had his fall: when he realizes he will not be going to Britain.

But that fall is cushioned. It may even be a lift as opposed to a fall. I sometimes think that the protagonist in *No Man in the House* is the character that Cecil Foster in *Island Wings* would have wanted to be. Howard is idealized. He does swimmingly well in school. I did alright, but I did not pass the entrance exam that is the highlight of Howard's attainment, for it's the first of the levers that lift you from the peasant class into the middle class. I didn't have the mentoring that Howard had. So, in a sense, his is the idealized life that perhaps Cecil Foster felt he might have had had he gone to England.

But I look at fiction in many ways. One of them is the tremendous scope it leaves for dreaming. In a memoir, if we are honest, we are constrained to be factual.

Precisely. It's all a question of form. Fiction certainly allows us to dream. Fiction, for one thing, might show the many possibilities that are, but also the fact that we can only choose one. One can always play around with the choices not made and the choices made. Play them off against each other and even vicariously live them. Of course I root them in the social consciousness that envelops us.

Nonfiction—the memoir in this case—is restricted to the specific choice or choices made. All room for speculation is removed. What we present is the product of decisions taken. We are even limited in our evaluation of those choices. This leads me to reflect on the various memoirs or autobiographies available to us, beginning with St. Augustine's. I'm thinking of specifically the point: I was a sinner saved by grace. Let me show you how grace saved me. With fiction we could pretend that there was never a fall and, consequently, no need for a redemption.

In Island Wings *you show your parents emigrating from Barbados to England to realize their dreams—your father to become a musician, your mother to become a nurse, I think; and more than that to distance themselves from the narrow insular class and colour restrictions of Barbadian society. But the end of* Island Wings *reveals the extent to which the dreams that took your father to England destroyed him psychologically, poisoned your parents' marriage, and destroyed your mother's health. There's powerful tragic irony here, and it's deepened further when your father remarks that you and your brothers were fortunate to have remained in Barbados. How did you feel about your father's statement?*

I thought this is quite generous of you—ironically of course—after all the trials and privations you've put me through. I had to conclude that in a sense he was right. But I need to add that my father is an idealist. Immigrants must be idealistic. The motives that underlie emigration make it so. I could use myself as an example—I'm referring here to the ending of *Island Wings*: the belief that six hours after boarding a plane in Barbados I would arrive in Toronto in order to spread my wings. Sometimes when I reflect on this—now of course that I've eaten the fruits of Canada—I acknowledge that there is some value to being naïve. If I'd known before coming some of the adjustments I'd have to make, I'd have been paralyzed into inactivity. So coming back to my father, I would say that he was idealistic, but not pragmatic. I think we must temper idealism with pragmatism. There are times when we must cut our losses and run, and other times when we continue because we feel that one more banging of the head against the wall would break it down. But when the evidence is there that the wall isn't going to crumble, we have to devise ways of scaling it or living with it. In that sense my father was a victim of his idealism.

In your second novel Sleep on, Beloved, *the immigration-emigration trope plays out in a Jamaica-Canada setting, instead of a Barbados-Britain one. If Howard is orphaned by his parents' emigration, the characters in* Sleep on, Beloved *are orphaned, metaphorically-speaking, when they leave Jamaica. Comment.*

One of the things I was trying to do in *Sleep on, Beloved* was to show the hidden costs of immigration—which in effect were not so hidden; in fact, they were quite visible. It was merely a question of focusing our gaze away from them. I wanted to look at the cost to these women [single Caribbean women on the indentured domestic scheme]: socially, they are isolated; they are cut off from friends and relatives—the women they bond with, the women who teach them how to socialize—those women who are vital transmitters of the culture, an essential part of Caribbean reality. One of the tropes I relied on to show this disconnection is dancing as a reflection of these characters' innermost spirituality. By the time the reader gets to the third generation of this family in Toronto, by then cut off from any form of spiritual revitalization, dancing is no longer for divine reasons, not for God but for money. That spiritual link is broken and the characters are bereft and must struggle to fill the void.

And Slammin' Tar*?*

I see *Slammin' Tar* as a companion work to *Sleep on, Beloved. Slammin' Tar* tells the immigration story from the male perspective. Men loving men (perhaps—and I stress perhaps—also in a homosexual sense, but certainly homosocially), and taking care of men—men as complete human beings, not needing to posture consciously or unconsciously as men do when women are present—some of them in roles Caribbean people define as female: cooking, caring for the sick, as well as mentoring and transmitting culture.

And these are roles that they have not been adequately prepared for.

Indeed. But they learn quickly. There's a reason why I chose the gender perspectives. My observations of Canadian immigration tell me that this is in large part how it happens. Excluding the smattering of immigrants that came at the time of the World Wars, the first immigrants to Canada from the Caribbean were indentured female domestic servants. It is primarily their story that I attempt to tell in *Sleep on, Beloved.* Via Ona, I imagine how one of those workers attempted to find her way into, and to come to terms with, the new society. Today when we examine the statistics on English Caribbean immigrants, we see that the women have adjusted better to this society. I wasn't aware of these statistics when I wrote either novel, but I must have intuited this, for, as you see at the end of *Sleep on, Beloved,* Suzan is making some very practical decisions. She puts aside much of her idealism as she plans how she'll make a place for herself within the society she is in, rather than the society she dreams of being in. But this is paralleled by the fact her brother Telson is on his way to becoming a ward of the province, and an outcast of the state. Whether Suzan will be able to rescue him is one of the unanswered questions of the novel.

In the case of Slammin' Tar, *the men are on the periphery, far from the urban centres where power is concentrated and options, however limited, are available.*

More than that they are not empowered. They can make no claims on the system. They aren't Canadian citizens, or even landed immigrants. I wanted to deal as well with the role of the Black male in Canadian society. Black males have not integrated into the society as fully as Black females. Much of the alienation that the Black community feels is centred primarily around Black males. If *Sleep on, Beloved* and *Slammin' Tar* are read along those lines, you'll be able to see some of the issues I was grappling with: for one thing, that we had an immigration policy that brought, and still brings, West Indians here as indentured labour—Black women as de facto house slaves, and Black men as de facto field slaves. This policy has created a legacy we are grappling with today.

Certainly in terms of how skin colour continues to be perceived in this society: as a marker for cheap labour when it is black or brown.

Immigration is traumatic for Ona Morgan, Suzan Morgan and Joe Morgan, the three most important characters in Sleep on, Beloved. *By the end of the novel, Ona is a patient in a psychiatric hospital and Joe is in prison, and it's the incidence of Ona's mental breakdown that probably saves Suzan from participating in an armed robbery and probably getting killed. You show racism in schools and the workplace—a racism your narrator attributes in large part to Canada's role in the colonizing process. A typical White reader might accuse you of saying that Canada is a cruel place for Black immigrants. How would you respond to such a charge?*

In terms of how I construct reality, what I show in *Sleep on, Beloved* conforms to reality. This system of immigration has destroyed a lot of people.

Let's come back to Suzan. She narrowly escapes madness. Remember that when the nightmares become overbearing she is institutionalized. Suzan, unlike her mother, who was so beaten down that in the end she collapses, was able to dig deep within herself and find some resources that enabled her to cope with absolute alienation—the alienation from one's own self. What at a deeper level stabilized her was the very thing that on the surface was driving her mad: the drums, the drums that embodied her grandmother-the-teacher. When she entered that space and embraced it fully without the earlier ambiguity, it becomes a stabilizer, a grounding force.

It's interesting that you say this because when Ona herself becomes insane, it is this same reality that she reaches for. She begins "journeying," the very thing that she'd given up in order to become more Canadian—and at the Eaton Centre, a space where journeying is construed as insanity.

But by then the spirit was not very forgiving of her, because she had a history of rejecting the spirit. In a sense, the reasons why Ona puts aside her faith are different from the reasons that Suzan initially does so.

Suzan does not really put aside her faith. What she does is compartmentalize her life. One half of it holds on to her faith, and the other half—the half that opposes her faith—puts it aside.

Whereas Ona jettisons it altogether; feels that it hindered her from becoming what she wanted to be: a successful Canadian. But if we put all this within the context of Diasporic discourse, we must acknowledge that change is inevitable. It is total negation of self that is pathological. We compromise our sanity when we attempt to erase the part of ourselves acquired during the formative years.

This is indeed my disagreement with Neil Bissoondath's argument against multiculturalism. You, too, seem to be quarrelling with him. He cites you in Selling Illusions, *and you seem from your comment on the citation (in* A Place Called Heaven*), to be quite upset by the use he made of the citation.*

I felt that Neil misused that information. I had come out against exclusive Black schools, and he concluded that my argument in this regard meant that I discredit the notion of ethnicity. First of all, I don't consider Blackness to be ethnicity. Blackness is a racial categorization. But that aside, my core view is that the school system must provide an education that is truly multicultural—for everyone. Therefore, for me, the setting up of separate educational institutions and calling them our version of multiculturalism is a misnomer. It's segregation. In concrete terms, I argue for a school system in which Black history would be taught on the same basis as White history—as de facto Canadian history. In this respect, Neil misread me.

In the end all three characters in Sleep on, Beloved *are locked in their separate realities and blame the others for their plight. How much of this can be attributed to a hostile society? How much of this is merely existential? I was faced with these questions after reading the work.*

If that's the way that the book left you, then the book works because that's how I wanted the story to coalesce, in spite of the particular situations we've already discussed. There's no formula for happiness. We wake up in the morning and expect a certain number of things to function in a given way: we expect the water to run, the electricity to be on, etc. But there are the accidents and the things that don't function at crucial moments when we expect them to. We're never totally free, nor are we totally enslaved.

I believe strongly in free will. If you look at my autobiographical writing, you'll see that the element of a free spirit is always implicit. Despite the flaws in immigration, it provides a possibility for freedom. And there is some truth to the fact that I grew up believing that I would have to leave Barbados in order to test my reality against other realities, my system against other systems.

Joe perhaps had some choices. He is perhaps the most unfortunate of the characters. He finds himself in a situation where all his points of reference have disappeared. He grew up with definite notions of what it is to be a man, notions he couldn't implement here. Ona is used up by the system. But

Suzan's double-consciousness is in a sense what saves her.

Your novel Slammin' Tar *is framed at one level by a journalist's reporting on a group of migrant workers who come annually to a tobacco farm in Ontario for part of the year. Your journalist narrator is the omniscient Akan spider trickster Anancy, and his employer is the Akan supreme God Nyame. There is an existentialist ethos to this novel inasmuch as defeat is the lot of all the parties concerned. Quite clearly, this is primarily your fictionalized delineation of the migrant workers' dilemma. I couldn't but wonder when I read* Slammin' Tar *whether you'd undertaken this initially as a journalistic task but ultimately changed your mind and transformed the story into fiction in order to enhance its meaning.*

That's true. You've tapped into something here. I first wrote about the migrant farm workers when I was employed by *The Globe and Mail.* I did the research and thought that perhaps I'd convert it into a movie script. That didn't quite work out. I thought about turning it into a novel, a linear, realistic narrative. But it didn't work. Eventually while reworking it I hit upon the idea of turning it into an Anancy story, one that would give the story continuity but would also place it within a specific tradition. It also occurred to me that I'd never heard or read an Anancy story in which Anancy is the narrator. Because the stories were about Anancy, we never fully knew whether the truth was being told about Anancy. So in *Slammin' Tar* I give Anancy a voice, a flawed one, one that reflects his incertitude about himself and functions as a metaphor of the state of Africans living in the so-called New World, Africans who've never quite found their stride, their voice.

A challenge I gave myself was to explore how the individual brings about change, how much our history imprisons us, how much of it should we discard, how much of it we need to launch us into the future, how idealistic we should be. These constitute Anancy's chief problems. For one thing, he remains totally grounded in history. He wants history to repeat itself. History does, in his view at least, but in the process Anancy is never any further ahead. I felt that was part of Marcus Garvey's problem. It is for that reason that the narrator so closely identifies with Marcus Garvey; indeed he refers to him as the greatest man that ever lived; moreover, he is awaiting a second Marcus Garvey. Meanwhile Mother Nyame is telling him that there'll be no second Marcus Garvey. Times have changed. There is a need for new stories. We want new stories.

I've observed in Slammin' Tar *as well as in the works of Nalo Hopkinson and*

Afua Cooper—all three of you being writers from the Anglophone Caribbean—that you evoke the Akan supreme being and the legendary Akan-Jamaican ancestor figure, Nanny of the Maroons. This is new in the works of writers of Caribbean origin. Is this your deliberate attempt to foreground Africa?

Yes. And a lot of this comes together in *Dry Bone Memories*, in the spirit of jazz, which permeates the novel and which, for me, is a figuration of African cosmology. In a way, it's existentialism of a sort that serves as a vehicle for the tragedy of the human condition. This cosmology is omnipresent in *Sleep on, Beloved.* Grandma Ned dances for her God; she dances at the Crossroads; she believes that she is a direct descendant of African kings and queens; that the ancestral spirits were around her, guiding and protecting her. Even while on the plane to Canada, Suzan senses these spirits about her.

In *Slammin' Tar* these ancestral spirits are on the boat. Even when characters go insane the spirits are there. Moreover, wherever you find a Black person, an Anancy-type figure, in whatever guise, is never far away. We acknowledge this fact when we throw our libations; it's our acknowledgement that the spirits preexist us, that we are their most recent embodiments, and that when we dissolve they'll still be there. I'm very much aware of this African worldview. It's one of the reasons why in *Slammin' Tar* there's a story of why the beaches in the Caribbean became white. They are the bones of a jackass that tried to swim back to Africa. Something of a humorous look at the Back-to-Africa movement. In *Dry Bone Memories*, the African presence is shown in the behaviours of the characters and in the Gods that are worshipped. And talking about change, of the same being different, you'd notice too that in *Slammin' Tar*, I deliberately gave Anancy the more common Caribbean spelling, rather than the "Anansi" of the more familiar North American version. What does that choice alone say about me as a writer and the stories I want to tell, even in North America? What am I saying about my Black characters, about Blackness in general, in a place called Canada? Yes, this Canada is Caribbean; so, you see, there is something very positive to be said about immigration.

You came to Canada to avoid political persecution; this was a reversal of your earlier position—the one in which you'd consciously decided not to emigrate, to throw your lot in with fellow Barbadians and help to effect the dreams of this newly independent nation. Much of Dry Bone Memories *is about what has happened to those dreams. The newly independent Caribbean nation, which is the novel's primary setting, is indebted to a sort of perverse capitalism and dependent on dangerous sources of capital. I wondered to what extent the novel was some sort of figuration of the postcolonial/neocolonial situation in today's Caribbean.*

If I were to group my novels, I would say that *Sleep on, Beloved* and *Slammin' Tar* go together, and that *No Man in the House* and *Dry Bone Memories* belong together. I think that *Dry Bone Memories* picks up roughly in a chronological sense where *No Man in the House* ends. The former reflects the sort of disillusionment that set in following independence. We might say then that the naïve, unconflicted Howard of *No Man in the House* becomes the Jeffrey, who travels abroad and returns home, after which all hell breaks loose—fictionally. That might not be a bad reading of these novels.

Clearly, one of the promises of independence was that Blacks would take over the "plantation" so to speak, meaning the economy. Consequently Blacks would be able to find dignified spaces within the post-independence economy; projects that would improve life on the island would come into being, etc. However, what the novel shows is that the capital isn't there for such projects, and so governments turn to the drug barons, and the result is cataclysmic. This leads me to see your novel within the prophetic tradition: you show possibilities that exist, that could exist, and possible outcomes.

Of course, a novelist deals with possibilities. The novelists don't write truth strictly speaking. What they might do is observe the way things are headed. Then they might connect the dots and prognosticate possible outcomes.

Let me say, turning to the plantation trope in *Dry Bone Memories,* that this comes through in the different views that Jeffrey and his father hold about the building of museums, for example. His father muses that the building of museums is tantamount to his going to his wife's (Jeffrey's mother's) graveside and spending the rest of his time there. For his father, museum-building is worshipping the dead—not that he is opposed to the traditional beliefs and practices, but as you know, beyond a certain point we consider this idolatry. In a sense, Jeffrey's position is a confused one. He is mixing up the practices we engage in privately with those we do publicly. In a way, he is copying what he has observed in North America.

*As regards technique—we began talking about that a while back—*Dry Bone Memories *is your most experimental form of storytelling. Much of the story is told in a surreal fashion and has the improvisational feel of jazz. Why did you choose to tell the story this way?*

I wanted to tell a story about life in much of its complexity. For me life is full of contingencies, a fact that is at the heart of African cosmology. African cosmology anticipates the contingent. Africans feel obliged to name phenomena, lest the unnamed force is usurped by something else with catastrophic consequences. So much so that much is made of negotiating changes that come in rapid succession. I wanted to confer some of this to the novel's structure, and I hoped that what I'd call a jazz structure would help me do it. You know, the basic structure with someone taking off on a solo performance. The improvisations, the riffs. So we have the universals, but we also have the particulars. I have seen this fluidity, not just in jazz but also in calypso and gospel music. Just as in life we might move from one level to another—or however we term it—I have noted the same thing with African-derived music. In each new setting it changes form. I am intrigued by circularity, and so the movement forward is also a movement back to the beginning, or vice versa: taking you forward in order to take you backward.

Books are now seen as part of the consumer culture and are published or rejected based on their revenue-generating potential. What implications does this state of affairs have for future Black voices in Canadian literature?

I used to think that the economics of publishing accounted for publishers' bringing out very few books by Black authors. Now I have changed my mind about that. Setting aside the Margaret Atwoods, most publishers will tell you that they can count on the fingers of one hand the writers who make a living from their writing. One thing we had, coming out of the 1960s, was a hefty state subsidy for publishing. We know too that most of the literary awards are a way of conferring honours on certain individuals. There are no objective criteria for determining that book X is better than book Y—I have sat on award juries—especially if you believe, as I do, that writers create out of their particular social ethos. Beyond the basic issues of form, etc., how do we determine what is a good book? That's always a subjective decision. What we are really dealing with is how society constructs itself—its mythology—and how it wants to see itself portrayed in narrative and by whom. I think that before we become accepted as writers, the culture has to see Blackness as inherent to its well-being.

Therefore you dismiss publishers' statements that books by Black authors don't sell. Are you also saying that cultural power and political power bolster each other, are interlinked?

Yes. I'll give you an example. This year [2002], there's a hectic ongoing debate about immigration. There are three notable publications on the subject that came out within a week: one by the Fraser Institute and two by two Toronto publishing houses. What's significant about them is whose voices and opinions they left out. That's their way of controlling the debate.

Cecil, thanks for letting me discuss your writing with you.

My pleasure, Nigel.

Claire Harris

How do you envisage your role as a writer?

The primary job, I think, is a groping towards truth, towards the real. Whatever I can find in spinning that is the world. I think reality is obviously viewed as a construct. What exactly is going on? How was it constructed? And in any case, why the world—physical, social and psychic? Why this planet? How did it come to exist? How did we get here?

And a new vision to suggest another way of seeing to people who haven't had to do this; who in fact have no way of thinking about this; society so rarely introduces us to other civilizations, other ways of being without trying to rank them. So writing is a relief. However, since I am a descendent of slaves, from one of the most thoroughly colonized countries in the world—almost five hundred years of unbroken colonization—I can't help knowing the human race. I'm from a deeply catholic, highly literate family, and I spent most of my life—from the age of eleven to the age of twenty-nine—in schools and university halls run by nuns. Then I taught in a convent school. I looked around one day and thought: here are these people, teaching with me, who taught me, who went to the convent, who went to university, came back here, and are still here ! And I had no intention of spending my life like that, and so I left and came to Canada, which was an accident. Originally, I was going to New Zealand. The weirdest things happen.

Now, I think what is important about my background, what I think people see in the poems is what I learnt from my great-aunts and my grand-parents. From them I learned the wisdom to counter what I was being taught about who I was. In school it was an education that concentrated on what the Europeans had done, the good things they had done. There was no discussion at all—ever—of slavery . . . and certainly no discussion of the Great Wars and the devastation of the last century.

Why do you think there were no discussions of slavery?

One of the functions of colonization was not merely to enslave you physically, but to enslave you morally as well. The colonizers couldn't claim to be civilized even as they engaged in slavery. Civilization and slaveholding don't go together. Neither can there be any acknowledgement of the fact that they are where they are precisely because they have benefited, and are benefiting, from slavery...and its aftereffects.

You put it so well ... NourbeSe Philip, Dionne Brand, Austin Clarke, Cecil Foster, myself—our writing is bound up with uncovering who we are as individuals and as societies throwing off the colonial yoke.

Exactly. Who we are! I think a noteworthy fact is that when slavery was abolished in Trinidad and throughout the West Indies, people walked off the plantations the very same day and would not come back. The plantation owners had to resort to bringing in the Indians. At the time, the British in Trinidad found themselves in a difficult situation: the French and Spanish accounted for the overwhelming majority of Whites in Trinidad at a time when the British were fighting France and Spain. They mistrusted them. Not only that: the Catholic Church had set up a Catholic school in every tiny little village for the purpose of Catholic indoctrination, and the British coming in had to counteract that. The only way they could break it was by putting up their own schools. And that was our foundation. They needed a civil service and couldn't trust the Spanish and the French so they had to educate Blacks for those roles. They needed tradesmen. They could not trust the Spanish and the French, so they worked with the Blacks. The training schools were set up, and the extramural department was set up to provide training for people who had not been able to go on to university. Then, because they had to put up their own schools, they had to train teachers. And that's why Trinidad ended up with quite so many secondary schools, more than Barbados or any of the other British West Indian colonies.

My impression is that the Black community expects the work of literature to be temple, community fair, and academy. Does this reflect your own experience?

In *Drawing Down a Daughter*, there is a section with a pregnant woman who has a serious argument with her husband and drives off leaving her husband standing on the pavement. I read this to an audience in which there were four Black people. Afterwards one of the Black women asked me: "Do you think these people know what mamaguy means?" I smiled and said, "It's a Canadian word now. I'm here."

It was evident from your two first collections of poems—both copyrighted in 1984—that you demand a very active participation from the reader of your poems. Would you like to comment on this?

Poetry began as an oral form—in all its aspects—from regular rhythm to rhyme. All the features we associate with poetry have to do with the mnemonic function. Paper, the page, has become a part of it. I wouldn't dream of publishing with someone who proposes altering my poems. Besides, there's nothing new under the sun. I use techniques present in the first third of the twentieth century. What's original is that I have combined several forms in order to say what has to be said. And I deliberately make it possible to read down as well as across. But apart from making it possible to read down and across, none of this is really conscious. I find myself sitting at the typewriter and the words come in a form on the page. The very first poem I wrote came like this. It's the poem "Seen in Stormlight," the last poem in *Fables from the Women's Quarters.* People said to me afterwards, "How did you know this was happening?" I was getting little bits of lines that I wrote down, and I had no idea what was going on. I had five pages before I realized that it was a single poem. The other thing that was happening was I would write it and would need to put some lines a little further in from the margin. After I'd finished the poem, I showed it to J. P. Clark, who was then my mentor. He asked me, "Why did you do this?" And I replied, "I don't know," because I didn't. And that almost has continued up to this day. I know that I would lose a poem if I try to force it to the form. I have tried it and lost poems.

So the poems dictate their own form. You are the scribe in a sense. The poem guides your hand.

Exactly. It's frighteningly sometimes like automatic writing, except that I know now what I'm doing, and after I get the poem, I spend ages, years, working on it.

Making sure that you've found the right word, the right sound . . .

That it's in the shape I want it, that I have spaced it, so that it says what I want it to say. It's in this that the real work is. Sometimes pieces of poems come years apart.

When I did *She*, I actually ended up sending my publisher one hundred and fifty pages. I said, "Look, I know there's a book here, but I don't know what belongs where." She pulled out some pieces and said, "I think this is another book." After that it was easy because I could see then what I had. As for the other pieces, I think I know what I'm going to do with them now. But earlier, when all the material was coming at the same time, I could not tell what belonged where.

Do your publishers push you to change the arrangements of your poems on the page, for publishers do want the largest possible audience for their books?

No, no one directly involved with my work ever has. Other publishers simply turned it down. Publishers want the largest audience for their books; but, in my case, they recognized that something relatively new was happening, and I think they foresaw the university-college market. But I'll add that Goose Lane has sold some thirteen hundred copies of *Fables from the Women's Quarters* and Williams-Wallace sold more than that; they had three or four reprints. *Drawing Down a Daughter* has sold well too. And I know it's not because people are going to the bookstores to buy them, but because they are being used in university courses. I credit that to the unusualness of the style. A lecturer in Britain has told me that she teaches it in an MA class, and the reason she does is that each year the class comes up with new interpretations. This is exactly what I wanted.

Because of the spaces you leave on the page and an absence of punctuation for the most part, you require the reader to hear your poems, to sift and connect the separate parts. What do you feel would be lost if you did not present the poems this way? If readers had an easier time of it?

I need that participation. I recognize it. But I think that reading isn't about what's on the page. It's what the reader brings to the page.

Except that the page must elicit what's already in the reader.

Yes. And so the poem is a guide. In the end the poem is the poem that the reader makes of this interaction. I provide a narrative and I leave spaces for the reader to fill in.

The spaces might be read as silences, as implicit statements in that they contextualize sound, are important, so that sound might be shaped by silence the way, in one of your poems, light sculpts darkness. Comment.

They are meant to shape, to interrogate meaning as well as history:

But
What would the dead have said?
My enslaved
Your colonized dead
My silenced
Your transported dead
. . . Let them whisper into our heads . . .

And remember, what has happened to one human being can happen to another again and again. Different actors, same story. We have a limited repertoire . . . . which poetry shares with those who are, those who were, and those who will be (I hope).

Your poem "Of Iron Bars and Cages," is in three columns, intended, I think, for the reader to understand some sort of simultaneity of the three interlinked poems—something like three actors on stage speaking at the same time. If my reading is correct, it seems to me that this way of putting the poem on paper is a protest against the limits of print . . . .

I never protest against a page—all that lovely white space. If it's a page you can always reread it. It's hearing that is limited. Moreover, what's there is not simply three poems. It depends on whether you read across for one line or two, then down, then up again, then across again, then down. It gives you choices, and you would be surprised by what you'll find once you do that. Moreover, it hedges the form on the page, and it constricts and strangles the speaker in the centre, especially where it is used as ritual. Hence the title. Especially because it takes place in the courtroom.

You are familiar with Rousseau? He had five daughters and gave them up for adoption. He didn't record their birthdays so when he came into some money and wanted to locate them, he couldn't find them. In learning this, one sees the damage the Catholic Church, Christianity as a whole, has done to the world. All because the church needed to have political control. Constantine did irreparable damage to Christianity.

His actions expunged the valuable, what I often call the soul of Christianity, the material contained in the four gospels.

The New Testament is the real Christianity.

The corruption of Christianity begins with Paul.

Exactly. The whole thing has become a mess. To me, that's a tragic characteristic of human beings. It doesn't matter who comes. They claimed that Jesus was the son of God. They created a cult around his teachings and his persona. The cult became a church. That conferred power. Power became the basis of the faith, and pervasive power stifles decency.

Once the power exists to force others to do our bidding, other considerations get elided.

It amazes me that these people still attended church. The slave owners went to church!

But that's because they saw religion as legitimizing their power and as a tool to consolidate and expand such power.

To return to "Of Iron Bars and Cages," one of the things I hope it does is sensitize people to what's going on, about the horror in such institutions. The very act of reading the poem in this way leads to the creation of a new poem. Every time I read this poem I read it differently. Whatever I think or feel, at the moment I am reading it, influences what's there, and, conversely, what's in the poem influences what I'm thinking or feeling.

And brings about a new way of understanding.

There's a Caribbean sensibility that the wife/mother in "Nude in an Armchair" brings to the trial. She says something to the effect that knowing her culture she wasn't supposed to leave her husband; she endured the beatings because she needed security for her children, etc. I'm sure feminists cannot accuse you of not being on their side, but I could easily hear some Black radical feminist woman wondering, why did Claire do that, why didn't she . . .

Because it's true. Actually when I wrote this, a child in our city had had a baby. She'd told no one that she was pregnant. She lived in an upper middle-class neighbourhood; her mother had left; she lived with her father. She had a brother; he was mentally challenged but was there for her. She gave birth alone. She and her brother wrapped the baby in a doll's blanket, placed it in a box, and put it on the doorstep of a woman who they felt liked children. The woman was away, and the baby froze to death. The judge removed both children from their father's custody.

These attitudes are not only Caribbean. We hear about them from Ukranian women, Polish women—women from many cultures. Imagine a woman today feeling that the most important thing is to get married! Five years ago I met a young teacher who felt this. Young women would go out with boys who have no intention of marrying them and have babies for them because they think that's a woman's job. So while a few educated women escape this trap, there's a huge mass of women who are still trapped by these notions; they still live by the old rules. They feel incomplete unless they have "a man to protect them." I think that if you have a man for these reasons you are in deep trouble.

But he could be complementary.

You could count such men on the fingers of one hand.

In the last poem in Travelling to Find a Remedy, *the speaker says something to the effect that I would have thought that my life would be richer, but this is what it is, etc. There your speaker measures everything in terms of cultural conflict: the roles that the woman would be obliged to play, the compromises that the man—*

. . . isn't prepared to make.

This underscores what you just said.

I think life is risk; one usually discovers the crux of the matter, whatever the topic, when it's too late.

In "Where the Sky is a Pitiful Tent," a poem, I would argue, in which your metaphors and imagery are used to deal with the pain the speaker feels about the atrocities that occurred in Guatemala (which I think you employ as metonymy for similar horrors around the globe)—you put in footnotes the data that inspired the poem and thereby engage in what's termed metafiction. Why?

To begin with, I got all the information for that poem from an Amnesty International publication. I am a member of Amnesty International. I had gone into the highlands of Mexico and seen how people there live—this was in 1972. What I wondered was how these women, given their culture, were dealing with their situation. This poem, like many of the poems I write, was written as a way of finding out. It took a long time to write it, to discover what one could do. A year after the poem was written, I read in *The American Poetry Review* the Rigoberto Menchu story, and realized that here was someone who had been a victim of the experience the poem explores. So I appended the Menchu story; and, of course, appropriated it.

When men go off to fight such wars, women are left alone with the children. They know what's happening. They see the tortured bodies at the side of the road. What can they do? Nothing! They are totally, utterly, helpless.

This poem and many of your poems seem to be attempts to give shape, voice, texture to suffering in order to highlight, in some cases, its tragic futility and, in others, its Sisyphean (existential) quality. I thought of Robert Graves' remark that the poem can be compared to the pearl the oyster creates to coat the grain of sand in its flesh.

I am the type of personality of whom that might well be said. I write often out of a sense of horror and immense curiosity about the human race. For a long while I wrote because I wanted to find out what human beings would not do. I see that many people, including some immigrants, are benefiting from the past horrors. I didn't go to live in the US because I didn't want to be taxed for their crimes. I can go home to Trinidad; my pension would once have made me relatively well off there, except that I would stop writing.

In this regard as well, many of your poems deal with a working out of problems, a coming to terms with change and betrayal, dying, loss of innocence—poems like, "In the Dark, Father," "The Fall," "This Fierce Body."

It seems to me, naïve as I then was, that human beings were capable of such beauty that, provided with slightly better than a living wage and better health care, we would all be better human beings. I had to disabuse myself of this.

Previously a good sentence, the rhythms of poetry, rhyme, etc., used to lull me into meaning. Before I began to write, I made it a point to learn to read, to recognize the nuances that hold meaning. Then it was that I knew that what I wrote had to be about the real world. I've always jotted, even when I was a little girl. I write to make things clear to myself. Narrative has a beginning middle and end. Personally, I think the passage [from life to death] might be interesting. For one thing, I want to know—and I hope I would be conscious when it happens—what happens. This energy has to go some place.

Well, you have a poem that deals, I think, with your mother's death, in which the process of dying is depicted. In the case of your father, the poem shows him already dead.

That's because my mother died more slowly; she had Alzheimer's. My father died suddenly of a heart attack. His was the first "real" death . . . the second actually. The first had been a girl in my class when I was eight years old.

In "Black Sisyphus" the father is presented as Adam. He is Adam enchanting the snake that is the colonizer. Racism implies an automatic devaluing. We are still colonized; they are still deluded. Every time we think something is okay—we know, this, at last—we discover that it isn't. Each generation has to bear the same damn burden over and over again.

You work extensively with personae. In The Conception of Winter, *there are the three women vacationing and the poet—a persona herself—recording them and herself. There are the personae in* Drawing Down a Daughter *and* She, *although I think you call these last two works novels in poetry. How do your invented personae aid you in organizing and shaping your material?*

It helps you envision it. That's really the thing. It humanizes what you're depicting. It imbues the subject with life, rescues it from being an abstraction. It does something poetry hardly does any more. When narrative poetry was the norm one learnt something. And it's much easier to decipher. People need narrative.

There's as well the empathy that the reader is able to develop for the characters.

You expressed an interest in multiple selves in your persona Jane whose Barcelona winter vacations transform her into someone else, and presumably she's healthier for it. But in She *you explore this multiple personality phenomenon from a point of view of pathology. Comment.*

I want to suggest, among other things, that there's a great deal going on in *She.* There's the deep colonization of the West Indian woman and, specifically in Trinidad, all the many personalities lurking in us and the relative ease with which we could choose. Which personality is one going to be on any given day? I think it's one of the reasons that Trinidadians are so creative—calypso, steelband music—an entirely new musical instrument that evolved into an orchestra. Some years ago our consul in Switzerland told me there were twenty-five steelbands in Switzerland. I asked if there were Trinidadians in Switzerland. She said no; moreover, the pans are imported from Japan.

Black Trinidad and Tobago has given the world a great deal. For an island with such a small population, there are such preeminent figures like CLR James, the historian and our late prime minister Eric Williams, Derek Walcott (who though born in St. Lucia) lives in Trinidad extensively, the Naipauls, and many others.

And certainly Earl Lovelace.

Lovelace certainly. NourbeSe [Philip] and Dionne [Brand].

One of the advantages that Trinidad had over many of the other islands, even Jamaica, is that several cultures came together there and cross-fertilized one another.

Indeed. It's a remarkable compliment for one small island. Remarkable really what Indian Trinidad has given to the culture. Consider the Naipauls. Then there's the music, the food and the fusion of the different societies. We don't as a rule shoot each other. Whatever violence takes place there is usually between members of the same ethnic group, as here in Canada.

One advantage of this is that Trinidadians can adapt easily to foreign cultures. Another is the clarity it gives about who one is and where one belongs. Somehow we have learnt that we cannot afford serious ethnic strife in an island so small. Think of all the groups: the Indians, the Chinese, the Blacks, the French Creoles, the Portuguese and all the others. That is why when the uprising took place in 1970 and the legislature was attacked—to begin with, there were about ninety of them, including women and children; eighteen were directly involved—when the government agreed to their demands but handcuffed them as soon they were outside—their exclamation was: "But, man, you promise me!" They felt they could take the authorities at their word. In a culture with so many possibilities for interethnic conflict, we have had to rely on each other's words.

But the language of Trinidadians—I'm speaking of the demotic—possesses an interesting vocabulary that suggests chameleon-like qualities. There's also Trinidad's unique vocabulary that many other islands have adopted. I can think of words like coonoomoonoo, boomboomber, mamaguy, warbeen, jackobat, mackoman, jamette, liming, etc.

That vocabulary is in part about fighting, about contesting situations, without putting one's self in a situation where one could be accused of actually saying what both know has been said. It's a way of answering the master without giving him the evidence to fire you. I think it's also about identity, particularly in the last thirty–forty years. Where before the educated used to speak British English, now they use the demotic, except in formal situations. In any case, everyone switches with ease between the two forms.

You are comfortable writing long poems. Most poets eschew them. What are the advantages of working with the long poem?

The long poem is valuable because of the space it provides to think things through thoroughly. It also allows space for varieties of craft that one couldn't do in a form like the sonnet.

Even so, many of your poems are short. What are they best for?

As fillers. In telling a story, there are times when I want to create moments of intensity, or to comment on the action, or insert emotional tinges, or provide setting.

Most of your poems position your speaker in two pivotal places: in a lookout above Bow River and at Lopinot—these being shorthand (synecdoche) for radically different/polarized realties. Indeed one could write whole essays about both pivots (maybe radii is a better word) in your poetry. Would you comment on the mythic dimension both places confer to your poetry?

One reason is that I like rivers: the light on the water, the sheer beauty of water, the flow, the currents, the movement. The fact that rivers are going somewhere suggests possibilities. Lopinot was our holiday home. It was a magical place. The Bow reminds me of it. But here it is a grownup's vision of escape as well as freedom from expectation. But that's not how I use it in the poems. In them, it anchors the speaker to a specific place.

I couldn't write in Trinidad because I felt confined. I would have been afraid to write because the readers would have believed that whatever I wrote had happened to me. I have had similar experiences here, one with a woman writer, herself a poet. People forget how large the imagination looms.

You have some secondary pivots as well; for example, the old man on the roof in what I call the Barcelona poems. Comment.

My notion of travelling in Europe at that time was booking a hotel here, and, when I got there, get up early and check out all the hotels before selecting one. When I got there they initially said that they had no rooms. I said nothing and eventually they told me that they had a couple of rooms but didn't know if I would want them. It's where their waiters used to stay, right up on the roof. I asked to see them. They were comfortable rooms that opened onto a large private balcony and gave a view onto the roof above the street. They were about three times the size of the regular rooms. When we got up there, this woman rolled her father out in a wheelchair onto their balcony and covered him with a blanket. It was a beautiful balcony with lots of flowers. She would come out and talk to him and go back inside. Then one morning he was no longer there.

His presence is pivotal in the poem.

I always think of death in terms of loss. It should also be seen as change as well. I want it to come when I'm ready for it. This man was dying, and he was loved. I am intrigued by the way death happens—one moment you're here; the next you're clearly not; the fragility of life and of time: the one thing we can't hold.

In Drawing Down a Daughter, *I was intrigued by the conflict—an irresolvable one, in essence—between Patricia and her husband. The conflict really is around what's the ideal society in which to raise a child. This novel foregrounds some of the major conflicts informed Black parents have about raising their children here.*

I personally would not raise a child here. We would always be engaged in an identity battle. The texts such a child would need to read are unavailable here. Multiculturalism is no help here. Black children here face daunting problems, especially the children of the expanding Black middle classes. It is doubtful whether such children could grow up whole. Most African students in the school system here perform much better than Black children from the Caribbean, and the reason is that they are more secure in their identity.

There are certainly the destructive roles that the mainstream society has reserved for Blacks.

Exactly!

And many Blacks are willing to oblige and become trapped. Of course, it's easy to understand why. Everyone wants to be accepted. No one wants to stand out except in the ways that please those who have the power to punish and reward.

And the roles they expect are the roles for which American TV has programmed them. They are cast as fools or criminals. I was at a school where Black and White boys were treated differently on the sports field. I witnessed a school baseball match in which the White boys threw the ball successfully and received modest applause. When the Black boy threw the ball and missed the school went wild with cheering. Unmerited, but it was their way of emphasizing what his role should be. He was also good in the corridor with the girls fawning over him. Becoming a doctor? Excelling at academics? No. That brings them no reward. What rewards them is being "cool"; the way they dress, the sports they play, and the cheap entertainment they provide. The number of Black Canadian boys lost because of such subtle programming is frightening. I know of at least a dozen, including one whose father was a senior engineer for one of the oil companies here—obviously he had to be outstanding. His mother taught at the college level. He is on the street busking. His sister on the other hand is a lawyer, and we know why.

But our female Black students also get chewed up by the system. Though, unlike the males, they are usually able to rise again after they've fallen. I have seen it in the schools in Montreal where I've taught—schools with over 20 percent Black population and in one, for a year, where the Black population was 60 percent. It was a very painful experience. I came to exactly the same conclusion as you: if I had children I would not raise them here. When I meet Black parents who've raised children successfully I want to ask them, How did you manage?

Exactly!

I know one such family in which all four children have been successful. It stands out because it is the exception. You and I are from the Caribbean. We know the heritage of education, how the society encourages us to surpass our academically successful relatives.

My father's refrain was, "We are teachers; now you get to be a lawyer." My father ended up being inspector of schools. All the children have been fortunate in that we have done partly what our parents wanted and partly what we wanted.

Of course, one could tie the conflict in Drawing Down a Daughter *with your widely anthologized: "Policeman Cleared in Jay-Walking Case" and, perhaps, with "this was the child I dreamt" (it is for the reasons implicit in these poems that the father in* Drawing Down a Daughter *wants his daughter raised in Trinidad).*

Exactly. The institutions that are supposed to protect everyone become part of the oppression.

History is an important theme in your poetry. And one way you evoke it is by challenging the colonizer's view of heroes ("Under the Feet of Heroes"), as well as the colonizer's impact on First Nations.

The colonizers are still here. And now they are many-hued. Immigrants continue to arrive and become colonizers. I think the situation is worsening. The First Nations are up against formidable forces. Their culture has been assaulted, the best of their land taken from them, the colonizer's god and values imposed on them, and yet they are expected not to be traumatized. They must get their languages back and take what they consider valuable in Western culture and weave that into the fabric of their real lives. They need their elders, not colonizers. We must never forget that this civilization was born in blood.

Women as bearers of tradition are lauded in your work. Comment.

This has to do with my own family. After the violent way we were brought from Africa, broken tradition was all we were left with. But we have been able to enrich those fragments with our own lengthening of the story. In my own family, it was the women who told the stories. My sisters and I tell those stories to our nieces. My brother asks: how can you remember these things? I had a Carib great-great-aunt, who when I knew her was already in her late fifties. She lived with a sister who had a Carib kitchen with all the implements. They lived on a small plantation that they owned. They cultivated cocoa among other things. When we were at Lopinot they were about a mile from us. We would take shortcuts through the woods. She took us walking and told us stories during the walks. She didn't know the Carib language. Her mother once did, but was now silent. She died at one hundred and three years old. I was around ten when she died and by then she was no longer speaking.
When I came to write *She*, I felt the need to explore what had happened to my Carib forebears. How could it be that someone lands on your island, you meet him on the shore with gifts—your traditions teach you to be generous to visitors—and his response is that you would make wonderful servants? These people are barbarians. I would say were, except that their despicable acts are ongoing.

"Framed" is an extended metaphor for two women whose destinies are different. Yet your poetry discourages any embracing of determinism. Comment.

People are entitled to their own fate even under the greatest adversity.

You employ two key words: "conjure" and "signify" that hint at how you create. Comment?

Conjuring is appropriate insofar as it is what I do. In signifying I draw attention to the thing—to make it mean. Both of these words are used to indicate commenting on, or reordering whatever story one has been saddled with. They indicate refusal of the way one is being "seen"/ "heard."

Many of your poems seem to depict mystical moments, epiphanies. I am referring to the way you "conjure" meaning/light from language as a way of expanding consciousness, of pushing back the darkness. In the end much of this must be Sisyphean with only the poem as proof of the journey/struggle. Comment.

One of the serious things I'm trying to do is never to repeat what I've already done. There are many books of poetry published in Canada, but upon reading them, one notices the vast similarities among them—the same themes and techniques over and over again. In the case of some writers, one also sees that they get to the entrances of places where they would not dare to go.

George Elliott Clarke laments the fact that the critics who've so far dealt with your work are not equal to the task. How do you feel about the critical response your work has received?

I have a rule not to read what critics say. I recall a review on *Drawing Down a Daughter* which said, "When I first heard the name Claire Harris, I thought of someone White." Imagine reading this! Think of the depth of historical ignorance in that statement! I don't want to spend my time responding to critics. I feel that my work will live or die on its own merit.

To what extent do you feel that power in the political and economic sphere affects power in the cultural sphere?

It affects it totally. We'd be naïve to think otherwise. I once heard somebody say, "What's the point of this book? It has nothing to do with me." Power is what counts in every sphere in Western society. When the work makes them uncomfortable, they reject it but give different reasons.

Most of the books by Black writers challenge the various national myths and are therefore unpopular with white readers. What implications does this state of affairs hold for the Black voice in Canadian literature?

I say we'd better make friends with the Europeans, continental ones. They are way ahead of Canadians in wanting to experience the art of other cultures. The Scandinavians and the Germans are extremely interested in what we do. I would say that Canadians, like Americans—and in fact the colonial powers *need* to see us in certain ways to justify their consistent, ongoing barbarism based on a profound and deliberate ignorance of people of colour. Human beings have to believe that they are "good," "sensible," etc. How can anyone afflicted with this history and its necessary shifts of vision live, if she or he is a decent person? How can a decent person accept and justify the material, physical, and, worst of all, psychological damage inflicted against people of colour? Look at what they've created in Africa?

How might we get around the marginalization some of us receive from Canadian publishers and book buyers?

I think it's time that we put together every five years or so an important conference where we bring together all the important Black writers and scholars of our literature from the US, from Europe, from everywhere. And the very fact that those voices would be here would provide the writing with the exposure it needs. We have to show Canadian publishers that people from elsewhere recognize the work we are doing.

Any other aspects of your writing I haven't addressed but which you consider important?

We've covered a lot of ground.

Thanks for letting me discuss your writing with you.

Lawrence Hill

Lawrence, since your work is set in Canada and the US, would you, for the benefit of our readers, provide a brief biography regarding your years in both places?

Sure. I am forty-five. I was born in 1967 in Newmarket, Ontario, about twenty miles north of Toronto. I grew up in Toronto. My parents are American immigrants. They got married in 1953 and came to Canada that same year from Washington DC. They raised their three children in Toronto. I grew up in Toronto and have lived mostly in Canada. I lived in the US for a year, pursuing a master's degree at Johns Hopkins University in Baltimore. I have travelled a bit in the States, working here and there, and I have lived in other parts of the world but only briefly—three trips to West African countries, one trip to South Africa, and various trips to France and Spain. I have lived in different parts of Canada, but Canada has always been my home base.

It's interesting to hear you say this, because in Any Known Blood, *you evince such a feel for Baltimore, one would have thought you'd lived there for a considerable length of time.*

During the year I was at Johns Hopkins, I tried to get to know the city well. I hadn't then written much of *Any Known Blood*, but I knew that Baltimore was going to be part of the setting for the novel. I visited a lot of Black churches and tried to ferret out much of the information I thought I would need. While working on the novel I made return trips to seek additional information.

How do you envisage your role as a writer?

As a writer? To write as well as I can. To write as honestly and meaningfully as I can. At the very least, write something that stands up to my own standards of creativity in imaginative writing. As a writer, I don't want to die before I nail down as much as I can. As a writer, I have the illusion of temporarily stopping the sands of time from slipping between my fingers. It's a way of defining and reshaping life in ways that are satisfying to me. It's an opportunity to reassemble the world in a way that has some resonance and meaning for me. It gives another run at things, and it gives me a chance to make sense of things as I work my way through them, so my role as a writer initially is deeply personal; it's to make sense of the world . . .

For yourself?

For myself. The first impulse to write is an entirely egocentric one in which I want to satisfy my need to grapple with the world. And I think I have many responsibilities—as a father and as a citizen of this country and an inhabitant of the world, who cares about a number of social and other issues. But my role as a writer is to listen to my muses and to run with them, and to be as honest and as piercing and engaging as possible.

Do you see writing as having a function?

I am sure it does—a major social function. It depends on the time and place where you live. There are many people in many parts of the world who'd think this question absurd because it would be obvious to them that writing is involved with some sort of liberation struggle: the need to bring apartheid to its knees—which, thankfully, has happened—the need to explore horrendous abuse in some system. Of course writing has a function. But its function varies according to the time and place. Even so, writers of the same time and place will have distinct interpretations of their obligations. It's not a surprise that many writers around the world are incarcerated—some tortured and killed—because of what they've written. Writing clearly has a function.

Let's switch to audience for a moment. My impression is that the Black community expects the work of literature to be temple, community fair, and academy. Does this reflect your own experience?

Well a lot of people have a lot of expectations about what literature should be. People of African heritage don't have a monopoly on trying to impose their demands on their writers. Thankfully these expectations vary from person to person and even from writer to writer. I think it's a very common expectation. When writers belong to racial minority groups in places such as Canada, there's often the expectation that their characters should be role models, that they uphold certain ideals. My grandmother, who was a very bright, university-educated, dynamic woman, detested the musical *Porgy and Bess.* She was born in 1896 and died in 1985. She felt it was defamatory to Black people. All that cavorting and carousing on stage. I understand why she felt that way. But I don't respond to *Porgy and Bess* the same way.

This is a long way of answering your question. Some people might argue, or at least expect, that books by Blacks should fulfill certain identifiable functions. I try not to listen to that. I don't want my writing to be influenced by the moral expectations of other people.

In the introduction to his latest book, Odysseys Home: Mapping African Canadian Literature, *George Elliott Clarke laments what he observes as a tendency by many critics to subsume African Canadian literature under the rubric of African American literature or to elide it altogether. A book like* Any Known Blood *might very well traverse those boundaries.*

As the son of American immigrants, when I moved from children's to adult literature and began reading what was on my parents' bookshelves, much of what I found was American literature: authors like James Baldwin, Malcolm X, Eldridge Cleaver, Langston Hughes, Richard Wright, Ralph Ellison. These were the authors I read as I tried to understand who I was and where I belonged.

Sorry to interrupt, but there wouldn't have been much African Canadian literature available then.

The only African Canadian writer I knew of whose work would have been on people's bookshelves was Austin Clarke. The explosion of African Canadian literature came after my adolescence. I think George has a point in that many Canadians—Black or White—know more (or think they know more) about African American culture than they do about African Canadian culture. There's African American music. Movies. Literature. But it's wonderful to see how African Canadian literature has exploded in recent years. Just look at the awards!

In *Any Known Blood*, I was interested in exploring what links the African American and African Canadian experiences. I was interested in the migratory element that connects these people. I was interested in the idea of movement backward and forward across the borders. While many Canadians know about the Underground Railroad, not many of them know that after the Civil War many of the Blacks living in Canada moved back to the USA. I wanted to write a saga that follows a family back and forth across the border for five generations.

Do you concern yourself with the issue of defining literatures?

What do you mean by that?

I mean giving an identity to literature. For example, an African Canadian literature, an African American literature, Romantic literature, British Romantic, American Romantic.

I don't. Remember I don't come to writing from an academic standpoint. I haven't a PhD in English literature. I am not an English scholar. Except for introductory courses, I didn't study literature at university. I read, of course, with great interest, and I take my work quite seriously. I come to the writing of others as a curious writer and reader.

But here I am calling you an African Canadian writer. Are you comfortable with my doing so? Moreover, definitions and identity figure largely in the issues you explore via fiction and literary journalism.

You could call me that, and that's fine. If you ask me to define myself professionally, I would begin first with the term writer. The words African and Canadian would usually get tacked on—by me or others—as a result of some sort of interactions or discussions.

How I define myself varies with circumstance. Do I at times see myself as a Black—African Canadian—writer? Yes. I am an African Canadian, and I am proud of it. But I don't think of myself in that way at all moments. Fundamentally, I want to be an alert and engaged person. I want to grapple with my ideas and my imagination, and to recreate the world in print in a way that satisfies me. So first, I think, is a person's humanity. Then come the shadings and nuances, which can include race, gender, sexuality, and so many other things. I think it's possible to diminish one's humanity by focusing too obsessively on specific aspects of identity. Consider two Canadian writers: one who is Black and the other, White. The first is likely to be defined, often, as a Black Canadian writer. But the other is unlikely to be defined as a White Canadian writer. He or she is simply a writer. That is all that matters. Do we refer to Mordecai Richler as a White Canadian writer?

Both of your novels, but especially Any Known Blood, *employ what I term an omnivorous form:* Any Known Blood *is documentary, romance, detective novel, family saga, identity quest . . . Comment.*

The only category I am not in agreement with is documentary, but I guess it depends on how one defines documentary. Certainly there are issues of identity; certainly there are elements of romance in *Any Known Blood.* They situate characters, primarily Black, who are searching for themselves.

When I say documentary I am referring to the novel's fidelity to history in those places where it adheres closely to history. This is especially true of your depiction of the movement of Blacks back and forth between Canada and the US.

Of course! I would be really disturbed if some historian were to read my novel and say, this is preposterous. It's part of situating my novel in its contemporary historical setting that reflects my truth and reflects my understanding of that history. If that's what you mean by documentary, I agree absolutely. Much Black writing seeks to explore history that has escaped the attention of others.

I guess you are asking me to comment on my novels. I think I hear you implying that they are somewhat sprawling, which is to some extent true—

I don't think I would use the word sprawling. Most people write in a single genre. You conflate genres, it seems to me, for your own artistic purpose.

I am interested among other things in exploring fascinating and important elements of the Black Canadian experience and exploring them dramatically. For example, what happened to the railway porters in Canada who were initially primarily Black? How did they get unionized? What were their jobs like? I was interested in recreating this dramatically in *Some Great Thing*. I feel that revealing dramatic moments in our lives is one way of showing people who we are.

This reminds me of Barbara Kingsolver's statement regarding her novel The Poisonwood Bible, *which, you probably know, deals with the assassination of Patrice Lumumba. Kingsolver says that if she'd merely written a monograph on the subject, six or ten people would have read it, but by transforming history into fiction, she gained a much larger audience.*

I think it's true. Dramatizing critical moments of our past can produce excellent fiction. Joy Kogawa comes to mind. Many Canadians might not have known about the experience of Japanese-Canadians during the Second World War if she hadn't written about it in *Obasan*.

How much of this is the result of your experimentation with the novel form?

I don't see myself as experimenting with form. So far, at least, I write in a fairly traditional manner.

Perhaps then you'd like to comment on the fact that your protagonist Langston dissolves into the character he is researching.

I had to give a great deal of thought to this section of *Any known Blood.* It was a novel that caused me a great deal of grief. I kept asking myself how I was going to tell the story of these five generations. How am I going to tell this story? How am I going to lay it out? After various drafts, it occurred to me to narrate in reverse chronological order. Now it seems so logical and so simple, but I sweated a long time before coming upon the idea. If you are going in reverse chronological order over five generations, you have to have some catalyst, some trigger to create a bridge from one generation into the previous one. So I was just looking for pretexts that would set up some kind of credible movement that would be interesting, that the reader could follow, that would lead one naturally from one generation to the other.

When you asked me about experimentation, I thought you were asking me about fantastical experimentation. There are writers who've done what I did in *Any Known Blood.* I can't think of any names right now. I was just looking for a simple and elegant way to do something quite complicated: that is, how to set the story up.

In observing the role humour plays in your novels, I could not but think of the two traditional functions of literature: to delight and instruct. Comment.

I don't sit at the computer saying I'm going to try to delight and instruct here. I'm not by nature a clown; I'm not the kind of guy who'll have five people rolling off their chairs with laughter in a bar room.

Some Great Thing *is a very humorous novel.*

It is. It is. It's probably funnier than *Any Known Blood.* Whenever I write, things seem to rise out of my subconscious and raise a flag and wave it hard. I seem to have a subversive, playful, disrespectful humour that comes to the fore at times. The more painful the subject, the more I need to treat it humorously. I'm part of a literary tradition here. Black literature, Russian literature, and Jewish literature explore painful themes with humour. I don't want my writing to be pedantic; I don't want to bore my readers. I don't want readers sighing and shutting my books because they feel they're being preached to. I hate sermons, and I don't want to insult my readers' intelligence. Humour is an excellent device with which to explore painful issues without being pedantic. Yes, I want to delight. I would love to write a novel that has readers roaring on the floor from the first page to the last.

Something of a twenty-first-century Mark Twain?

I have mixed feelings about Twain. Yes, I want to delight, and yes, I want to instruct. I don't want, however, to be seen as a preacher.

I suppose what I am asking really is a question about your craft.

Plot is a hard thing to manage. It's the last thing developing writers get. It's important to my work and I think it will continue to be. It's certainly true for the novel I'm working on right now.

One of the hallmarks of your fiction is the parodying of genres: the slave narrative, for example, in Any Known Blood.

Let's just stop for a second. In what way do you mean that *Any Known Blood* parodies the slave narrative?

Normally the standard protagonist in a slave narrative is someone of unimpeachable moral standing: a church-goer oftentimes who has been delivered by God. Your character is at times egotistical, morally ambiguous, certainly as regards sexual matters.

First of all, I'm no expert on the slave narrative but I've read many of them and find them fascinating. As part of the research for *Any Known Blood* I read many of them and I had read some of them before. Slave narratives were written by ex-slaves in the 1700s and 1800s. I am writing in the twenty-first century—we're in 2002 right now—so I'm not going to recreate a form that was pioneered for a very specific purpose, by a very specific people, in a very specific social context. I'm not going to reproduce what they've done. I have to acquire my own contemporary understanding and combine that with my own intelligence and sensibility. I am not the best judge of these things; I'm not the best person to evaluate my own work, but I don't consider *Any Known Blood* to be a parody of the slave narrative. I accept that it contains elements of the slave narrative, but I very consciously wanted to create a fictional narrative of a slave who did not lead the life of a saint and who led a fallen life. Of course, we look so much to create heroes in the Black community. In this family, Langston Cane V is discovering the slave narrative, fictionally-speaking: everybody holds up his grandfather and great grandfather as heroes. He struggles against this because he perceives himself to be a failure. He wants to know about the first hero in this line of five Langston Canes, and he discovers a man who is very much like himself.

Inadvertently that's parody.

I don't see it that way. I see it as my attempt to create a layered and thoughtful three-dimensional narrative of a character who has failings as well as strength and courage. For me, the illustration of character failure does not constitute parody. I don't want to turn this into a debate, but I felt that I was diverging from what might be expected of a slave narrative. I'll certainly grant you that.

There are several role reversals in your writing. I'm thinking, for example, of what I suppose one might call a master Black narrative in which women are depicted as the moral leaders of the household. Your characterization of Louise is the exact opposite of that.

I take pleasure in subverting the expected. I like the fact that Louise was trying to thwart Ben's efforts to inculcate a sort of nationalistic pride in race. I was tickled by the fact that she felt it was a lot of nonsense and didn't want him focusing on quote-unquote "Negro pride"—this is her language: 1960s language. I take pleasure in subverting stereotypes. Remember, I was raised by two sociologists, who were always looking for exceptions to the norm. They were always examining stereotypes—poking holes in them, shooting them down and showing all the times when they didn't apply. I suppose that that carried over to a certain degree to me. I like the fact that here we have a fellow from Africa who is parodying and poking fun at the whole concept of a race riot and people of colour (playing with the language there). I am attracted to characters that subvert expected roles.

You even evoke a taboo subject without deflating it (the sexuality of Langston Cane I), one that would have been topical because of the Rushton controversy raging around the time that Some Great Thing *was published.*

I'm aware of the controversy. Let's be clear about one thing here. Phillip Rushton was advocating a racist view in which he was categorizing races on a hierarchy of morality and intelligence. In my novel *Any Known Blood*, I draw a slave—Langston Cane I—who has escaped to Canada. He becomes an unfaithful husband. He returns to the US partly to flee his family and partly to join John Brown's crusade. I show him in a state of moral ambiguity because I feel that was the richest way to create a three-dimensional character.

I didn't want to create a superhero. Much later in time, in the same novel, Langston Cane V struggles to make sense of his life. In coming to terms with his own failures, Langston Cane V is encouraged by the discovery that his own great-great grandfather wasn't a saint himself, even though he has been treated that way in family lore. The discovery of the complex humanity of his own great-great grandfather helps him settle down.

Some people may take offence to what I've written. You talked earlier about some of the things one expects of Black literature. I'm not saying that it wouldn't trouble me emotionally to face harsh criticism, but it would be unproductive to fixate on it or to allow it to diminish my own creative flame.

One has to take his lumps too. I am the brother of a singer-songwriter who was hammered over and over again at the peak of his own fame. I haven't attained that level of celebrity so the need to take shots at me isn't as great as it was with Dan. To a certain extent, if you are going to stand up and write something you have to be prepared to come under attack. I suppose the challenge is to take the criticism and learn from it, when that is possible, but not to be silenced or discouraged.

In fairness to you, however, your parodic characters are more than balanced by positive, even heroic characters. Louise's superficiality and self-hate is more than compensated for by Ben's race pride and paternal diligence. But that too is a reversed narrative albeit positive.

I'm curious about your father's[1] *reaction to your depiction of such characters. I am assuming that he is still alive.*

Yes, but he is very ill.

I have in mind the Black community's outrage at William Styron's depiction of Nat Turner—an issue not unlike some of the ones you explore in Mahatma's experiences at The Herald*: his exposure of Judge Melvyn Hill, much to his father's displeasure.*

My father has been functionally blind for a number of years. I have read to him parts of my books that I thought would be of most interest to him. My mom would read parts that she thinks might interest him. He understands the difference between sociology and fiction. He was an avid reader of fiction.

He joked about a character in *Any Known Blood* who was of the same generation as one of his sisters. I remember him saying, did you have to make her a prostitute? And we laughed about it. He knows there's no relationship between that character and any sister of his. He helped me out with details, and he was happy to see me doing something I wanted to do. There were

[1]Daniel Grafton Hill III, Lawrence's father, died in 2003.

always questions I had for him: for example, Could a Black man get a taxi at the Penn Station in Baltimore during the Second World War? I used to be able to bounce things off him. But he never really engaged in a serious literary way with me about the way I create characters. He was glad that Dan was writing songs and that I was doing something I want to do. Like me, he knows you only live once; like me, he is an atheist.

A hallmark of both of your novels is their multiple plots. What's the advantage of multiple plots?

Well, it's playful. Part of it is I am naturally of a rambling nature in my writing personality. I spend a lot of time on plot. I consider it to be central to my own notion of my writing. I realize that the value of plot is downplayed by many writers and critics of contemporary fiction, but I'm not among them. This doesn't mean that every book that I read or love has to be plot-driven. I can think of many books that move me that are not at all heavy on plot. But when I write I tend to be very interested in plot. And I can attribute that, partially at least, to my reading of African American literature: works I read when I was thirteen, fourteen, fifteen and that I've been carrying in my memory since—by James Baldwin and Richard Wright. Especially Wright. No writer, when I was a youngster, could pull me into a story faster with very few strokes than Richard Wright. You know something important is going on five or six lines into a story. I was very much influenced by this.

I find plots difficult to manage. And I like multiple plots. I like expansive novels: big stories, and I seem to like to write that way. Of course, I like them to make sense, resonate, interrelate, hold together, and be tight.

Sort of like Hemingway's For Whom the Bell Tolls.

I love that novel. I read it a couple of times.

Setting and a welter of detail are very important for you. Even in dramatic situations, your narrator notices the details, mentions them.

I agree with you about this. Setting is very important for me. I do like details but don't want to numb a reader with too many of them. As a reader I often skip over excessive details, so I don't want to go too far in my own writing. I like to write things that are grounded in specific social and political geographic settings. I like my readers to know where they are socially, politically, historically, and geographically.

As you speak I'm visualizing some of the settings in your novels.

I've lived in Winnipeg, and got to know the city quite well. I was a reporter there for two years, and, believe me, you learn a city well when you're reporting in it. I got to know almost every street in that city. When I was writing *Some Great Thing*, which was years after my reporting in Winnipeg, I went back there and walked the streets for a few weeks to explore it because I wanted to make sure that my details were correct. I wanted my reader to think, Yes, that's Winnipeg. I couldn't imagine setting a novel or a part of a novel in a place that I haven't come to know from actually living there or from doing research. At the moment I'm writing a novel that's set in the 1700s[2], so obviously my knowledge comes from research. I'm very partial to setting; it's an aspect of fiction that interests me. I like to put my characters in clear, visible spaces.

So your details are designed to give concreteness to your characters and surroundings, not necessarily to confer symbolic meanings.

Remember you're talking to a former reporter here. I've been influenced by that. Detail is vital to the work of a journalist or reporter, and I'm sure that has influenced me.

You continue the character of Yoyo from Some Great Thing *into* Any Known Blood. *(Incidentally, I read* Any Known Blood *before* Some Great Thing.*)*

I don't know. I don't have a responsible answer for doing so. I could say that he refuses to be put down. But if I take a more serious approach to your question . . . (long pause)

You interlink your novels.

Yes. Yoyo isn't the only character that makes it into both novels. Mahatma Grafton the protagonist in *Some Great Thing* makes it into *Any Known Blood* in a minor role.

Oh, yes, he's the reporter in *Any Known Blood.*

I guess I didn't want to let go of Yoyo. He had something of a hold on me. I almost felt a sense of relief to bring him back again. I felt that *Any Known Blood* needed Yoyo and other minor characters such as Aberdeen Williams to give the reader a break away from this long family line of Langston Canes. The minor characters help balance the narrative.

An interesting aspect of this is the role you make Yoyo play towards the end of

[2]*The Book of Negroes*, forthcoming in February 2007 from HarperCollins Canada.

Some Great Thing. *He is back in Africa and things seem to be working out quite well and then suddenly we find him in Baltimore, and therefore know that things have gone sour for him. In a sense this functions as a corrective to any vision that the reader might have had of his returning to some panacea. Mark you, I'm not implying that* Some Great Thing *depicts a panacea. There are the children who live in rather squalid conditions.*

Yoyo is sort of innocent in *Some Great Thing*. He has never been outside of Cameroon before, and he is a little bewildered in an amusing way in Winnipeg. But by the time we meet him in Baltimore ten years later, he has a more sophisticated understanding of North American society and he knows how to survive in it.

You do some interesting things with him, as with Mahatma. Each is able to see the society from the perspective of the Other. Much as the Westerner sees Cameroonian society from the perspective of the Other. And in both societies there is much that appears ridiculous to the outsider.

I was interested in depicting one culture through the eyes of the Other. It's both entertaining and meaningful to see someone from another culture reflecting on North American values. I think it's a great way of parodying some of the more absurd elements of life in North America.

The things we take for granted and therefore never subject to scrutiny.

Some of the observations are insightful. Yoyo can't understand why Helene would interrupt her lovemaking in order to answer the telephone.

Your novels are intricately wedded to history. Even Yoyo helps in some small way to do this. History itself is a trope in your novels. The true stories of the lives of your characters are paramount and must be told.

For sure I'm very interested in history. It's more evident in *Any Known Blood* than in *Some Great Thing*.

There's a lot of history in Some Great Thing.

Yes, in the experience of the Black railway porters before and after the Second World War. There's the aspect of retelling their story fictionally, dramatizing the lives of Black railway porters in Canadian society, among other things. Black Canadian history is full of fascinating unexplored nuggets that deserve to be dramatized and made exciting and interesting and engaging to draw people into the story. We still have probably twenty-five million Canadians who know extraordinarily little about the Black experience in the world and the Black experience here in Canada. The fact of the matter is that it is a fascinating history and I don't care to have it forgotten. The novel is one way to accomplish that.

It is an open form.

Your bio states that you taught creative writing at Ryerson. You also studied creative writing formally. This means that you've spent much time reflecting on technique. How does assemblage of technical detail impact on your own writing? Do you at times find any of this to be an impediment?

I don't like to be reading a lot of student work when I'm in high gear. But I don't find my training to be an impediment. I have an MA from Johns Hopkins University, and I've taught creative writing over the years and enjoyed it. I have much to share with developing writers, and they seem to appreciate it, which is gratifying. But what studying creative writing means—at Hopkins at least—is that you write a lot and share it with other writers, some already published and others not. They read it, give opinions, and you go back and write some more. It's not as formal as a classroom lecture. You can take or leave their suggestions. It's like what you would imagine happens in a painter's studio, with the accomplished painter functioning as mentor to the beginning painter.

It's just that in my own encounters with creative writing instruction, the focus has always been on technique. Sort of like the exercises John Gardner says he gives his students so they'd write in certain forms and modes ostensibly for the development of technique.

I've done that kind of thing when I was younger. I studied creative writing as an undergraduate at the University of British Columbia years before going back to study it in a serious way. But these are writing exercises to limber up. There are lots of things the creative writing teacher can do to help emerging writers develop, and one of them is to get people to experiment and play on the page. I'm not sure I'm answering your question satisfactorily.

How do you get your students to fuse (the Dionysian) the inspirational with the (Apollonian) more technical aspects of writing? Do you find that one interferes with the other?

I try not to tell students how to write. In my case, I look for ways to fuse the two. In the initial phase I let my inspiration dictate. Later I rewrite. I'm an ex-journalist so I have the stamina for rewriting. I begin by trying to write fast to get at the things that are richest in fiction: quirkiness, unexpected changes in character, humour and things that shoot up out of nowhere. After the raw explosion, I return for rewrites.

It's exactly as Toni Morrison describes her own writing process. In my own case, most of the interesting things come during the rewriting phase.

And then you fill it in. That's interesting.

Anyone encountering Mahatma and Ben after he or she has read Black Berry, Sweet Juice *(which is how it happened in my case) cannot but see how traits you attributed to members of your family show up in your characters. In a recent interview I heard Victoria Glendenning refer to herself as a magpie. She added that her children then told her that she was now stealing from her own nest.*

What writer doesn't draw in some way from the life she/he has grown up in? Of course I draw from the people I've seen around me. There is no strict correlation between what members of family or I have done and what my characters do. I invent their stories, but I certainly draw from the world around me. That's only natural that you draw from the world you know and have come to love.

Some Great Thing, Any Known Blood, Black Berry, Sweet Juice*—all deal with the who-are-you/where-are-you-from role non-Whites living in Canada find themselves cast in. One of your short stories also deals with this obsession. Is there anything you would like to say about this?*

I am interested in identity issues. I am fascinated by the dramatic elements involved in the quest for identity, and I think Canada is a fertile ground for this because there are so many identities that run together, sometimes happily, sometimes not so happily. I remember a bit of advice given by a creative writing coach some years ago: explore your obsessions. I think there was some validity to that bit of encouragement.

Some writers—M. NourbeSe Philip, for example—would argue that all serious Black writing is an exploration of identity. Temperament aside, her treatment of the identity quest would be different from yours if only because she grew up in a British colony. I guess I'm deviating somewhat. Any comments?

Yes, much of it does. I don't know that I would agree that it is exclusively that. There are lots more things to write about that are interesting and important and that are no less serious. But issues of identity are a constant feature of works written by Blacks. Why shouldn't it be? Identity is fluid and is evidently evolving. Initially other people tried to tell us who we were and tried to brand us with their own views of who we were. We have spent a few centuries trying to climb out from under that and to assert how we see ourselves. But our environments are ever-changing, and so are our efforts. Even in the way the language we use to identify ourselves as Black people in North America has evolved over the years. This reflects an overriding societal interest in identity issues—certainly among Black people. Part of it is reclaiming one's identity and rejecting imposed definitions. Part of it comes from an endless dissatisfaction with our own efforts at self-definition. It makes sense to me that our debates will never end. My own children will not accept my language, verbatim. And why should they?

That said, exploring issues of identity is not exclusive to Blacks. People everywhere are caught up in exploring—from the standpoint of ethnicity, gender, or even generations. I would hope that the identity issues that I explore are of interest to other readers regardless of their race because fundamentally they are universal issues.

You are one of the few very successful African Canadian writers, so your opinions on the literary marketplace for African Canadians are especially pertinent for this project. You are one of the few African Canadian writers who have managed to reach a large audience. I am sure Black writers tell you about their woes.

It's hard. It's really, really hard to break in, to persist, and to keep going. I think the most single determining factor in whether or not you make it as a writer is persistence. A thick-skinned pigheadedness is needed. More than talent. You have to keep going when you are turned down. It's especially difficult when you are unknown and just starting out. I would advise developing writers to believe in the value of what they're doing regardless of how their work is perceived by others, and to keep going. It's important to find other ways to survive while they're writing and developing their craft. Most writers, even those who've attained a measure of fame, can't live off their royalties, so they have to find supplementary sources of income. It's somewhat easier now than let's say twenty years ago.

Publishers are putting out Black literature because they feel that it is new and fresh and that it meets a need for a more diverse body of literature. Things are better today than they were ten years ago. But there is a dearth of Black editors and Black critics. I am delighted to see the work of Rinaldo Walcott. He is writing quite critically about Black culture in engaging ways that haven't been done before. Maybe some of us should start to think of starting up our own publishing ventures. For a long time Sister Vision Press did a great job.

And prior to that Williams-Wallace, which came on the scene in the early eighties. Apart from Austin Clarke, who'd been published by McClelland and Stewart—and by then McClelland and Stewart had stopped publishing him—no publishers were publishing Black writers. Some of our stellar writers today: Dionne Brand, M. NourbeSe Philip, Claire Harris, for example—were first published by Williams-Wallace.

It's not that publishers are more openhearted. It's just that they've seen that books that explore minority experiences can sell. Fifteen years ago, it would have been difficult to find many of the major Canadian publishers releasing work by Black writers. But Black writers still face hurdles.

How do you feel about the critical response your work has received?

On the whole *Any Known Blood* received some very positive reviews.

Well the serialized reading on CBC of Some Great Thing *was quite a feat.*

It was wonderful and exciting for me to hear it. I loved it. *Black Berry, Sweet Juice* had a more mixed reception. I anticipated that. We talked about it a little bit earlier. It contains material that would bother some readers. I think on the whole, I've been treated quite generously. People seem to have been quite receptive and encouraging. To date I've been relatively lucky.

There remains one topic I'd like to have your opinion on. I somehow cannot get away from the perception that the groups in society that hold power are the ones that get the better jobs, the promotions, political offices. In Canada Black culture seems to be on the margins. I have on occasion wondered whether enhanced political involvement might alter that. Or is it the other way around: culture consolidating at the base and claiming some sort of concomitant political space?

You mean would a larger presence of Black Canadians in positions with political influence open up cultural possibilities? I think it's important for Black Canadians to have opportunities to involve themselves and be engaged at all levels of society, including municipal, provincial and federal politics.

It's extremely important that we be present at all levels of decision-making: in the media, in politics, in business, and in so many other spheres of policy-making. Certainly, if Black Canadians occupy socially important roles, that can't be bad for the arts. I don't draw a direct line between them though.

Other people have drawn a direct line. A few of the Black writers in Toronto have told me that once the Toronto Arts Council made it its policy to have multiethnic representation in its juries, the number of grants to minority writers increased substantially.

Absolutely. I think it's very easy for Black writing to be shoved to the side by jurors with their own agendas. Balance in that sense is important. When I am invited to be a juror, I try to be open to writing from different backgrounds. I have the impression nowadays that arts councils try to make their juries ethnically diverse.

I hope you did not find my questions awkward or confrontational.

Oh, no. Not at all. It's touching to see the attention you paid to my work, and I'm glad to have talked with you about it.

Nalo Hopkinson

Have you always lived in Toronto since leaving the Caribbean?

Yes, I have. I've been here since 1987: twenty-five years. I've visited others parts of Canada but not much. I was born in Jamaica and we moved around, kind of doing a triangle amongst Jamaica, Trinidad, and Guyana, and did a detour to Connecticut because my dad was in the graduate theatre program at Yale University for a while. But you can probably tell from what is left of my accent that most of the time was spent in Trinidad.

I identify bits and pieces of the Trinidadian and Jamaican demotic in your writing and the occasional Guyanese expression.

The Guyanese is more in the expressions than in the accent.

How were you as a child—with your siblings, your schoolmates? I ask this question because there are times when your narrators move seamlessly from the adult world to the child's world.

I was a combination of tomboy and egghead. I devoured books. I was reading beyond my years at an early age. My dad being who he was and my mother working in libraries meant that the likes of *The Iliad, Gulliver's Travels* folktales—Philip Sherlock's collections—were all in our house. That's the kind of thing I was reading, but I'd be up in a tree reading them. Climb the tree with a book between my teeth, so I could have something to do when I get up there. I was very quiet. I didn't have a whole lot of friends; because my parents moved about so often, I didn't get the chance to have a social circle. I get to do that now as an adult. So I was a quiet kid that mostly lived in her head but who was very active.

So you had to be self-sufficient.

Yeah, until my brother came along (laughs). That's a different story.

Why do you write?

I write partly because I have the fortune to have had the experience given to me of people who write. In other words, I grew up knowing that writing was something that people could do, because my mother worked in libraries, because my father was a writer and was surrounded by writers, and that made so much possible. I also write because I like telling stories, and I like having stories to read. As a child I preferred to read stories because storytellers told them too slowly. I was a very fast reader.

I write, too, because it is the only career I have found that I could stand to do. I mean I've tried the treadmill thing: I've spent most of my adult life working fulltime. And I've spent most of my adult life depressed, because that sort of treadmill—I didn't realize this until a few years ago—that treadmill is akin to slavery. The treadmill of waking up every morning at the same time and going to the same place to do the same thing for most of your life, for most of your day and most of your weekend.

So from a point of view of scheduling your time, writing gives you the freedom to choose your hours. Of course, this comes with restrictions.

Income.

Why science fiction as opposed to realist fiction?

Science fiction because it was so much of what I'd grown up reading. My father taught the "classics." *Gulliver's Travels* was, for me, a work of fantasy. Years later I understood that *Gulliver's Travels* is also a work of social commentary and satire. But as a child, these were wonderful stories that resembled nothing in my life. Partly, too, it's a temperament thing. Without being sarcastic, I'd say that a lot of fiction mimics reality: you're born, people treat you like shit, then you die. I had figured that out quite early on. So I was looking for work that took me beyond that. Science fiction and fantasy are in some ways about the archetypes that anchor our lives. I found that really rich. They also imply that our lives could be different; they present the possibility of change. And that is really exciting because so much of life is drudgery. It's also literature that explores the fact that we are, as a species, always manipulating our environments to suit ourselves; it might be something tangible like a piece of revolutionary technology, or it might be something intangible like a system of beliefs or laws or social rules; we are always fiddling. That fiddling—that creation—changes us as we are changing it. Science fiction and fantasy explore how our actions change us and how we change the world.

How does the fact that you were born in the Caribbean and lived there until age sixteen influence your writing?

I think that being from the Caribbean and being in the environment where my parents were very creative is significant. My mother was the one trying to feed a family on a small income; wherever we moved to, instead of relying on the grocery store, she would find a market. She would not only find a market, she would find the people who lived and worked there because she needed somebody to teach her what this or that strange-looking vegetable was, and how to prepare it. So I was surrounded by that kind of creativity and, more particularly, one with a Caribbean flavour: one where we put together, for good or for ill—some of us by choice and most of us not—a diverse mix, a diverse culture. You know, "You cut your coat to fit your cloth." We're very used to taking what we have and making something beautiful of it. That, I think, that hybridity, that making something new from the tatters of the old, very much informs my aesthetic.

Looking at the mythic figures that appear in your fiction—the rolling calf, the lagahoo (loup-garou), soucoyants, etc., I see that you've made extensive use of the folklore from the different Caribbean places where you lived.

Yes. I absorbed the folklore. Mostly through reading the books on my parents' bookshelves. Not from sitting around some fire or from somebody's grandmother telling them to me. I came from a really urban background. I was reading them in books in the library or listening to them on "Rikki-Tikki," which was a Jamaican television program for kids. But, yes, I absorbed those stories; they were ours. I remember a couple of books of Caribbean folk tales; tall, thin paperbound books with line drawings. The stories scared me shitless as a child, because none of them turned out well; they were always about frightening you, and always about, if you don't behave, if you're looking at the wrong woman, or you're looking at any women, bad things are going to happen, and la Diablesse is going to come and get you. Reading that literature and going to the library where my mother worked, I ended up, because I was reading at an adult level, discovering science fiction and fantasy. So I discovered a genre that takes all of that stuff, that takes the folklore, and creates a genre to tell stories in that mode. But the stories that I wasn't finding were our stories; you could find science fiction that is based in folklore from the British Isles; you could find nothing that's based on folklore from the Caribbean.

Our writers are very much in the realist tradition.

Yes. So when I started writing fiction, part of what I was trying to do was a little bit of covert subversion and in some ways just kind of infusing the genre with some of the possibilities I imagined.

How does the fact that you've lived in Toronto since age sixteen impacts on what you write?

That was like being dumped onto Mars. I came from a culture where the weather varies maybe five degrees year round, where in some islands the beach is never more than an hour's drive away, where there are many, many, many colours of people, but predominantly brown and black people—to this huge city that could hold the population of Guyana a few times over, and which at that point was comprised largely of White folks. It has changed rapidly: it's now 30 to 50 percent people of colour. The most culturally diverse city in the world, we're told. That's a bit of an apocryphal story, yet living in present-day Toronto, it sure feels true. But back then I ended up in the suburbs in Toronto where, to me, every blade of grass is the same size, shape, and colour as every other blade; and in a very, very different culture: I'm the one who is strange; the language sounds strange; I'm ignorant of all the cultural codes; and for eight months of the year I have to wear a spacesuit in order to go outside. Even the music. I remember my first term in University I wore a T-shirt that said "Triumph." I thought it was a positive affirmation. But it was the name of a heavy metal band, and people looked at me very oddly. Black people weren't supposed to like that kind of thing. Dunno why: Geddy Lee has an amazing voice. The aesthetic here was very, very different; the aesthetic in the Caribbean is very much about melody and colour. I couldn't even understand the humour. I remember watching SCTV and I just did not get it, I did not see what was funny . So it was very much a "bouleversement"—I can never think of the English word for that—"Disorientation" sort of does it. That took me about another two decades to recover from, and so I think science fiction is again very much the literature of being an alien.

In a sense you have voyaged from this strange but real reality to one you invent and in which you incorporate mythic Caribbean components.

Yeah. It would hardly feel any stranger than where I had found myself living; and in fact it was a way to return home a little bit, because I could invent a world that looked like the world I'd like to be in.

Who have been your mentors? The first time I heard about you, it was from a short-story you read on the CBC, and Olive Senior had recommended that you read.

In terms of spiritual mentors—I mean in terms of reading his work and being inspired by it—foremost is Samuel R. Delaney, the first Black writer in this genre on this continent. Kamau Brathwaite is another. I was very very fortunate that he was a friend of my father, so he is someone I maintained a contact with. Lilian Allen, who was one of the first people to push me to send my work out. Libby Scheier here in Toronto. She died a few years ago. But before that, I'd registered in a workshop she was running and when I couldn't afford the money, she let me pay by the week. Judy Merril. She actually got me started writing. She was an American who came to live in Canada partly in protest against the Vietnam War. She was at that point among the most influential science fiction editors in the field and one of the people at the head of the feminist wave in science fiction. She donated her collection of science fiction and fantasy books to the Toronto Public Library. The collection began what was then called "The Spaced-Out Library." That collection is now the Merril Collection in the public library near the corner of College and Spadina. She got me started on writing and got me into a writing group. There are so many: my friend Kelly Link, whom I went to Clarion with, is a woman who's just on a star level; her writing blows me away constantly. There are so many.

Do you have what I would call a theoretical framework out of which you create?

If I do I don't know it as such. I write in genres that have conventions and have genre protocols, and I work within those. But part of the practice in both those genres is to break the protocols, to see what you can get away with, screwing around with them. So if I am understanding your question, I am not sure I do have a framework. It's an academic concept, but I got published well before I had academic training as a writer; I am the literary equivalent of—what do they call it—a naif artist.

Your influences have been many.

My influences have been many, and coming out of science fiction, as I do, I don't—even though I just got an MA in writing popular fiction, but that came after I'd written three novels—have a whole lot of formal academic theory writing. You don't need that when you're writing popular fiction. Or rather, it's difficult to get formal training. Academe as a rule still turns its nose up at popular fiction. So we create our own mentoring networks.

But your writing is highly literary, and, in fact, I know that two or three years ago somebody actually gave a paper on your earlier work—in a CACLALS panel (Canadian Association of Commonwealth Language and Literature Studies) in which she was exploring whether or not you are a postcolonial writer.

I'd love to know more, because I have no idea how you define that. If I am, a lot of the stuff I kind of picked up and absorbed has been by reading it, and living it, so when I sit down to write I am not following any sort of formal structure.

Which incidentally is excellent training for a writer, because once you've studied literature your voice gets confused with other people's voices, and literary theory begins to interfere with literary craft.

And I've certainly read a lot, lots of fiction, and that's where much of it comes from. But it's only in these latter years that I'm beginning to read some literary theory.

How do you feel about the label African Canadian Writer?

That's one of my hats. I once discussed it along with André Alexis and Djanet Sears at a roundtable chaired by Toronto literary critic Donna Bailey Nurse on the subject of racism in publishing. André said he does a constant dance: if someone says he is Black, he says yes, but amongst all these other things, etc. And if they try to erase his Blackness, he makes sure to put it back in the picture. I really understand how that works, because I find that I'm always trying to work against people's assumptions. I have no trouble being called an African Canadian writer as long as I am called a Caribbean writer, as long as I am called a woman writer, a science fiction writer, or just a writer.

I have conflicting feelings about these labels myself. Some years ago, I think '97, CELAFI had its celebration here in Toronto, and I was asked to talk about the African Canadian aesthetic.

What would that be?

I came to the conclusion that there was no such definable thing. Too much depended on the temperament of the particular writer and a host of other things. But I went on to say that people see literature, writing, as having several functions, and it was up to the particular writer whether he or she responded to one, many, or

none of these functions. But most specifically as African Canadians we get ourselves into phantom quarrels about these things.
Are you aware of the lawsuit between M. NourbeSe Philip and one of Toronto's radio stations? (I ask the question because the opprobrium poured on Philip by the station reflects in large measure part of the baggage that comes with the label, as well as what I think is a desire by the dominant population to restrict the themes we explore.)

Yes, I know a little bit about it, yeah.

This is part of what I mean about being identified as an African Canadian writer. There's a lot of baggage there—it's unstated, but it's very much there—concerning what we write and how we should write it. It's censorship of the themes we explore. Yeah, you folks, you come here, you come from where you come from, you didn't have this or that opportunity, you come to Canada you have opportunities and then you shit on the country and that sort of a thing. To me this is part of the label.

That is what you get to do as a citizen of a country, or a citizen of the world.

I am in many ways lucky that I have managed to sidestep a whole lot of that, by coming through the science fiction genre, which practically meant that I couldn't have been published in Canada. If there are few Black publishers here, there are also few science fiction publishers. Only one small press is doing science fiction in Alberta, run in part by my friend Candas Jane Dorsey, and a few other magazines publishing the short stories, but there is no infrastructure of science fiction publishing, and Canadian publishers specifically won't touch it, neither would Canadian agents. So I've escaped a whole lot of the baggage; what I have to fight is people calling me an African American. If I were American we would be having a whole different conversation about identity. But genre does not prevent me from having a voice and saying what I want to say. I criticize Canadian politics. It's part of what my first novel does. And often criticism is what science fiction does.

There is no significant Black presence in the publishing industry. What are your feelings about this?

That really bothers me. Because there is such wonderful Black production going on—some of the work is getting out there anyway, through self-publishing, for instance—but yet I know the value of having an editor who knows what you are talking about, who can edit your work properly. And, if the community doesn't own the means of production, then we're not going to get our own face out there.

The politics and economics of publishing certainly seem to be working against us...

Another facet of this phenomenon I find is that when we do get published by mainstream houses, often the work has the feeling that it has not been properly edited. You read the work and you think, yes, this person clearly has talent, but this manuscript has not been through a critiquing, editing and rewriting process to the point where it sparkles. A publisher has just slapped two covers onto their manuscript. At some level that starts to feel, to me, contemptuous. It feels like the mainstream is saying, "Well, you know, this is the best Black people can do."

You're absolutely correct. I can think of a few novels that came out in the last few years that fit this description. You're right: writers need editors who'll push the writers they work with to excel.

I have such a relationship with my editor. We've gone through a kind of a mutual learning process. With the first book, I don't think that she tried to edit me much at all; perhaps because she knew she didn't have the background in some of the cultural and linguistic elements on which I was drawing; so at some level there was a certain amount of respect there, but I found that I was a young writer and I could have used a bit more critique from her. With the second book I could see her take her courage to the point of saying, here is what I think. And I would tell her the bit about the culture or language or folklore that she didn't seem to know, and she would say, "Okay, I see why it needs to be there, but if you want someone like me to be able to follow what you're showing, it might work better if you did X or Y." And those comments have been very, very helpful. So it is possible. And it's work that both sides have to be willing to do. But it would be so sweet to have an infrastructure here of our own work and our own editors. Just a few days ago I went to talk to a bunch of people: Black folks who are starting their own writing group. One of them who knew me from years back had asked if I would come and talk with them. It's the kind of thing I don't often do, because, frankly, for me it takes time away from the immediate activities that put food in my mouth, and I'm still struggling to do that; but they are four or five aspiring writers and I thought if I could help in any way—more of this needs to happen—so I went.

In conventional literature we talk about protagonists, but in your two novels I have to call your protagonists heroes.

Do you?

Yes.

Because there are science fiction writers complaining that they were too introverted.

Really, that's interesting.

They don't save the world all by themselves. In fact the second protagonist Tan-Tan doesn't save the world at all.

The reason is that, for me, the battles they fight and win are archetypal battles.

Yes. Yes.

And so my question is: Do you create your protagonists with this in mind?

Partly I do, but I also make their battles very very personal. When it comes to people of colour writing in the genre, women writing in the genre, queer people writing in the genre, often we're kind of digging at that convention of the heroic tradition, because the heroic is often White, often male, often Western guys who save the whole world.

Or think they do. And from privileged backgrounds, and so on and so forth.

Yes, very much. So, we're still doing that heroic thing, but we're messing with it. In my first novel, my character saves a whole city, but she does it with the help of the marginalized people in that city. She does it with the help of the street kids, the poor people.

And certainly ancestral wisdom.

Yes, very much. All of that tradition that she has been looking down her nose at is what she has to call on finally. And in the second novel, my character doesn't save the world; she makes a change, but it's a very small change.

In a sense what she is trying to save is in fact herself.

Herself.

Though as she is making her difficult journey, there are all sorts of specific acts of injustice where she intervenes. For example, there is a fellow—I can't remember his name now—who is beating a woman and she intervenes.

She is forever being reminded that she may have this heroic notion of herself, but she is human.

That's right. You do have her being helped by the Douens. But even so, in the final analysis, as you said, the responsibility is still her own, because there is only so much that the Douens can do.

The big change is that she tells her own story.

There, of course, you do have an oral storyteller. The novel is fitted within that frame. I'm curious: Is it for experimentation purposes that you do this—as opposed to, let's say, the first novel?

Partly it was because the second novel is actually the one I wrote first. At the time, writing a novel felt very, very big to me. Then I was working for the Toronto Arts Council and seeing other people's book projects that were linked short stories, and I thought maybe I could do that. So that's where the three "folktales" came from. Then I got older and wrote another novel, and the experience showed me, in terms of structure, how to pull the stories together. I still wanted to keep the three core stories. I knew that I was going to have a mystery to be solved at the end, and the answer was to have a narrator who would tie everything together, so it was experimentation that I stumbled into.

Defamiliarizing the familiar is something writers are taught in most writing programmes, but few writers go on to do so in any notable way. You are one of them: what is the aesthetic benefit of doing so?

Sometimes that's just me being pissed off. I had to pass through Detroit on my way to Michigan State University to attend a science fiction and fantasy writers' workshop. It was on Mother's Day, and I was travelling with my friend Brent, who was also attending the workshop. We were standing in the Detroit bus station holding on to everything we had brought with us for six weeks, because otherwise it would have been gone. There were people marauding around the bus station. There was one extremely drunk man who accosted Brent when I was in the bathroom, and Brent apparently told him that "his friend" was going to come and beat him up. Brent neglected to mention that the "friend" was a 5'5" woman. For somebody who comes from a fairly orderly city, there is plenty of poverty to be seen in Detroit and plenty of anger. Detroit is frightening; there are broken buildings that you can tell have not been inhabited the way they were created to be inhabited for years. They are boarded up, though I'm sure many of them have become squats. The streets are filled with potholes. So that was one experience.

On my return to Toronto, there was a discussion at the Toronto Arts Council about how to avoid what had happened to Detroit. The phrase that an economist used regarding Detroit is the "hole in the doughnut—" meaning that the government cuts way back on services to its residents, which means that it's more expensive for industries to remain in the city so they leave, so there's lots of unemployment and poverty, and well-off people leave because it's become dangerous; and pretty soon you'll have an empty city. And I felt, actually, you don't have an empty city; people are always going to be there. Who are those people? Detroit is not empty.

Years later, I went back to Detroit for a conference and found myself in a little bar: a Black working-class bar, Friday night. I mean going through the city of Detroit, you could practically see the tumbleweed—the city felt so deserted. But this little club was packed full. Everybody knew everybody by name; it was like a family gathering. And you had this real sense of community. When I was about to go back to my hotel, I went to stand outside to wait for a cab as I would do in Toronto, and half an hour later nothing had gone by. I went back in and the bartender said, "Oh, no darling! Cabs don't just come by. I'll call one for you. It will take about an hour to come; in the meantime, go back and sit with your friends and have another drink. I'll call you when he comes." There is a community there; it doesn't have much money; but they're people that are making lives for themselves, and who're sometimes treating each other well, just like anywhere else.

You do not hesitate to employ Caribbean English (the versions I identify in your work are Jamaican and Trinidadian). Given that the presence of Caribbean nation languages in our writing is something publishers frown on, why is using it important for you? In fact, in Midnight Robber, *standard English is referred to as "patois" (an interesting inversion).*

Again, ignorance is bliss. I grew up with people like "Eddy" Kamau Brathwaite, and so the whole notion of nation language is very, very familiar to me. The whole notion of the first time that Miss Lou [Louise Bennett-Coverley] got up to perform, when somebody said, "Is that yuh mother send yuh a school for?" I was already politicized around language, so I just wrote from that place. And again, I go to somebody who is from the outside; I go to a publisher where what's valuable to them is: Can you bring a fresh vision of the world to our readers? So, they read it, and if I am able to make it accessible to them, and it's well written, they are going to like it—if all goes well, that is.

In Brown Girl in the Ring, *the evil to be destroyed is a monstrous father-grandfather who is the embodiment of an inverted beneficent Voudun force, as well as pernicious patriarchal power; and in* Midnight Robber *it is an incestuous father who is also an imperious husband-lover-politician. This places your work in the context of what I would call the writing of Black women's liberation. Would you like to comment?*

You aren't the first person to ask that. If I were to rewrite *Brown Girl in the Ring*, I would probably put more into the character of Rudy. I actually felt more for him than came across on the page, because, again I am learning as I go. About three quarters of the way through the novel I asked, why is this man like this? I thought through circumstances that would make him like this. And I had a whole other storyline—very little of which made it into the book which I actually wrote—about someone poor, Black and male coming from the Caribbean, where he is at least in the majority, coming here and being reduced to merely another Black Jamaican, with even less than he started out with. He's not very politicized and the anger and the helplessness he feels are vented on the people close to him, which are the women and children in his life. So I was writing kind of a very old story I think. Would I have to do that now, I would probably try to do Rudy the kind of justice that I actually did feel for him. But then the sort of energy that I wanted the story to go over with and end with yielded the character he is. I think I did that better in the second novel, where I have a better feel for some of the pressures on the character of Antonio.

He is certainly nuanced. In fact one is horrified by one's own reaction to him. The reader is prepared to forgive him, even when he uses the poison. One can say that he is a jealous man; moreover, revenge is such a natural thing in the human condition, etc . . .

And it's tough because I wanted to write a story about incest, and I ended up looking at how incest happens, and the fact that it's often perpetrated by men. I tried to counter it by presenting male images that were positive, such as the man that Tan-Tan ends up with—Melonhead (Laughter)—I love him! He is one of my images of a good Caribbean man. Of course, there is the alien, Chichibud, who is not even human, but who is also male and is also capable of expressing a fuller range of himself.

Part of the problem I'm dealing with is, if I'm writing about the oppression of women, very often that means that I'm writing about the oppression of women by men. So I try to balance that. One of the ways I do this in *Midnight Robber* is with the woman who is one of Tan-Tan's antagonists. Janisette, and she is a piece of work (laughs). I would not want to meet her on a dark night, no matter how good her outfit was. So I tried to balance it, and I don't think I quite have it yet.

Both are driven by their territorial instincts—the sort of, You've taken my man and I am going to get even with you. In Rudy's case, You've taken my woman and I'm going to get even with you.

You are mine and I can do whatever I want with you.

Have you received any adverse criticism for creating such antagonists?

Yes, not by too many people. What I usually do is point them to the whole body of my work, which gives you a better sense of my sympathies for both women and men. On the whole the critiques have been good.

I ask the question because I know the sort of criticism women writers who've explored this theme receive: Alice Walker and Gloria Naylor among others. So much so that Naylor resorted to writing The Men of Brewster's Place.
Your short stories, are they sort of the best pieces that came out of your apprenticeship writing?

They are the only short stories I've written. I think there's only one—maybe two—that I haven't published.

I am impressed. It seems to me that they are the matrix for the rest of your writing.

I started out as a short-story writer, partly because that's the usual introductory path to this genre, and I still find short stories easier to write—well, not really. A novel might take you a year to twenty years; a short-story might take you a week to a year. There's also the learning curve: you can take what you have learned from a short-story and move on to another story, whereas with a novel I might take a year to twenty years to do that. Also because they are shorter, you can see the structure of the story more easily. So I've been able to experiment more with them.

I meant to ask you about closure. You do like your stories to end (laughs).

You think so? I'm more often told that my stories are way open-ended. Again, it's something that I'm sort of fighting in the genre because it's very much a plot-driven genre and you have to have your beginning, your middle, your climax, your resolution.

Aristotelian.

Yeah. Very much.

Which brings me to the business of craft. You must spend an incredible amount of time crafting, finding the right word, the right musicality, the right sound combinations.

It is hard to tell, because when some writers write a story, they get a draft then they rewrite it. I don't. I write a little bit, move back and rewrite it, then write some more, then go back and rewrite it, like that. So I can't actually tell you how many drafts I do. But, when I get to the end, I usually don't need to rewrite that last segment. I have built the story up to that point, so that by that time I'm near the end, it has its shape, and I just go.

So, in a certain sense, if you write something today, you go back to it tomorrow. If doesn't sound right to you…

I'll fix it right then before I move on. So I think this is the boon of having a communal community where . . . . you know my dad was an actor, a playwright, a poet.

Indeed, I remember you mentioning in a CBC interview that your father worked with Derek Walcott, and I see the various epigraphs from Walcott's Ti-Jean and His Brothers. *Moreover, there's a strong theatrical influence in your work—a strong reliance on dialogue, setting and gesture.*

Very much. I grew up in the theatre. I grew up with Shakespearian theatre as well as Caribbean theatre. I got to see a lot of theatre performances. I remember as a child, one of my favourite performances was done by Dem Two: two travelling Guyanese performers, Ken Corsbie and Marc Matthews. They still perform Caribbean works; and one of the first stories that I saw performed was Wordsworth McAndrew's poem "Ole Higue." So there is very much the sense of drama, of the power of words, of the power of little details to draw you into a story, and the poetry, the rhythms. It's been wonderful to have that.

It seems to me as if you genuinely believe that words can be the equivalent of the magician's wand. Would you like to comment?

Yes. And that comes from being a child who could disappear into a book. I would literally not know what was going on until I would pick my head up and I would be surprised to find my book back in the world.

I'm relieved to hear somebody else did that (laughs). You'd call me and I would not hear.

Exactly. And people think you are being rude.

And my final question: there is a loose notion that Black writers should write works that are relevant to the Black community. Does that impact on your writing in any way?

What has happened, as I got developed as a person and as a writer, is that I found that I can't really make one clear statement about anything. I find that my background is so diverse, everything about my personal map is so diverse that it is really rare that I can say this is my definitive position and it will never change. So when it comes to writing about Blackness, I don't see how I could help it. Because I'm Black, because no matter what I do I'm drawing from my experience. It would take an effort for me not to write about what it's like to be Black, or female or terrestrial. Even though writing science fiction, I couldn't get away from my own perceptions; they are coming through my filter. On the other hand, part of what I write and why I write is to explore some of the injustices I see. The ones that have to do with being Black and being female are very personal to me.

I know there are critics who say that a writer like André Alexis elides the Black experience here in Canada as opposed to someone like Cecil Foster, for example, who underscores it.

I don't know. André and Cecil come from such different worlds. I wouldn't say that André elides the experience of Blackness. An uninformed reader could read his novel *Childhood* and not know that the protagonist is Black. Yet to me that characters' experience as mixed-race, Black, growing up in "back-a-wall" Ontario—I apologize to Petrolia—feels so very Canadian, so very Black in a way that does not get told. And no, André doesn't make a big deal of it in that novel. Yet I've read stories of his that are very much a Black man's story. André's position—if I remember correctly from the last time we talked about it—is more: I am first and foremost a writer. I happen to be a Black writer and sometimes I'll be talking to you about Blackness. Whereas someone like me, I feel like I'm trying to put it all on the plate one time, and trying to make sure that you forget none of it. So I think it's just different positioning.

On the other hand, one cannot accuse writers like Dionne Brand or NourbeSe

Philip of not writing about the Black experience. Though I often hear the comment that Dionne isn't accessible to the mass of the Black reading public.

That's true. Dionne would not be accessible to the mass of any reading public—and I love that. I like having that range, from Terry McMillan to Dionne Brand.

It is probably a very good thing that we have that diversity within the African Canadian writing community. It's a sign to me of the maturity of the literature. The different public quarrels are signs of a diverse and vibrant literature, one secure enough to make its quarrels public.

I think it's a healthy thing. Dionne should go right on being erudite and Terry MacMillan should go right ahead writing about middle-class Black women in Florida. All those experiences need to be out there.

And you should go right on writing science fiction or in any other genre you choose. Thanks for letting me discuss your work with you.

Suzette Mayr

Suzette Mayr, how do you envisage your role as a writer?

My role as a writer is just to be one voice in that huge dialogue that is going on between a culture and the art within that culture. I would never assume that I am representative of anybody but myself. However, being who I am, and being a writer, my voice is more likely to get heard over the voices of people who aren't writing. That's one of the things I think about, but I never assume that I'm speaking for anybody. I am one part of that clatter of voices that comprise the culture.

Do you see writing as having a function?

Yes. I think that writing does have a function. I think art has a function. I think it was Althusser who said something to the effect that art is one of the few ways in which people can get outside of their ideology. I think that art, and therefore writing, is essential for a culture to be self-aware and, hopefully, self-critical, and therefore as beautiful and as useful as it could possibly be.

You are both a novelist and a poet. Would you like to talk about the restrictions and advantages of each of these forms?

I actually started out as a poet and came to writing prose and novels quite late. What I love about poetry is the fact that it works at the level of the word rather than at the level of the sentence, which is what prose does. Prose obliges you to work with basic syntax: the subject, the verb, and, maybe, an object. When you have dialogue, you have to set that up in a specific way. Poetry is free of that, and you can explore the tiniest moment without having to worry about the larger elements of story, character, plot, and all the other requirements of narrative. I love too the aleatory aspect of poetry, where you can put a single word, then add another word, and the meaning completely changes, because somehow the context has changed even though the word itself remains the same. Prose became useful at a point where I wanted to have plot and to explore character. But I wasn't interested in the epic poem, so I turned to prose. I try to bring to prose some of that poetic language. But, of course, I can't do that as easily. Right now I move back and forth between the two forms. At the moment I am putting together a poetry manuscript.

As you were saying that, I kept thinking of three writers that combine both: Claire Harris, who has two novels in poetry, She *and* Drawing Down a Daughter*; NourbeSe Philip, who says that* Looking for Livingstone *is really a novel in poetry; and George Elliott Clarke, whose* Whylah Falls *is, he says, a novel-in-verse.*

What's gorgeous about those books is that they blur the boundary between prose and poetry. And I hope to move in that direction eventually too. I find that readers are a bit more resistant to them, but, you know, I think they are excellent books.

There are sections in Moon Honey *that read like poetry. Both of your novels reject linearity in the telling of their stories. What's your reason for this?*

I tend to reject linearity as a writer and also as a reader. I'm not really interested in reading straight, linear texts, although this is not to say that there aren't some that I enjoy. I'm interested in how a writer conveys time on the page. Your 5:30 yesterday and my 5:30 yesterday happened at the same time, but they were radically different experiences. And it's not that one is more 5:30 than the other. So how do you convey that simultaneity of action and of time on the page? And the same goes for memory. We don't remember chronologically—at least I don't. I remember in flashes, more like sensory photos. So, I am really interested in the fragmentary nature of memory and the illusion that somehow we remember in a chronologically linear way. And the fact that this completely fragmented organization, or this fragmented structure, informs who we are now, in the present time, deeply interests me, and that's why I go for that.

Clearly, then, you have high expectations of your audience? You expect your audience to create the story out of these different pieces …

I know some people are resistant to that. When I got translated into German, it was extremely difficult for some German readers to understand that fragmented approach. What I'm asking readers to do is to suspend their disbelief. I'm much more interested in the notion that there are many, many truths and many versions of events, so that if at the end of a text, readers come up with a different reading from what I intended or a different reading from somebody else because they filled in the gaps in a way that's specific to them, then that's perfectly fine with me.

But really, you're saying that you're writing for a literate audience.

Yeah, I guess so, or a patient audience. A writer whose work I adore is Michael Ondaatje. He is the king of fragment. He seems to be doing okay. I don't think he has only a literary audience. Do you?

Well, I don't know. I'm not sure that The English Patient . . .

No, not that one. I mean books like *Running in the Family.*

Or Coming Through Slaughter. *No,* The English Patient *seems quite straightforward to me.*

Yeah, that's true. You're right.

One senses a strong authorial distance between you and your characters.

Meaning?

Your narrator narrates with an almost objective eye, doesn't become involved necessarily in the characters' emotional plight. For example, at a point when Carmen is crying, the reader can see that the narrator is poking fun at the way Carmen is expressing her grief.

That's a good point. I think partly what motivates me is kind of selfish just because I like being able to swoop and dip into all the characters' heads whenever I want. It is a tremendous challenge for me to write from a focused third-person or even a first-person point of view and not have access to those minds. I'm partial to the idea that there is no such thing as a villain or something like that. Different characters have different motivations for what they do, even when what they do seems malicious or evil. So, it's partly that. I guess the other thing too—and I don't know if it's necessarily a convincing reason—is that I want to stay far away enough from the characters so that the readers can pass their own judgements on them. It's not about the narrator informing the readers how they should feel about the characters.

Your novel The Widows *incorporates the fictional and the historical, and it reminded me of Claire Harris'* Fables from the Women's Quarters, *in which Harris provides in footnote form the historical acts out of which her poems took form. Nowadays there's much discussion of the metafictional . . . I better let you comment.*

Combining the historical and the fictional. With that book specifically, I combined the two because I was in part dealing with Annie Edson Taylor, who was the first woman to go over Niagara Falls in a barrel. Initially I intended the book to present her as herself, and maybe, in a prologue or in some sort of excerpt in the book, establish her as a historical character so that people would know who she is. But while I was researching the book I found that there were many versions of her, in part because she misrepresented herself. At one point she gave her age as forty-three when she was actually fifty-three, all kinds of things. But the historians too gave conflicting accounts of her personality, even different versions of what she wore when she went over the falls. So it came down to which of these were more or less accurate—and I was not prepared to choose. I preferred to include it all, and show that Annie Edson Taylor, even though she was a historical personage, is also a construction—that writing is an act of construction or reconstruction. So much subjectivity went into the written accounts: Pierre Burton calls her Pudding Face; others called her other names; I felt I should include it all.

Annie Edson Taylor is quite an inspiration for The Widows.

Oh, *The Widows*, yeah. They have their nonfiction pasts too. They came of age during the Third Reich and were part of that generation that imbibed Nazi ideology and believed it for a large part of their lives. That was the central theme in earlier drafts of the book. Niagara Falls wasn't in it at all. It was taking place in Germany, and it was from their points of view on issues such as immigration, coming to terms with kids, moving, and stuff like that. What happened is that the nonfiction started dominating the fiction, and I found myself writing a book that had been written before. I wasn't interested in that sort of writing; it was quite depressing. So I moved it to Canada and tried to find a Canadian figure, but could only come up with Annie Edson Taylor, who is American, but who was a nice sort of borderline Canadian-American figure.

Both of your novels contain multiple plots. Why?

Let me just remember. In *Moon Honey* it was Carmen using her lover, then turning into a Black woman, and then there was a metamorphosis.

And you certainly do have Renata and Griffin. I guess you could add Miko's relationship with Renata.

I think it probably goes back to the same impulse to resist linearity. There are many events going on all the time and they all impact each other, even though they occur completely separately from each other. Sometimes I wonder if I shouldn't go into film or some other sort of medium that would let me get that across. Not that it's not working fine for me in text, but I know there are other ways to do it, like on film, for example, with split screens . . .

Though something is always lost, in the sense that if you have it on screen, you can only look at one scene at a time.

It's true.

Though, now that there are videos, one can always go back to what was ignored.

Maybe it's because I'm looking for a reader who can do three things at the same time; so ideally I think what I would do is have a video installation where I would have three television monitors playing at the same time with different things happening on each one, and the person in that room had better be able to see all these things at the same time (laughs).

I asked Claire Harris a similar question yesterday about some of her poems. She has the poems in three columns very often, so I asked her if she intended some sort of simultaneity in reading, and she said, "No, what I really would like is for people to read down and across."

You obviously made some deliberate choices about the degree to which both The Widows *and* Moon Honey *would be realistic. What are your views about realistic fiction?*

I have many views about realistic fiction. I appreciate a lot of realistic books that are written in a realistic way. But, for me as a writer, I think it's a total shame to be working in a medium where if I wanted to I could make somebody levitate and burst into an explosion of flowers, and to not use that; so that's what is appealing about writing. It's creating your own world where you could defy gravity if you want to. And it's also connected to my love for magic-realist works like Gabriel Garcia Marquez's. Magic realism enables you to explore your place in ways that an outsider might not appreciate. So I love the fact that for Marquez writing in a magic-realistic way—I think he says that he doesn't; he says that he is writing in a realistic way—was a means to examine the politics of a place. For Robert Kroetsch, it's a way to examine the myths around Alberta and how Alberta was constructed. In *What the Crow Says*, he has a winter that lasts two years, which is kind of what it is like in Alberta a lot of the time; so even if it comes across as this completely magical thing, it's just a further extension of the real, of making the real an apt metaphor for describing something.

In Moon Honey *such magic realism is attained in large part via metamorphosis. Why metamorphosis?*

When I was growing up we always had a lot of books in the house, and my parents were very encouraging of our reading any kind of book. We knew about the Greek myths the way other children know about fairy tales. I was always fascinated by the transformation stories and the interspecies stories like "Leda and the Swan"—Leda's laying eggs that hatched into people… I just loved that. As I got older and I read Ovid's *Metamorphosis*, a recurring question for me was: What happens after the transformation? I know there are a few kinds of transformations—I think Salman Rushdie brings this up in *The Satanic Verses*—there's the transformation where, let's say, a woman gets turned into a tree. She becomes a tree, and that's the end of the story; or she's still a woman, but trapped in the tree. So, for me, what was happening in so many of those metamorphosis stories, particularly those in Ovid's *Metamorphosis*, was that they are centred around female characters who are in a place of crisis, and the way they get out of such crises is to be transformed into something like a bird or a tree or a stone or whatever. But I wasn't satisfied with those endings. What happens to that woman's grief? What happens to the bird that she becomes? I wanted to finish those stories.

I thought about Kafka's "Metamorphosis" in which Gregor becomes an insect. But I think Kafka's narrator is showing us all along that Gregor is, in mentality, probably an insect. I wondered whether, in a sense, you were using metamorphosis here as a way of pointing out what some of these characters fundamentally are.

Yeah, it's like Circe's pigs. She turns the men into pigs and determines that that's what they were all along. In Carmen's case—people have read the book in so many different ways because of that transformation. They say to me—because, supposedly, I have all the answers—Was she actually a White woman who turned into a Black woman, or was she a Black woman all along, or is it a metaphor for mixed-race, or did she…?

I can see why they were asking you such questions because you are of mixed-race heritage. You probably were annoyed by some of them.

I don't know. Usually I tell them that it's whatever they want it to be; that if they can find the support for it, it's fine.

I think though that at the very end of Moon Honey, *the narrator hints that she was always what she becomes, just that she just never thought herself so. But you leave enough ambiguity for readers to bring their imagination into play.*

Absolutely.

There's metamorphosis in The Widows *as well. The going-over-Niagara is something of a second life, never mind their purchasing the café.*

You know, that's one of those things that didn't actually make sense until the book was written, until I heard people talking about it. The very first review that came out was the one in *Quill and Quire*, where the reviewer talked about the book being entirely about sex, that Niagara Falls was this big sexual moment for these women that resulted in a rebirth. You're raising your eyebrows (laughs). You know with the egg shape and all. So that was one way to look at it. While I was writing the book, I saw Niagara Falls or Niagara River as this boundary between a whole bunch of things. You know, it's the boundary between the US and Canada; for the characters, it's sort of the boundary between life and death; for Annie Edson Taylor, it was the boundary between life and death, or destitution versus material comfort for the rest of her life.

Or being a somebody as opposed to being a nobody.

Yeah. Somebody wrote a paper on it, arguing that it is at the Falls that Hannelore comes to terms with her Nazi past. So the Falls are definitely this focal point. You can call it a symbol, whatever you want to call it. They are the focal point where all these things happen.

The names of your characters in Moon Honey *are allusive. Godfrey (God's brother or friend, I think) shortened to God, is used ironically. Frey, Scandinavian god of fertility and fruitfulness; together with Francie they give birth to Griffin . . . etc. Your use of names reminded me of Pynchon's* Gravity's Rainbow. *Would you like to comment on the onomastic dimension of your fiction?*

For Godfrey I just needed a long version for God. I love names and I love knowing what the meanings of names are, just because they offer so much possibility for character. Quite often I do head straight back to origins of words and I go into babies' name books and stuff like that. In the case of *The*

Widows I wanted authenticity. I'm not a native German speaker, but I wanted it to be as authentic as possible, and also to give myself freedom within that structure. I wanted German names that reflected certain things. Frau Schnadelhuber is a name that my father made up. I asked him for a name that is prototypically Bavarian. He said that all Bavarian names end with Huber or Guber or whatever, and came up with Schnadelhuber, which was great. I get responses from German readers who adore that name because it's so specifically Bavarian. In English it has been interesting too.

When I wrote *The Widows*, I didn't know that the fact that she is called Frau Schnadelhuber all the way through the book is characteristically Bavarian. I later found out that women call each other by their last names even when they are friends. Clothilde is a name that I guess is utterly archaic; it reminded me of Brunhild: a woman in armour, a sort of a female warrior. Hannelore is just one of those names—in this case the name of a woman I worked with, a woman I liked; coincidentally, it's the name of Helmut Kohl's wife.

How much of a ludic (entertaining) quality do you feel your own fiction must have?

When I write, it's utterly serious, and I have a serious intention, but it comes out as being funny. It's like having a speech impediment, because no matter how serious I'm trying to be, people think it's funny. Sometimes it might just be because of a couple of factors: like the omniscient narrator, who supposedly sees everything, but who doesn't actually make enough of a comment; therefore people feel freer to laugh. I, certainly when I think about the things that are appealing to me, love to laugh, and I love stupid sitcoms on television at night. You know, I have a real delight in satire, in putting across really heavy messages by making them funny so that people accidentally swallow the pill.

Until it's digested.

Yes, hopefully, hopefully. So I guess whenever I do it intentionally, it's for that reason.

I remember opening Moon Honey *quite at random, and remarking, this is a distinctly funny book.*

Some people think it's not funny. And other people have called *The Widows* quite cruel—a cruel depiction of German Canadian women: that it's stereotypical, that it pushes the stereotypes too far.

Do you introduce aleatory elements in your fiction to see what effects they'll produce?

In my fiction not so much; in my poetry, definitely. Actually with *The Widows*, after not liking the first draft, as I mentioned earlier, I abandoned it and started work on an entirely new text, which was more of a prose poem about water. I found out about Annie, and did some research. And then, I said, oh my God! This is perfect. It was this very weird cosmic moment.

Perhaps this is the appropriate place to ask you about those writers who have been models for you.

I guess mostly British and Canadian writers, now that I think about it. I didn't come to writing until I was in my early twenties. But before that I read all the time, and, as a good Canadian kid, I read Margaret Atwood and loved her work, loved the sarcasm in her work, which I saw reflected in a lot of British fiction like Fay Weldon's. But it wasn't until university that I came across various writers of colour. I remember being just blown away by *The Colour Purple.* The fact that it was this just hugely tragic, gorgeously written book with a ridiculously happy ending. It was a revelation to see that. I don't write a thing like Alice Walker, or Toni Morrison, who is also one of these incredibly rich writers, but, hopefully, I'm some sort of synthesis of the writers I have read and the writers who have come before me. And there's Michael Ondaatje, whom I've mentioned before. He's one of those writers who when they write prose it's still poetry, and he has such an investment in his creations.

Do you see any merit in what used to be considered the task of novelists: to delight and instruct?

Yes, I do. What are you doing it for if it's not fun for you and fun for anybody else? Regarding instruction, I think the longer I go, the more I realize that you can't know what things people learn from fiction, what things they take from it. So you know, I can't instruct them in one particular way, but I hope they benefit from the experience of occupying someone else's point of view for a few hours.

You just have to be faithful to your vision.

Yeah, exactly.

You are one of the persons Lawrence Hill interviewed for his book Black Berry,

Sweet Juice, *a book that explores identity issues of Eurafrican Canadians. Does your Eurafrican identity inform your writing?*

Certainly, definitely. I tend to localize it a bit more because my mother is from the Bahamas. So I think of myself more in terms of Caribbean Canadian because African Canadian seems so far away, not that I'm not part of the African Diaspora.

All that African means is Black.

Pretty much. Yes, my identity informs my writing. I can't articulate exactly how, but it's essential for me that I present my version of that experience. It's just that everybody has a different story.

Hill states that you also define yourself as lesbian. Does this bear upon your writing?

Yes. Certainly. In my books it mustn't be taken for granted that heterosexuality is a default position. It also questions that idea of sexuality, because I don't think that heterosexuality is defined by the fact that it's not homosexual. What do heterosexuality and homosexuality actually mean? What happens when you take away the comparison?

Yes, but it's like so many things that are defined by saying what they are not.

Same with race too.

I'm thinking of one of Faulkner's characters, one of the Compson children—Benjy, I think—whose definition of himself is: I'm not a nigger.

Exactly. What I really liked doing in that book was looking at how comfortable Clothilde is with her sexuality and her desire for it. She isn't defined by stereotypes. And Hannelore, who belongs to the dominant culture and therefore should be comfortable, is uneasy. And it partly has to do, certainly, with lesbian sexuality: there were no ways to define it; it wasn't a question of what you should or shouldn't do, because you shouldn't do any of it. So you can pretty much make up your own rules. Whereas with heterosexuality in *The Widows*, the rules are preestablished: you shouldn't sleep with people before you marry, etc.—all the rules that Hannelore is bound by; and so Clothilde's relationship highlights Cleopatra Maria's anxieties around sex and sexuality.

Do you see your writing as sharing in the thematic concerns of other African Canadian writers? The theme of identity is a central one for, I suppose, obvious reasons.

Yeah, that's a really good question. For a long time I believed that all the African Canadian writing in Canada was Torontonian, until I read *Childhood* by André Alexis. Even though it comes from central Canada, the story could occur anywhere in Canada, as opposed to just in Ontario or specifically in Toronto. And I think it takes place around Ottawa, which I thought was really interesting.

It begins in Petrolia of all places. I thought it was an invented place.

In Petrolia! Exactly! Well it resonated because there are so many places in Alberta with equally stupid names. So that's what I loved about that book, and I am definitely thinking about issues of identity. What I like though is that you can have Dionne Brand, you can have George Elliott Clarke, you can have André Alexis, and all these writers who aren't necessarily writing about the same things but are kind of writing about the same things. And I love George Elliott Clarke's thesis that all of us are writing in different places and have this multitude of ideas that are contributing to maybe one larger concept. I don't know if he has figured out what that is yet.

Well I think the metaphor he uses is the Odyssey, *post-voyage. In* Odysseys Home: Mapping African Canadian Literature, *George discusses your work in terms of such identity issues. And I think it's in the section where he is dealing with zebra poetics. He has probably spoken to you about this.*

No, but I heard about it in passing. I don't know very much about it. Do you mean in terms of hybridity?

Yes, mixed-race.

It's called zebra poetics?

Yes, it's called zebra poetics.

Really! I think it's one of those images that work perfectly. *Zebra Talk* was the name of my chapbook. The other day I was looking through a copy of *West Coast Line*, and saw that some other poet had used the zebra image to describe being of mixed race. I mean, it resonates.

On another issue, George argues for an African Canadian literature distinct from its US counterpart. There is a tendency, he feels, to merge African Canadian literature with African American literature. Have you any thoughts on this?

I think he is absolutely right. I think that they are absolutely distinct. I don't know if I can comment much further than that, but I don't like the notion of Canadians being mistaken for Americans at all.

Though in the East we sometimes think that Alberta is an extension of the US.

Well, it is in a lot of ways. It's true. They say Calgary is Canada's most American city. It's because of the history too, and the oil interest in the US and in Canada.

You are now a writer-in-residence at the University of Calgary. What effect is it having on your writing?

I'm getting so much writing done. Even when I'm not writing, even when I'm just doing basic things, I get to be in that writing headspace.

As opposed to teaching at the college.

Teaching sucks your brain out of your head. You go home and are consumed by marking and preparing for class. I only have time to write in the summer.

How do you feel about the critical response your work has received?

I don't want to be a whiner, but I think that it's been noticed mostly by people in postsecondary institutions, and it didn't get reviewed a lot. That could be for a number of reasons related to the fact that it was published by a very small Western press. Content, too, may be a part of it. I remember reading a critique by a student that was partly about me. She said my work was about being Black in Canada, not as a first-generation immigrant from somewhere else, but as someone indigenous, and that somehow people have problems wrapping their heads around that, especially in the West.

That's surprising. I found your work refreshing. Different. Setting aside George Elliott Clarke—and even his work is similar in many ways because it is rooted in Nova Scotian Black reality, which in many ways resembles Caribbean colonial reality—a lot of us: NourbeSe Philip, Dionne Brand, Cecil Foster, Claire Harris, myself, we all write that first or second novel that deals with coming into alien space. All of that to point out why your writing is refreshing. On the other hand, you mentioned André Alexis, whose Childhood *has turned out to be quite controversial for some Black writers and literary scholars.*

Oh really. How?

For me, Childhood *is a fine novel; it's beautifully written and crafted. However, there is a feeling among some writers that André deliberately avoided dealing with the experiences of Blacks growing up in Eastern Canada, and that he did so to pander to the marketplace. I heard a reviewer on CBC praising it because "it does not feel Black."*

Interesting.

To what extent do you feel power in the political and economic sphere affects power in the cultural sphere?

I think there's a direct relationship. Let me make sure I understand your question. What do you mean by power in the political sphere?

The people who hold political power control funding and can, and do, exercise censorship.

I think writing would happen anyway, but having the funding sure makes it a lot easier; and, frankly, I think that back in the days when the Canada Council had significantly more money, there was a type of writing done that isn't necessarily receiving the same support and space now. And this post-September 11 pall that we are under—even though it was American—it has affected everything, even the way people speak. Calling Bush a moron, for example. I think that was an incredibly literary moment myself, you know, calling Bush a moron—and then getting fired for it. In a pre-September 11 atmosphere, it would have never been a problem. Somehow I wonder how much the present climate is affecting what people are writing.

I think it's frightening how low a priority the arts are. They are so essential that whenever somebody achieves something artistically challenging, then the politicians are out there and talking about it. It says to me that art has a tremendous function, but is rarely recognized.

If it were up to the Alliance Party—

There would be no art. I remember Stockwell Day saying that we should put the money that goes into arts funding into health care. In Alberta, arts funding comes out of lotteries anyway.

Most books by Black writers challenge the various national myths and are therefore unpopular with White readers. What implications does this state of affairs have for the Black voice in Canadian literature?

Well, it could result in Black writers not wanting to write about the Black experience or erasing race from their work. I've had students of colour who want all their characters to be White because they think nobody would be interested otherwise; and maybe they're right. That's the scary thing. Maybe people won't be. I like to think that this is multicultural Canada with an audience that's literate in every way—a utopian vision, no doubt. I hope writers don't let any of this stop them from writing what they want or need to write.

Well, I know NourbeSe Philip has been publicly insulted, because of her attempts to challenge systematic racism in Canada's literary institutions, including the Canada Council.

What's horrible about that too is that she's writing about really important things, and doing so with a tremendous amount of craft, but somehow her skills as an artist get ignored because she is saying things that people don't want to hear.

Any thoughts about how we might get around the marginalization some of us receive from Canadian publishers and book buyers?

Well just from what that I've seen, what seems to happen is that people get published by small presses, and they get picked up by the big presses because big presses are lazy. They don't want to take the risk. I don't know, I think it's just that we writers have to keep on writing and keep on publishing, and at some point we will reach some sort of critical mass where we won't be ignored anymore, I hope.

Though someone was saying to me the other day—I think it must have been George Elliott Clarke—that there is no guarantee, that certain years you have quite a lot of books, other years you have none. And there is no guarantee at any point that this is going to continue. Lawrence Hill stated something quite similar the other evening. My view on that is that we should get into publishing.

Absolutely.

But usually writers don't have the personality for that sort of a thing.

And also now it's such a horrible climate.

Any other comments that you would like to make about your writing?

No, I don't think so. That was pretty thorough, very thorough.

Thank you.

Pamela Mordecai

Pam, you are an extraordinarily prolific writer of poetry and children's books, an anthologist and a cultural critic. May I ask how many books you've written?

About thirty books, Nigel. They include over a dozen textbooks, four books of poetry, five children's books, and a collection of short stories, as well as several anthologies. And there's a reference work, *Culture and Customs of Jamaica* that Martin and I did together.

Since your works, even those that are set outside Jamaica, are informed by a Caribbean ethos, would you talk a bit about how your being Jamaican informs your writing?

I was born in Jamaica in a house around the corner from the General Penitentiary on Tower Street in downtown Kingston, so I was a city child from the beginning. I grew up in Kingston and was middle aged when I immigrated to Canada, so I'd spent most of my life in Jamaica. I did spend time abroad, going to college in the US, for example, but I never was away for very long. It seems that I was a lucky Jamaican, too, for at school I didn't endure the full colonial brainwashing that many of my friends were subjected to—some of them tell grim stories. I went to a Catholic school, Alpha Academy, where I was spared English history, which we weren't obliged to study. Alpha was a downtown school, not one of the uptown schools. Though we didn't know it at the time, the school was special in that it stressed the performing arts, with a strong Jamaican focus. In *The Jamaican Stage, 1655–1900: Profile of a Colonial Theatre*, the late Errol Hill mentions that the Alpha Cottage, as it was called at the time, was among the first to develop indigenous theatre. That tradition was still very much alive when I was at school. We took part in the annual All-Island Drama and Speech Festivals, and there were sections in the speech festival for the performance of dialect poetry, and of Jamaican poetry in English. There was great competition to qualify to represent the school, especially in dialect poetry. Caribbean plays were performed in the Drama Festival, where there was sometimes highly creative use of dialect. So I grew up surrounded by very Jamaican noise—I think of language as a crucial element in being Jamaican. Whatever we call it, Jamaica Talk, Jamaican Creole, the vernacular—that's my heart language. Of course, I am a native speaker of English too, I like the language, and I think I use it well.

At the moment you're speaking in English and doing so impeccably.

Thanks, Nigel. My Pa would be happy! But I couldn't write outside of my Jamaican self. And I haven't lived outside of Jamaica long enough for that absence to make much of a difference to how I write or what I write about.

Which poets would you say have had the greatest impact on your writing?

You're going to laugh when you hear my answer. From the Caribbean, it's Kamau Brathwaite and, preeminently, Louise Bennett. Otherwise, Chaucer, Shakespeare—can you imagine!—Coleridge, the Romantics, Gerald Manley Hopkins, and Dylan Thomas. And Dr Seuss! But I don't think of myself as "a poet" who has been "influenced." One gets asked these questions, though, and they are helpful because they force me to look at my own development in ways that I otherwise wouldn't. My acquaintance with these poets came partly as a result of a lot of theatre and reciting of poetry at school. Learning poetry by heart became a habit. I can still recite poems by Miss Lou, and certainly chunks of Shakespeare; you'll recall how we in the Caribbean studied Shakespeare. Given all that, it's impossible for the voices one knows so well not to infiltrate one's subconscious. It's in this regard that they are influences.

How do you envisage your role as a writer? For example you evoke the term griot a few times. Do you see writers in such a role?

A writer is a person who tells stories and sings songs. Writers are minstrels—that is one word that we need to rehabilitate. Writers are griots. A griot passes on the story, lore and heritage of the tribe—another word that needs to be reclaimed. Like the griot, the poet or writer preserves the tribe's myths, histories, languages, wisdoms; the writer shows the tribe to itself: its virtues, its vices, its accomplishments, its failings. This is what Louise Bennett did so brilliantly.

Pardon my interrupting you. Do you feel that society, society as it now is in the Western world, is sufficiently literate to read and understand literature—to garner from it the "wisdom," etc.?

I think everybody is literate enough, or can be helped to be so. Look, for example, at the fans that reggae, dub poetry, hip-hop have garnered. These have become our literature. So there are ways of making people pay attention to song and story. But it's not in the interest of those in charge of us—I am sorry if I sound like a conspiracy theorist—to have us understand who we are, and what we have done, and how much more we can do. If we understood, we wouldn't buy, both what they sell and what they say—certainly not as much or as indiscriminately—and it's very important that we be unthinking consumers of things and information. Literature is an excellent tool for helping us to understand. What do songs and stories do, beginning with Anansi stories and Aesop's fables? They construe experience; they help us not to move blindly through life.

Today, however, the broad rubric under which you placed literature has been broken down into other disciplines or subdisciplines. Hip-hop, for instance—popular music on whole—is relegated to the discipline of popular culture. "Those in charge of us" would argue that popular culture is distinct from serious literature insofar as literature is inaccessible to vulgar untutored minds.

Chaucer and Shakespeare catered to the common folk in their time. We have an Institute of Reggae Studies at UWI, which probably no one ever thought likely when Bob Marley and the Wailers first began to sing their songs. Study reggae? Ridiculous! I see these things as running along a continuum, though I admit there are rabbity jumps and points where it thins. I think we all can, and should, understand most of what's out there to be understood.

The elitists would argue that Shakespeare functions at several registers. There's enough in his plays to make them interesting to people at all intellectual levels. Some would respond to the crude jokes and puns, others to those plus his philosophical concepts—

The fullness of meaning.

Thank you.

Let's use the example of Louise Bennett. The first article about her work, if I am not mistaken, was Mervyn Morris' "On Reading Louise Bennett, Seriously." It is an article that probes the work beyond its easily accessible humour. Louise started out as, and people took her to be, "just an entertainer." In time, it became clear that she was fabulously that, and a great deal more.

Even now, she hasn't received enough serious attention for what she was doing. Like Shakespeare, there's something in her poems, stories, commentaries, for the frivolous to relate to, but a great deal for the thoughtful person as well.

My next question, Why do you write? has been answered already, unless there's anything you'd like to add.

There is. It has to do with writing for children. There's very little writing for Caribbean children, either poetry or prose. Our writers have ignored them, so the children are largely feeding at alien troughs.

Are you sure you want to use the word trough?

At this point, we all, adults and children, largely consume the fare provided by the ten men who decide what shall and shall not be published in the world. That's a trough if ever there was one! Trough is a nice farmyard term; it's grounded. It reminds me of feeding chickens in the coop in our yard. I think it helps to be earthy in how we understand things. And I'm certainly there, at the trough, gobbling it down with all the other little piggies.

Do you see poetry as having a function?

When I was at university, I was warned away from any utilitarian view of poetry. They said that if poetry were political, it was likely to be proselytizing and propagandistic. If it had a message, it was almost certainly bad poetry. But I think poetry does have a function. As Jamaican poet Edward Baugh says, "There's no such thing as 'only literature'./ Every line commits you." And that commitment to honestly represent people to themselves is sober and demanding.

My impression is that the Black community expects the work of literature to be temple, community fair, and academy. When I say temple, I mean a place where we celebrate; community fair, where we're entertained; and academy where we're instructed. Does this reflect your own experience in dealing with audiences? And do you think your work manages to fill these needs in some or all of these respects?

That's not an unreasonable expectation. Where young people are concerned, I do think my work serves as celebration and entertainment and instruction, whether they are of Caribbean heritage or otherwise. As for the wider audience, regardless of where I'm reading, or where my work is being read (insofar as one can gather this from reviews, and people's comments), I know it is entertainment. The elements are there: humour, rhyme, rhythm, story—not always together, of course—sometimes even music, and they seem to work. I think it's celebration for my audiences as well—of what's familiar and treasured on the part of Caribbean people, and of what is energetic, honest and earthy on the part of non-Caribbeans. I'm going to take the easy way out and say that if it entertains and is a celebration, then it's instructive too, "instruction" being a complex and complicated business. And it finds its way onto high school and university curricula, so presumably it is instructive in that sense. I know the performance poem, *de Man*, works extremely well as celebration and as entertainment. It's theatre, contains humour, tells a tragic story. I have to conclude that it is also instructive because it continues to be performed during Lent, people use it for prayer and reflection, and it's used for spiritual direction. And the first time I read an excerpt (it's entirely in Jamaican Creole) in a Toronto school, my first reading at a school here in Canada, a whole section of the student body erupted—in celebration, in recognition, and, I think, because they'd never heard anything like it before.

Your poem "In Verse" reflects on the colonized state of English Caribbean writing. Writers are seen as worthwhile only after they have published abroad (quote: "So we look out and bless and curse/ our outward looking: so we verse/ourselves in that plantation twin-/ingness of view, our primal sin. God, what a trade to ply/distilling cris de coeur/ with one sly eye/ on metropolitan market conditions").

Why do you think literary culture is in such a dismal state in the Caribbean?

I've just had a conversation with a distinguished Jamaican writer who was lamenting the fact that we still look abroad to be published.

But we have to look abroad to be published.

We don't always have to. This writer was telling me of a fine Caribbean poet who deserved to have a collection of poems published, and wanted to know whether our small press, Sandberry Press, would consider doing it. She strongly felt that if we invested more in the few publishing houses we have, there would be better publishing opportunities there in the Caribbean. Happily, we now have many more publishers than we once did. I can think of perhaps ten Caribbean presses right away: Ian Randle, LMH, Twin Guinep, Mill Press, Carlong, Sun Zone, Arawak, MEP, The Press (UWI), our own Sandberry Press. However, to build these presses, we, the writers, must support them. You've used the term literary culture, and by that I think you mean the culture of reading books. Right?

Yes. The culture of reading, and reading as an informed reader.

One of the difficulties is with the schools of course. For as long as literature is taught by teachers who don't especially like, or who positively hate teaching it, we will fail to create an audience of eager readers, and, much worse, we will deprive young people of the enjoyment of song and story.

This brings me to the following personal observation: that the English-speaking Caribbean never made it to the literary phase. We no longer need to read for information or entertainment, and that seems to suit us just fine. We started out as an oral culture and just as we were about to enter into a literate culture, we were upstaged by the new electronic oral culture. Literacy and literary culture in its profoundest sense have been obliterated. Except for a tiny elite. A high school teacher in St. Vincent told me that she found the teaching of literature so painful that she was going to ask that it be removed from the school curriculum. Of some twenty-plus secondary schools in St Vincent and the Grenadines, only four teach literature. And in none of them is literature compulsory beyond the Grade Nine (Form III) level.

Well, you're using Vincentian statistics to support the point I was trying to make. It's sad because we all like to tell stories, to make up stories, to listen to stories. Perhaps it's left over from a time when we learned about songs and stories that were foreign and so made little sense. Or perhaps it's that we've succumbed to the siren song of North American movies and soap operas.

Let's focus a bit on the conflict between literacy and masculinity. You know that's a huge part of our problem.

What can I say about this notion that it's not cool to be literate if you're a man? Errol Miller says that, at a certain point, the colonial powers closed one of the teachers' colleges in Jamaica because they feared that Black males, if educated in significant numbers, would eventually subvert the power structure. So those imperialists certainly understood what literate men would be able to do in their own interest and the interest of their societies.

Similar observations have been made about the situation in the US and the fact that it has resulted in more Black men in prison and on probation than in college or university.

We are different from the US, though, because we in the Caribbean have always had predominantly Black or of-colour societies; African Americans have never been in that situation.

What do you see as essential in a book for young children?

They should see themselves celebrated.

What about enchantment and reassurance: enchantment in the metre, for example; the right not to be conformist as shown in the behaviour of the characters' irreverence—your "Ezra's Goldfish" being an excellent example?

Caribbean children—all children—need to see themselves, their place, their culture, and their language celebrated in song and story. That's an important kind of reassurance. And if that happens, magic will be present, especially since for us in the Caribbean, magic is inherent in our folklore—in its incantatory, or tricky, or riddling qualities. Not to mention the magic of "Anansi-bad-behaviour," which I think we should also celebrate.

Nonconformity?

Yes. All those things combined make for good children's writing. But I come back to my first statement: that children should see themselves celebrated.

Writing that helps to anchor them.

Right. My late writing collaborator of almost thirty years made a decision to homeschool her children after her daughter began saying she wanted to have blonde hair and blue eyes. Why? Because at school she was using an American reading book in which all the children had blonde hair and blue eyes. We set ourselves the task of making some suitable textbooks and spent twenty-five years doing that.

Bruno Bettelheim would have been delighted by your work. His theory, expressed in The Uses of Enchantment, *is that fairy tales help children mediate the frightening reality that surrounds them.*

Do I see any such function in my work? I think so. "Ezra's Goldfish" is a poem about a goldfish, who is in fact silver. It's a poem about prejudice, about being treated as different, as needing to be fixed. "Jemima" is a poem about a rambunctious little girl who has to tell her mother that all she really needs, in order to settle down—not change, but be less disruptive—is the reassurance that she's loved. *Rohan Goes to Big School* is a story about a boy going to primary school for the first time who is rescued from bullies by a little girl who is brilliant at playing cricket. I don't know if Bettelheim was talking about monsters and atom bombs as sources of terror, but I try to write poems and stories for children that describe difficult realities but that also deprive those realities of their terrorizing power, and offer the children a way to overcome them.

Some of your poems deal with tragedy; for example, "Convent Girl" (hatred for difference, raw testosterone power) and "Sky Jazz" (genius the consequence of a flawed being). Others are not exactly tragic but depict the flaws, the "cracks," of humanity. Comment.

"Convent Girl" is a poem about serial rape; "Sky Jazz" is a poem about a musician whose personal and professional lives are destroyed by liquor. I want to write about our failings, to address the breaks, the fault lines, the places where we don't treat each other very well, or where individuals don't hold together well—probably because I don't think I hold together too well.

Freud's theory about artistic creation is that there needs to be a state of imbalance within artists to propel them into creating. Robert Graves and Langston Hughes said as much about their need to create poetry.

Well, I won't speak for anyone else, but I'd bear witness to my own lack of balance. It's a challenge to write about imbalances, especially the most imbalanced imbalances. I struggle with how well "literary" writing copes with that task in this apocalyptic time and space. I think I can be clever; I know I can be crafty. I want to put cleverness and craft at the service of a bald dissection of human experience. I can't prettify it.

But a refusal to prettify human experience might well be a substantial part of the definition of a serious writer.

Okay.

Several of your poems—"Easy Life" and "Dust" are examples—deal with the difficulty we have reconciling ourselves to our human limits. Comment.

I think of it not so much as reconciling ourselves to our limits, but maybe more so of effecting catharsis: Aristotle's catharsis, the idea of purgation, relief. One gets relief from simply hearing the story told. The narrator in "Easy Life" lays it out for the woman who complains that she hasn't had an easy life. She asks, "Which way you walk that you didn't choose?" and then she recounts the life of the complainant and sets it against other really hard lives, including the life of her mother who "set her back/ against the world to plant/ you deep for long life." The woman in "Dust" sees the man to whom she is making love as a "downpressor," but admits she hasn't yet managed to learn the lessons of "a decent chastity." So she keeps on making babies for him. Life happens. We go on. Sometimes we learn. Notions like "reconciling ourselves to our situations" and "closure"—I don't know how much I believe in them. We trudge through step by step, hour by hour, always bearing the burden of being decent human beings. We devise ways of containing the breaks and cracks and ugliness (I don't mean limiting them, I mean taking them into ourselves) so that they become part of the decency each person carries inside himself or herself. I hope that is what good poetry, good literature, helps both reader and writer to do.

You therefore see the self as a matrix holding together and managing all sorts of warring forces.

Yes, I guess so. Perhaps one problem I have with the idea of reconciling ourselves to things is that it strikes me as too rational, too calculated. That's not how it is.

There is as well your theme of transcendence: in "Catch the Wind," "I Want to Go Up Rivers," for example. Comment.

The persona in "Catch the Wind" hopes to extend a hand far enough to catch the wind, which is a Spirit wind. The persona in "I Want to Go up Rivers" isn't trying to discover or map anything. Instead he or she longs "wet, naked, to move farther in/ to water, rock, sky, innocence." There are different ways we can understand ourselves: as people who make money, have lots of knowledge, power and control, do brilliant things, people who can be young forever if we work hard at it. But there's a way of understanding ourselves as creators, makers, kin with the transcendent Creator/Maker, however you conceive of that Person. It's obvious that we create: offspring; language; civilizations; art; song and story. But the most important thing we make is ourselves. That's our big project: to understand ourselves as creators and to make ourselves into the best creators we can be. You know the poem, "Ode" by Arthur O'Shaughnessy, "We are the music makers, and we are the dreamers of dreams…" I think that's a good way to think of ourselves, a good thing to want to be—makers who forsake consumerism and capitalism and instead move and shake the world with song and story.

But the very possibility of our discovering and developing ourselves outside of the consumerist context we're born into is a very difficult one. The state and civil society conspire to work against such self-growth and culture. Here's an example: in the province of Quebec, where I live, to this day literature isn't taught in the French schools, a heritage of the Catholic Church that once administered them and kept out literature, precisely because the Church sought to ban all ideas that might challenge Catholic teachings. I have been shocked to discover students in my introductory university literature courses who have never read a novel, play, or short-story.

Nigel, that can't be true.

At first I didn't believe it could be. Later I read in a series of articles about the dismal state of the French language in Quebec that the exclusion of literature from the curriculum was one of the reasons for this.

I think that literature is the place where God makes his last stand, so to speak.

The place where everyone with or without religious faith might encounter God.

Of course! So the idea that literature would be forbidden in the school curriculum in Catholic or any schools makes no sense to me.

Some of your poems function as disputations of other poems and establish a sort of dialectic: "Easy Life" vs "Going Home"; "Tell Me" with "Exeunt." Others express a tension, an uneasy coexistence, between the desire for self-reliance and the need for companionship: "For Eyes to Bless You." Obviously you are seeing the poetic space as a place for debate. Comment.

Some of the poems consider different aspects of the same thing—that's inevitable. So, to take one of your examples, in "Tell Me," a woman issues a challenge to the man with whom she is embarking on a relationship by telling him what she's prepared to invest in it, while in "Exeunt," a relationship is nipped in the bud because the man makes sex a necessary condition. I am interested in the back-and-forth in things, the alternatives, good and bad. Life is that type of motion, isn't it? That tidal wash, the ebb and flow, and its inherent tension—enables the negotiation of those spaces where we discover things about ourselves that help us further our self-creation.

I would like you to comment on two subjects that you treat with startling difference: one is the feminism of Virginia Woolf (as seen by a less privileged Caribbean woman) and the other is the figure of Caliban, which, I think, you're employing subversively. In any event you're taking him out of the space Shakespeare and colonialism have assigned him.

Feminism is all very well, but one has always to think of how many of the women in the world it can mean something for. One has always to test a perspective, a point of view, in that everywhere-in-the world way. I've no quarrel with Virginia Woolf. She's an outstanding writer and very likely deserves a place among the great writers of the twentieth century. Moreover, there are things I share with her.

Given your earlier comment about wanting your writing to be accessible to the average reader, quite clearly styles of writing—I'm thinking of her novel To the Lighthouse—*isn't one of them.*

No, it isn't. I'm thinking of her life, and death. My family has a history of mental illness—wandering off into water—so I'm certainly not dismissing the pain that oppressed Ms Woolf, and the life experience out of which an important body of work came. But I am saying that her view of woman and how she occupies her space in the world could have been larger. Her privilege needn't have constrained her vision.

Five hundred a year, metonomymically speaking, does indeed confer privilege. To begin with, it pays for a space of one's own.

And the ability to occupy it alone. It don't have to "pack-up" with twenty people. Most of us in the majority world don't have rooms of our own. As for Caliban, I suppose we in the Caribbean can't avoid being preoccupied with tempests. Some people would wonder why I didn't focus on Sycorax—

You didn't exclude her.

No, I didn't, but it is "Caliban Calypso." There was a point at which I recognized—it was probably when I was writing *de Man*—that in a very real way, Creole gave me my writing voice. That voice is Caliban's voice: the language used for cursing, with all the ironies that implies. Those glossalalic syllables that he is depicted as using in "Caliban Calypso," and that making of pan, they are resonant symbols for me. Pan is a voice we have made. Creole is a language we have made. Calypso is a music we've made.

How would you relate your experience under colonialism to the way you depicted him?

I don't think I ever felt colonized, but I felt like an outsider from the start. If you are outside, then you aren't part of anything, not even an oppressed community.

You are referring, I suppose, to your being of Jewish, Black, and South Asian ancestry.

And more too besides! We need a community of mongrels, I suppose. But I never fit in anywhere, from the beginning. I had very few friends in school. I was always the youngest in the class and among the brightest, and praised for it by teachers—not a situation conducive to making friends. I was untidy, bright, earnest, transparent, weird in a lot of ways. But they did teach me language, and I like to think that I eventually turned it to its Calibanic purpose. I love the image of Caliban as a pan man with the power to "disturb [his] neighbour" and to imbue that disturbing noise with melody, meaning… Quote: "… him tongue twining with curses?/ Muttering glossalalic nonsenses/ him find him can decline/ him pain in verses, start spirits with words,/ and the birds, if him call dem, will come." And you see, the sound "make him head start rise." You know what that means?

The proud feeling of achievement.

Right. Also, insight, the ability to see into the spirit world. Caliban is empowered by his ability to curse, as also to make nonsense noises that others will dismiss as glossalalia. But glossalalia is the ultimate way of communicating with God, beyond words, spirit to Spirit. Also, "Him bruck a stick and start lick galvanize." With his language, his pan, he can beat down the oppressor: galvanize=Babylon.

Your way of conquering it.

Thank you, Nigel.

Your poems about Caribbean residents in Canada show them in conflict with the culture. I'm thinking particularly about "To No Music," "Serafina," and "Blessed Assurance." These are poems that use humour to say a great deal about cultural dissonance. Would you like to comment?

I think that we "Caribbeans" come here aware at some level that we have the task of what Louise Bennett calls "colonization in reverse." We bring plenty; we don't come with our two long, empty hands. Serafina, for example, is a health worker, who has the discernment to listen to God's messenger, never mind that he arrives in an odd form. When an incontinent White patient in the hospital where she works joins battle with her, she routs him with her rhetoric and her Bible knowledge. Whether they fire her from the hospital, whether she never finds another job, hers is the triumph of being who she is, of standing by her choices. The "warner-woman" in "Blessed Assurance" is equally fluent and discerning, aware of her role as prophet and preacher "in these latter days". The worker in "To No Music" concludes "They [the people in 'this country'] walk to no music/ and that is misery."

A big part of what we bring is not just our culture and language, but how we inhabit the culture and use the language. Edward Baugh has a great poem, resonant with that culture, that rhetoric, those sounds, called "Old Talk, or West Indian History." So if my poems end up showing immigrant and adopted cultures out of kilter, that's because they are. I would prefer to say, using your terms, that these are cultures in negotiation, and that we immigrated Caribbean people negotiate with power, and with humour too…

Talking about humour, it along with language, especially Jamaican language, enriches your poetry significantly. How consciously do you employ it?

I want to write funny because I hope that I am writing tough, and, in the Caribbean, the two things go together. In the Caribbean we say that, "If you don't laugh you cry." We speak of "taking serious thing make joke," because that's how we cope, that's how we face life. So to write about us truly, I have to employ humour.

In an earlier conversation, you and I spoke about reality being the frontier that the creative artist must traverse. This is very much the case with your poem de Man. *Would you like to comment on its genesis?*

I like to say that it was commissioned by my parish priest at the time, a wonderful man, a Jesuit and a literature scholar. At the end of a Good Friday service one year, he asked if I would write something for Good Friday the following year. I think he was thinking of that frontier of reality that you mention. He wanted something for Good Friday that was part of our Jamaican reality. I said yes. When Lent began the next year, I had written nothing. But I don't like to break a promise, so I knew I had to do this. Catholics have the ritual of the Stations of the Cross—I think Anglicans do too—in which we follow Jesus through the journey of his crucifixion. I thought that I could use that as a kind of structure. When the first line "came": "Unoo see me dying trial!"—it fit so well that I knew that the rest would "come" and would be in Creole. And most of the poem followed quickly enough. In fact, the first twelve stations were performed that Good Friday.

If we need proof that language transforms rather than translates content, it is here.

Okay. (Sceptical)

You take the biblical story and you render it in another tongue. And the semantics of that tongue transforms the story.

The last time I performed excerpts from that poem was to a church full of non-Caribbean Canadians on Good Friday this year. The response was overwhelming—very much as if the congregation were hearing the story for the first time. And the Creole transforms other Bible stories too. The story of Jesus changing water into wine at the wedding feast in Cana has always seemed stiff, unreal to me. But listen to it in creole: Mary comes to Jesus and says, urgently, "Son, them no have no wine!" He looks at her, mischievously, and says, "Ooman, me no business wid dat. A no fe me time yet." And she looks at him, raises her eyebrows in mock exasperation, and then instructs the servants, "Unoo just do what him tell you." And of course, he obliges. (Laughter) Suddenly the story has meaning.

The cultural references are impressive. I'm thinking of the order that's given there that isn't even stated.

Exactly. But, you see, it isn't merely a question of language; the language effects a kind of cultural shift, expresses a whole new way of seeing and being.

You seem to be showing how the tale alters when it is told with another tongue and framed by another zeitgeist. Here, for example, the tale is framed by the socioeconomics of Jamaica. Comment.

An insight I got while I was writing *de Man* was that the language Jesus spoke on the street was not Hebrew, the language of the priests. It would have been the vernacular, Aramaic. Both his language and the culture in which he was raised no doubt resembled that of ordinary Jamaicans. It's easy to miss this, because the Gospel makes a point of his erudition: at twelve he is disputing with the priests, in the temple, presumably in Hebrew. But he was raised in Nazareth, a grotty little town, and he grew up speaking the language of the common folk. It seemed to me that all the parallels were there. It felt right.

Your poem with the title "Poem" speaks to your understanding of the birth of poetry. Would you like to comment?

"Poem" is dedicated to Kamau Brathwaite. I met him just about when *Rights of Passage*, the first book of his first trilogy, was about to appear. I took part in at least two early performances of that book, so I know it well. It was just at this point that I was beginning to write poetry seriously. *Rights of Passage* was a tour de force, unlike anything that I'd ever met before, having, as "Poem" says, "secret" meanings, the sound of which I heard, but many of the significances unfolding afterwards. The images in "Poem"—of the poem as a sounding drum, and of insight as "the wind.../sifting the long grass"—relate to that whole culture and history and heritage that I was increasingly coming to appreciate, in part through my encounter with Brathwaite's poetry and his work as a historian and aesthetic theoretician. So "Poem" is both a thank you and a homage poem that witnesses to the fact that one writes best out of who one is, and that the creative act is informed by that who-ness.

I often say that I admire the Enlightenment for the corrective it brought and for the impetus it gave to the natural sciences, but I'm glad the Romantics dethroned it, in literature at any rate. The Enlightenment reduced everything to mathematics and the senses, and there is so much more to reality than either math or the senses can measure. After all, mathematics measures only what mathematics can measure.

I like that. Mathematics measures what mathematics can measure.

And what mathematics cannot measure is the domain in which creative artists and mystics labour.

Absolutely.

To this one might add "Poems Grow" and "Starapple Tree," in which you (seem to) imply that poetry is linked to what Jung calls the shadow of the psyche, that part of ourselves that cannot be accessed via logic.

We talked earlier about this, Nigel. I don't at all countenance (to use my Granny's word) the idea that logic and science are paramount. African and Eastern cultures affirm the realm of the shadow, a realm of spirit, an immanent and mysterious world. The image of the starapple tree expresses that mysterious otherness: its leaves are coloured differently on each side: as the wind blows and the underside of the leaves is exposed, a different tree emerges. "Poems Grow" describes all the unlikely, ordinary places ("window ledges," "slightly dirty kitchens where rats hide") where poems lurk. The "Griot older than time on Zion hill" lives in all those places, continually making the ordinary extraordinary, and inscribing the temporal into the eternal.

Now I'd like to turn our discussion to form in your poetry. Let's begin with orality. Oftentimes one hears the speaking voice in your poetry.

The speaking voice was always there, in poems like "Protest Poem," "Last Lines" and "Easy Life" in the first book, *Journey Poem*, but it's increasingly present in poems written after *de Man*. Many of the later poems tell stories featuring real people with individual voices. This change probably has to do with what I was more and more wanting to say in the poems. My sense is that the world is ending, in terms of the speed with which we are destroying it ecologically, the deliberate use of divisiveness and war to express national policies and our rush to create weapons capable of obliterating humanity. I badly want to spread that news, and the live voice has that urgent, compelling quality.

Would you say that "Sky Jazz" is a ballad in non-balladic form? How conscious are you about working against form?

I agree that "Sky Jazz" is a ballad although the form is not balladic. On occasion, I do deliberately work against form. "The Story of Nellie," in *The True Blue of Islands*, for example, sounds like a nursery rhyme but tells the tale of Nellie's abuse as a child and young adolescent. That counterpointing is deliberate. "Sky Jazz" is a ballad about a jazz musician, so it attempts to be musical in a modern way. The poem in fact contains two sequences that are meant to be sung in jazz style.

Whole poems of yours—"Caliban Calypso or Original Pan Man," "Dust," even in the frightening subject of "Deadly Beauties," "The Angel in the House," especially the line "pum-pum politics"—rely on wit for their effectiveness. But your use of irony is really what interests me most in this case. Would you like to comment on this?

Poets often speak about the poem writing them, Nigel. I think the poem in Jamaican language writes me. And it's a mistake to think of the Creole as a vehicle for just belly-laugh humour. Puns, double entendres, sarcasm, irony—these are all devices that the vernacular employs. Jamaican proverbs offer ready proof of all this. So I'm going to give the credit for wit, if there's any to be given, to Jamaican language and culture and to that way of seeing things. I don't think "pum-pum politics" is original. Nor is the man's springing "ting-ting" in "Caliban Calypso." True, the woman in "Dust," who considers her man a "downpresser," is giving an already revised term a further shaking up, and, until the imaginary woman in the poem thought of it, I'd not heard breasts spoken of as "Deadly Beauties." Still, I'll take any blame, and give a lot of credit to the language.

You are its servant.

Definitely.

Some of your witty effectiveness is achieved through a very distilled and carefully chosen alliterative and profoundly significant metaphoric diction, for example, in "Cane Juice & Other Vinegars," particularly the stanza: "So heaven for poets/ is good grass/ and a new wasp-waisted wife." But it's used with deft satire in "The Angel in the House." Comment.

I think theatre made language something delicious. Rhyme and rhythm, alliteration and onomatopoeia, double entendre (the term itself stresses the aural aspect of the device) are mother's milk to me. It's wicked, I guess, to suggest that heaven for poets, these sensitive people, should be "good grass" and "a new wasp-waisted wife." What manner of poet is this? What manner of heaven! What manner of wife! The title signals the perverse point of view—we don't normally think of cane juice as vinegar. "A new" suggests he's had this kind of wife before; "waisted" also means "wasted": if she's been wasted by wasps, this implies something about her character and his choice of wives. The same perverse point of view applies in "The Angel in the House." If you're going to take on Virginia Woolf in Jamaican Creole, you'd better come good, as we say. The thing is, it sometimes happens that at a certain point one feels the poem lift, like a kite, and this one did. Its diction is tea-meeting-style erudition. So the Cherub in the house "accept the job/ to jook and cook" and "This Miss Woolf/ take a simple/ view of pum-pum politics,/ she make a crass construction/ of the sweet domestic life." Hopefully it works.

In some of your poems every strand is an image weaving into other images ("Island Woman"). Others are very spare in imagery as in "Farewell" (Piarco). What determines one or the other approach?

Maybe it's that "Farewell" is an actual experience, set down just so. I don't know. Some poems—I think especially of "My sister muse" in *Certifiable*—absolutely depend on images. I agree that "Island Woman" is one of those. It's mostly not a poem about me; it's about a woman-island, woman as an island, the capital P, Poet, as a woman-island—not so easy to write sparely about.

Any comments about your prose work?

I have been writing prose for a long time. I have the MS of a novel that I started when we lived in Trinidad in 1978–79. So writing prose isn't new. But it's not something I have practised the way I've practised writing poetry. I find that, as in writing poetry, I'm not just interested in telling the story, I'm challenged by the possibilities of form. The use of both standard English and Creole has turned out to be a challenge too. One is shopping for publishers in North America, after all, and they do balk at the use of Creole.

Is there anything that writing stories gives you the opportunity to do that poetry doesn't?

Develop characters more fully, round them out, see them operate over more extended periods of time, follow them into situations and watch them work through challenges, throw more of them at one another in the same space. It's been a sort of natural development, in a way: poems, the performance crucifixion poem, which is where the storytelling began, more storypoems, and now short fiction.

So do we expect a novel in time?

We'll wait and see, Nigel. It not good to talk too soon.

To what extent do you feel power in the political and economic sphere affects power in the cultural sphere? You know the problem we have as Black writers to get published in this society. We are told point blank by publishers that our works don't sell.

Publishers say our works don't sell, but it isn't true—even our poetry is marketable, and that's a notoriously hard sell. Goose Lane reprinted *Certifiable*, my third collection, never mind that many of the poems are in Jamaican language. *de Man* sells steadily as well, with more and more people discovering it ten years after it was published. I do think we need to flex our political and economic muscle more, though we are getting better at this. And we need to strategize. When we started our small press, we focused on publishing first collections, because one of the hardest things, especially for a poet, is to get a first book published. This gives beginning writers a foot in the door that makes it easier for them to approach other publishers with their second manuscripts.

But if the sales for the first book are poor, writers generally have trouble placing their second book, much the same way film makers, if they bomb with their first effort, have trouble raising money for their second.

That's why presses like Sister Vision, Williams-Wallace—unfortunately now defunct—TSAR are so vital. There's another component to this: I think we need to be more aggressive in marketing ourselves. I think of Third World Books and Crafts, which is no longer in business. We should have found a way to keep Third World operating. When Gwen and Lennie Johnson ran it, if a writer walked in there with even a self-published book they would stock it. Getting the book published is one thing, getting it into the readers' hands is another. We have some Black bookstores, but we could do with more.

How do you feel about the critical response your work has received?

If individual readers like my work, that's the best critical response for me—critical too in the sense that the book gets bought! I've earned my living almost exclusively by writing for a long time, and not many people can say that. I'm not on the conference circuit, and that's a constraint, and because I haven't had a very easy life (ha ha!), and am by no means as good as I should be about networking, I'm sort of isolated here in my little backwater. But readers have a duty to find writers, too, and God willing, the work will find an audience. My writing for children is pretty well known in the UK, and is used in textbooks and anthologies there, in the US, Canada, West Africa, and the Caribbean. When it comes to criticism in the sense of what has been written by academics about my work, I'd say that response has been positive too.

Most of the books by Black writers challenge the national myths and are therefore unpopular with White readers. What implications does this state of affairs hold for non-White voices in Canadian literature?

That's a difficult question. Again, those ten men who decide on what we read! I think that where our literature goes depends on how energetic we are in creating, producing, and distributing it, as also in mobilizing our own audiences to support it. I see, for example, Rabindranath Maharaj's success with Knopf as a positive thing for non-White writers. When writers like him succeed—and he's relatively new—they create a beachhead for others. Winning prizes helps too—Austin Clarke's winning the Giller, for example.

But Clarke's Giller comes after thirty-plus years of writing.

His photo with the Giller prize in his hand is a very positive image, nevertheless. Dionne Brand's succcesses, too, are very encouraging.

Have you any other suggestions about how we might get around the marginalization we receive from Canadian publishers and book buyers?

We need to go more often into the schools, colleges and universities, not just in February but all year long. We need to get our books on the curriculum. Perhaps we should create opportunities for our writers to read together, by, say, organizing Festivals of Canadian Writers of Colour. One hopes for a time when we are all "mainstream" writers, but until then, we probably need to do those things. And it's the readers who have the last word. We are fine writers. We just need to let them know we're here.

Thanks for discussing your writing with me.

M NourbeSe Philip

More than any other Black-Canadian writer, you have theorized extensively about the relationship between language and the self. This seems to be a mission, an obligation to yourself.

Do I have a choice? The relationship of language to self? I think for me as a Caribbean person, and for us as Caribbean people, people of the Antilles, I think language is central to the way we are, to the way we be, to use a Black expression, the way we interact with our environment and others. And it is a project that chose me; I didn't choose it as a writer. I may have said this to you before[1]—I think projects choose writers and then they spend the rest of their lives working on them. You know the history of how language came to us—European languages, that is—overlaid, I think, on a deeper language that we continue not so much to speak as to express and which is often in conflict with the European language. I agree with the poet Kamau Brathwaite when he says that the language of the African Caribbean is among other things the language of the howl, the shout, the machine gun, a wave . . . There is a lot of energy and violence in those images, and they reflect a certain reality for New World Africans today. It speaks to a deeper issue that is still running throughout our communities wherever we are: the issue of what happened to us Africans—how we were brought here, what has happened to us since; how we make sense of an event about which we can never fully make sense.

Silence as trope and as historical fact preoccupies you. How have you been able to deal with this in your creative works?

I think the first thing I need to say is that I don't believe that we as a colonized people were ever silent or were ever silenced. I think that often when we appeared silent to the colonizer, we were doing something else. Having said that, however, we have been written in as silences.

How I have dealt with it in terms of writing? *Looking for Livingstone* was

[1]See, "A Rejoinder to Prospero: An Interview with M. NourbeSe Philip," *Kola* 8:2 (1996), 38–55.

one way, because at one point during the writing of that work, I realized silence was a very abstract construct, so I felt I had to ground it in something tangible, someone real. Livingstone, then, became the metaphor for silencing. But another way that I deal with it on the page, one I learnt when I did *She Tries Her Tongue* and *Looking for Livingstone*, was through the use of space on the page—isolating words and learning how not to fear the empty space, the silent spaces, because it is that "silent space" that actually helps to give voice to what is said.

The last paragraph of your essay "Ignoring Poetry" made me see the blank page as a metaphor of a silent whiteness and the Black characters on the page as fracturing that silence. I suppose what really matters is how those characters get configured.

I think there is an interesting tension happening. As I said before, we were never silent, and that's what I say in the paragraph there. But we, too, have to learn how to read our own silences, our historical silences. At the same time, I talk also about trying to fill up that space. And that is one of the contradictions, and it leads to tension because I think sometimes we feel that we have to fill up that space to prove that we are who we think "massa" wants us to be. What I am saying is that maybe we don't always have to fill the space up. Instead we have to learn how to read the silences.

You argue though that the aesthetics of silence makes reading your poems difficult, and you give the example of an occasion when you had to read after Linton Kwesi Johnson and you didn't quite know what to do. Have you thought since of how you might resolve that problem?

With some of those poems—I don't know if I told you this years ago—what I figured out was that the performative act was very important. I felt that when *She Tries Her Tongue* and *Looking for Livingstone* were done. They need a choral, collective voice. And, depending on the context, I can achieve this. If I am in a university class, for instance, I will ask the students to actually come and read them with me, and a mini-dramatic performance happens. Where I see the "problem," however, is that it's not the kind of work that we usually associate with Black writing. Even though the work is within the same project as the more accessible works like "spoken-word" and Hip Hop—those spoken word artists who are politically charged and understand what we are about—it is not in as accessible a form for such audiences. And, for me, that's a challenge and a problem. Because a part of me would really love—and I say this in one of the essays—to feel that the work is being read and understood, or heard and understood by the ordinary men or women (if there is such a thing), the people I talk about in that introductory essay. But I don't fool myself: it's not. And I think that's a function of the education that I have come out of—a function of all the forces that have produced who I am. And I have to accept it, live with it, enjoy it, and make the most of it. But there is an issue there. And I can't pretend otherwise. I still think that writing in the Caribbean is not embraced with the same level of enthusiasm and comfort as the oral arts are.

Writing has been so closely associated with demonization and put-downs.

And there is good reason why it should be viewed with suspicion, because it is through the mechanism of writing that our lives were made hell on earth. So I think there is every good reason for the suspicions. I was really struck when I was living there in 1990, and was reading George Lamming's *Pleasures of Exile*, to see how similar the situation still was for those of us who make our living through the written arts—all these years after so many Caribbean people have shown themselves to be consummate practitioners of the written arts.

In Looking for Livingstone *a desire to end silence drives the novel. Is it more successfully handled in this form? In fiction rather than poetry?*

I have always considered *Livingstone* a poem in poetry and prose. It was the publisher's decision to market it as a novel.

That is interesting because that is part of a question I have prepared for Claire Harris. As you know, her novels Drawing Down a Daughter *and* She *are written in poetry. In the question, I mention* Looking for Livingstone *as another example of a work that does this.*

So I think that it can be handled really well in poetry.

Yes, and you can see why it could be marketed as a novel because there is a quest, a story line and the prose passages. But it was always intended as a long poem in prose and poetry. And, as I said before, I felt that I had to ground it in something very real and tangible, hence Livingstone.

In "A Genealogy of Resistance" you tell us that Harriet in Harriet's Daughter *and some of your other characters were created out of a need to fill the silence about your ancestors. You say, as well, that writing comes out of the self. Most authors say that their writing is not autobiographical.*

For me writing comes out of the body. And, therefore, the Self, because the body is a part of the Self. This is, of course, counter to the European Enlightenment tradition of splitting the body from the mind. But this does not necessarily mean that the writing is autobiographical. When I say writing comes out of the body—and I speak only about myself here—I mean that I have a sense of sacrificing a part—an aspect, if you will—of my body every time I produce work. Further, I am often reminded of that quotation by Carlos Fuentes about "imagining the past," and "remembering the future." We usually think of it as the other way around, but for us New World people, us Africans, that's what we have to do. We have to imagine the past because it is not in the official text. And in the imagining of our pasts we are remembering our future generations for whom we are laying down a foundation.

Exorcizing much of what is toxic to self in the colonial language that was foisted upon us is a theme of your poetry, especially in She Tries Her Tongue, *but it is as well the concern of your essays in* Frontiers *and in some of the essays in* A Genealogy of Resistance. *Let me quote you: "The place we occupy as poets is one that is unique—one that forces us to operate in a language that was used to brutalize Africans so that they would come to believe in their own lack of humanity. No language can accomplish this—and to a large degree English did—without itself being profoundly tainted."*

Some of the more obvious things I think about when I think about how English works is the passive tense. For example: the natives were subjugated. By whom? Who did it? The language functions to remove the agents of these atrocities and we the users of that language are all the poorer for it. I am at present working on a set of poems in which I am using the report of a court case to make the poems. The case itself is a famous one involving the slave ship *Zong*, from which the crew threw the slaves overboard. Murdered them, in fact, to collect insurance monies. It is a very short report, just one and a half pages long, but I believe the legal language is actually a cover for the story, or stories, that happened on board that ship. You can say the story is lodged within the words of the case.

Language and the female body in patriarchal societies is the subject of your essay "Displace: The Space Between." I wonder if you would comment on this.

I think this essay began, before I was conscious of it, in a letter I got from Carol Boyce Davies regarding an essay I had sent her. I believe it was "Managing the Unmanageable." I replied that I hadn't wanted to make reference to women just for the sake of making reference to them. But that stayed with me and no doubt germinated in me. Before I began *She Tries Her Tongue*, I was very interested in the idea of how women take up physical space in society. The fat woman is still seen in Western society as unattractive and inappropriate—health considerations aside. Fortunately, in African societies that is often different. Here in North America, it is only when pregnant is the woman seen as legitimately taking up space. Even travelling on the subway you notice this, in the differences in the way men and women sit. Often the man will have his legs wide open. So how do we as women negotiate space? It occurred to me as well that when a woman asks: "How safe is this place?" she's basically asking how safe the space between her legs is, or will be, in that particular place or space. In other words: "Am I going to be raped?" She is not asking whether or not she's going to be killed.

Your essay reminded me of something I read or heard—I think it was from Pam Mordecai. She asked a group of women how many of them had been raped, and more than half of them indicated that they had been.

Regarding the Black woman's body, we have to remember that one of the reasons that Black women were brought to the New World was to pacify men; it's there in the recorded documents. Later Black women's bodies were reaped, very much the way that land is reaped. So I became interested in that link between the outer space and the inner space—the Black woman's womb as one example of that inner space. I was also interested in exploring how women had historically negotiated the outer space in ways that suggested that they weren't always victims. That led me to the erased histories of the jamettes in Trinidad. I recall as a child, my mother used to say to me when I was loud, "Shhh, you sound like a jamette." A jamette was a loud woman and a woman who occupied the street in an uncompromising way. My research revealed that these groups in Trinidad—in Port of Spain—formed themselves into gangs of women who fought off their adversaries and protected one another. When I presented that paper at the Second Caribbean Women Writers' Conference in Trinidad, it was not very well received. Some participants were concerned that I had dared to mention Nanny of the Maroons in the same breath as I mentioned jamettes. Was I suggesting that Nanny of the Maroons was a jamette, I was asked. They missed the point, of course. Nanny, as you know, was a leader of liberation warriors, the Maroons, who fought the British, and I was interested in exploring how she negotiated and manipulated the space of war. Interestingly enough, after the presentation, a colleague informed me of the belief in Jamaica, that Nanny caught bullets with her behind. Nanny was not raped; on the contrary she turned that space between her legs—so the story goes—into a place of resistance. She caught the bullets in her behind.

You believe that a liberating poetry requires a new language and a radicalized form. And you provide an excellent example of this in your poem "Discourse on Language." It's more than a decade now since you wrote She Tries Her Tongue. *Have you any afterthoughts on this. Whenever I talk with my colleagues in the US, those who are familiar with Black Canadian writing, they mention it.*

I am aware that interest in *She Tries Her Tongue* remains strong over the years. It's been more than ten years since it has been out and people are still asking me to send them copies; professors want it for their classes, etc. It is rewarding and fascinating that it is still being discovered. I have said this to you before—that I had learned a lot from those poems after their publication. I was conscious that I wanted to destroy the lyric voice, as I worked on *She Tries Her Tongue.* Then the poems became very difficult to read, particularly those in the second half of the book. Until a student said to me "Can you read 'Universal Grammar?'" And then the answer came: "If you read it with me." And then I knew that I had replaced the lyric voice with the voice of the multitude—a sometimes cacophonous chorus of voices, all clamouring to be heard.

Your experimentation with form has certainly continued in the essay. Here you not only incorporate multiple genres: poetry, fiction, drama and fragmentary sentences, but you disrupt the traditional linearity and rigid logical structure of the standard essay, and in many cases, resort to montage. ("Whose Idea Was It Anyway?" for example)

I love writing essays and I have certainly become increasingly aware of the need to bring a poetic to and poetry into the essay. I think good essays have the elegance of a good poem—the economy and the elegance.

But essays tend to follow Enlightenment restrictions, in the sense that they have to be logical, absolutely logical.

One of the things that I have had to work against within myself is the legal training to be logical. And I think that it's that desire to disrupt that logic that creates a space for the poetic voice.

In some cases I resorted to metaphors to picture the essays. One I thought of was interconnecting ponds fed by underground tributaries.

I think a lot of that goes back to what we began the interview with: silences, and voicing the unvoiced. I think that your metaphor about the interconnecting ponds fed by underground streams is apt. I think it's a desire to understand where and how these ideas connect: the need to explain them to myself and to effect that explanation forces me down to subterranean depths to discover the links and interconnections.

In "African Roots and Continuities: Race, Space and the Poetics of Moving," diction, constitutive metaphors, and axial allegorical personae (Maisie & Totoben, for example) create a framework into which you pour historical data. Comment.

In "The Absence of Writing," what I argue is that we possess language; we, Caribbean people, live within a spectrum of language. I wrote the first page and a half of that essay in the Caribbean demotic or vernacular. But then as the essay goes on, I shift into standard English which I even address within the essay as a kind of failure—the need to resort to standard English..

In the Caribbean we move from demotic or vernacular to standard English and back again without even noticing and often within the same sentence. But I have always been interested in using the demotic or nation language to write something serious in an extended way. Usually when we read the demotic, or hear the demotic in the theatre, for instance, it's often humorous or comedic. But I was convinced that carnival did not happen in standard English. It doesn't happen in any of the European languages. We return here to that idea I raised in the beginning that the European languages have been thinly overlaid over another deeper language. And that is the language Carnival takes place in.

For me to write about it would be to put another restriction on this event that throughout history had been the subject of so many restrictions—written ones at that. For myself I was very interested in seeing whether I could write the history of Carnival in demotic. That was the genesis of that essay.

Reading your essays, I have wondered if you have come to the conclusion that the poem by itself cannot execute your intention, but that the poem in the context of a radically altered essay form might achieve it. Comment.

For me, I think it is a follow-through on what I just trying to do with "Discourse." If you recall, what I said in "Discourse" was that I was putting the poem back in the mess and the morass and the matrix as opposed to sculpting it out of it. I think that is what is happening there. It's putting the poem back into its context. Because for us in the Caribbean, and being of the Caribbean, we do not have the luxury of these divides between the genres—poetry, fiction, social and political commentary: they all bleed into and onto each other as our lives have done.

In the preface to your play Coups and Calypsos, *you state that your temperament does not fit you for writing for the theatre. Yet you chose to write this play on a theme your work had up to that time overlooked: Indian-African relationships in Trinidad & Tobago. Would you comment on the genesis of* Coups and Calypsos*?*

I was there [in Trinidad] during the attempted coup on the government and I saw theatre in the way we performed the coup. The biggest players being the politicians, of course (laughs).

It's spontaneous.

It's theatre 24/7 and everybody, to some degree, is on stage. The news of what was happening during the coup was limited to the three radios that I had. It was a very oral and aural experience. I knew I was going to write about it, but I knew it had to have something of a three-dimensional quality; it couldn't be just on the page, so it had to be the stage.

Now, in terms of the race issue, you can't be from Trinidad or Guyana and not be aware of the tensions between Africans and South Asians. It has always fascinated me that when the issue of interracial relationships is dealt with, as in the films *Jungle Fever* or *Mississippi Massala*, it is always the Black male with a female from another race. And it seems to me that this is an area of deafening silence as it relates to Black women. Of course this is a reflection of the patriarchal society we live in as expressed in the ultimate threat: Would you let your daughter marry one of those. However, during slavery, during the days of colonialism, the mixing of the races was primarily between White males and the Other: African females, in the case of slavery; Aboriginal women, in the broader colonial sphere. So I was mainly interested in putting myself, the Black woman, at centre stage—she would be the desired one, the loved one, and her partner an Asian man, who would be prepared to break with his family for her.

It's a play that lays bare the various ways in which both Indians and Blacks have sought to demonize each other. But it is also about the challenges and suspicions in interracial marriages, the sort of issues Lawrence Hill explores as well in Black Berry, Sweet Juice. *Comment. For instance, one of the subjects he touches on is the exasperation that Black women feel about Black men who marry outside the race. And he argues that their feelings are to some extent justified.*

I very much agree with him. The Black female is still by and large at the bottom of the totem pole of desirability and it is, therefore, upsetting when Black men in increasing numbers appear to prefer non-Black women. In an indirect way, *Coups and Calypsos* was an attempt to reply to that situation.

And it's a play that explores issues of loyalty to one's birthplace.

It comes down to: where is home? And for those of us who belong to what I call the Afrospora, do we go back to the Caribbean as Césaire and others like Lamming have done; do we go "back" to Africa; do we stay in North America? And always there's the feeling of having been ripped away from something, of having lost something. There is a psychic wound that we all carry and that we all struggle to heal.

A missing dimension.

It's interesting that I have not seen this longing in the works of African Canadian writers whose forbears have been here for centuries. I'm thinking of the writing of George Elliot Clark and Lawrence Hill.

Actually Lawrence does in a small way, via an African character, Yoyo, that shows up in both novels, and the protagonist in Any Known Blood *actually makes a trip to Niger.*

Today when you look back on your first two collections of poems: Thorns and Salmon Courage, *how do you feel about them?*

I look upon them with great fondness.

Do you see them as your apprenticeship pieces?

I think the poems by and large stand on their own. I am not ashamed of them. They are milestones along a way, aren't they? And they contain all the issues I would later deal with.

You are generally seen as an activist campaigning for greater inclusion of minorities in Canada's cultural spaces. I think of the campaign that along with others you mounted against PEN's racism, and the fallout with the June Callwood episode, but also of your piece in FUSE which analyzes the disingenuousness of the reforms the various arts councils sought to undertake in the early nineties.

You have had to undergo quite a bit of opprobrium for this.

I think you said it all. The irony for me, the contradiction, if you will, is that the work that I have done, I could only have done here in Canada. George Elliott Clarke and I disagree on this, and he has critiqued me on this: the feeling that when I began writing here in Canada, there was no body of literature by African Canadians ahead of me to follow or not follow; to write with or against, as there exists in the US or Britain. He talks about the written sermons in Nova Scotia; they constitute a wonderful tradition, but that is not what I am talking about.

It's not what you mean by literature.

No. And so while I agree with him to a certain degree that there was a written tradition of some sort, I still maintain that it looked pretty bleak to me. Who was writing at that time? There were Austin Clarke and Sonny Ladoo—a brilliant writer who died very early, shortly after the publication of his wonderful book, *No Pain Like This Body.* There was also Lorris Elliot. I believe Claire [Harris] had already started writing, but we knew nothing of each other. I felt that I had to write or else I would be crushed by the emptiness around me, and the absence of a tradition—a clearly articulated one—meant simultaneously that I was rattling around in a large space, but I was also not burdened by that tradition. I was on my own, on the margin, which is another word for frontier. Now, in trying to make the shift from margin, in trying to create a more hospitable space and place for African writers from the Caribbean or Canada or wherever, I came up against the system that then tried to disappear me. Fortunately for me, my work has always been valued and welcomed in the US and abroad, and that has sustained me over the years.

Well, as you know, they've coined their own term, "victim art," to dismiss the social justice concerns we raise in our art. I was the member of a writing awards jury some years ago where one of the jurors said regarding one of the pieces: "My antennae went up, because immediately I saw this as victim art." My response was: "What's wrong with writing about oppression? We laud Solzenitshyn, Vaclav Havel and Arthur Koestler for it. Why draw a circle around it when it's about racial oppression that occurs in Canada?" Moreover, they have no problems promoting Rohinton Mistry, who deals with it in an Indian context.

As long as it happens elsewhere it's acceptable.

I have a distinct feeling that the literary establishment (the large publishers, book reviewers in the print and electronic media, award juries, arts councils) feel that we quarrel with their policies only insofar as we've been left out. But after a few grants, a few awards or nominations for awards, we have nothing to gripe about. It's classic Marxist theory: co-optation by the superstructure. So far you have not been co-opted and I think the superstructure resents that.

That is true, although I don't think of it only in terms of getting grants and being satisfied, because, if you go back to what we discussed earlier on in the interview, it's not just about getting grants, at least not for me. Yes, we need grants to live, and I don't teach anywhere; I don't have a straight job. So grants are important.

But then grants are from taxpayers' money. You are a legitimate writer, you are a writer by occupation, and writers are eligible to apply for grants, so you are entitled to apply.

For me the project is larger than that. It is about reclaiming who we are and bringing to voice, imagining the past and locating myself in a tradition that has always resisted that attempt to wipe us out.

But, you see, in doing so, we must of necessity do a certain amount of debriding, and in the process those who think they are the guardians of culture sometimes feel the need to impede us.

I agree. But I never lose sight of what I think my writing is all about.

But they see themselves as having the power to silence, and certainly one of the things that power always does, when it is able to, is silence the voices it does not want to hear.

They do have a certain amount of power.

When I interviewed you in 1991, we spoke about the literary marketplace for African Canadian works. At the time there existed Williams-Wallace, and Sister Vision. Today there is no African Canadian publisher. How do you feel about this?

It is a tragedy. We don't have a publisher; we don't have a magazine where we can debate issues that are important to us. Sometimes I think that if I had the energy I would try to start a magazine.

NourbeSe, thanks for giving me this opportunity to discuss your work and the state of African Canadian literature with you.

Althea Prince

Althea, since your work is set in Antigua and Canada, would you, for the benefit of our readers, provide a brief biography regarding your years in both countries?

I came to Canada from Antigua in 1965. I was sponsored by my sister, who'd come here as a nurse. I did an undergraduate degree here, then some graduate work in Baltimore, then went to England for a couple of years, and returned in 76–77; in the mid-eighties, I returned to Antigua to live for four years, after which I returned to Canada.

The prism through which I write is comprised of the geographies of Antigua and Canada. Of course other issues from other geographic spaces are absorbed into these two spaces.

How do you envisage your role as a writer?

I don't see myself as having a role. I write because I have to write. I write because I've always written since I was a child. I hear people say that my writing impacts in this or that way, or is committed to this or that political position. I see writing as spiritual, and if no one ever bought my books, I'd probably be cool with that too.

Do you see writing a having a function?

I see writing as a spiritual experience. So I see writing as an expression of spirit. I know that some people see it as a therapeutic experience. I've never seen writing as a solution to pathology.

There are many writers who believe it has a healing effect. That writing too initiates in trauma. Auden's elegy written at Yeats' death contains the line: "Mad Ireland hurt you into poetry . . ." Robert Graves likens the poem to the pearl the oyster creates to palliate the pain from the grain of sand buried in its flesh.

And Van Morrison says that if he didn't sing, he'd probably grow boils. Perhaps, if I didn't write I'd be an angry person. However, it isn't anger that impels me to write. And from writing, it seems that I'm healed. But the one isn't related to other. When I feel bad I don't write.

My impression is that the Black community expects the work of literature to be temple, community fair, and academy. Do you think your work manages to fill these needs in some or all of these respects?

I really don't know and I really don't care. I'm not trivializing anything here. I really feel that if my writing becomes linked to people's needs I would lose interest in it. People criticize me for not finding what they want in my writing. When *Ladies of the Night* was published, a few men who were very critical of it were present [at the launching]. In their view I was airing our dirty laundry in public.

If there is some sort of redemption that Black people look for in the work of their writers, and they don't find it in mine, that's just too bad. I'm not saying that it's wrong for them to look for it. But that's not why I write. If accidentally they find it there, then that's fine by me too. I have had redemption through reading people's work. They weren't necessarily Black and not necessarily women either. I'm thinking of people like Carlos Castaneda, Rumi, Wilson Harris, CLR James. However, I found no redemption in Naipaul, and that was fine. I wasn't looking for that. I looked to him for what he provides, which is to say excellent writing. I think Black audiences look to all their writers for that redemptive experience, and I understand why they do it. But I don't write to provide it.

Your collection of short stories Ladies of the Night and Other Stories *explores in a very unsentimental, frank way marital relationships, parent-child relationships, aging, and folk beliefs in Antigua, for the most part, although two of the stories, "Junice and Stanley" and "Body and Soul" are set in Toronto. Would you like to comment on the genesis of these stories?*

These stories came at the crossroads of my life. They were not the first things I published but they were the first things I wrote seriously. All of the stories were written in Antigua between 1984 and 1986. I'd returned home to Antigua thinking that I was going to settle there and never leave. But after four years, 1983 to 1987, I did want to leave. Some of the stories in *Ladies of the Night* came as a result of the people I lived among. Some came out of things that bothered me—like the absence of social services for the aged population. There were no child advocacy groups, no attempts to rescue children who were living on the streets. I was the cofounder of a home for street children. I was struck by this new phenomenon in the Caribbean: homeless children. There were no homeless children in Antigua when I left there in 1965. In 1983, when I returned, there were homeless children. And there were blinkers on the eyes of many people, who actually denied that there were homeless children. The increase in the rape of children by adults alarmed me. One such incident stands out in my memory—the rape of a child by her mother's ex-boyfriend. He came to the school she attended, told her that her mother had been hospitalized, and that he was taking her to visit her. Instead he took her into a field and raped her. She was thirteen. "Ladies of the Night," is, I think, the way my imagination chose to deal with this incident. I combined this incident with another in which a woman immobilized her daughter while her boyfriend raped her. The judge threw the book at them. Of course such aberrations are not restricted to Antigua. They happen here as well. I'd thought that our societies didn't engage in such depravity. I am sure such things must have been going on while I was growing up. It's just that I didn't know. Some of the other things, especially as regards the stories set in Toronto, reflect what I consider as horrific relationships between Black people from the Caribbean—they are the people whose lives I can write about knowledgeably. I was very concerned about the way the men treated their women. I felt exasperated that the women were not more aggressive in doing something about it.

Your story "Henrietta" contradicts the belief by Caribbean people that the aged in the Caribbean are cared for by their children or by the community.

That's pure nostalgia. The problem of the aged, as I've mentioned before, is something that those who should know better ignore. The story came out of my wanting to deal with a situation that I knew about. It isn't altogether similar to Henrietta's. The real-life story involves a woman who was an amputee, someone I knew well since childhood. She did the laundry for some of my maternal relatives and sometimes helped my mother with hers. She and my mother were age-mates and were quite close, a family friend in fact. But my mother eventually came to live in Canada; this woman's children and grandchildren were no longer in Antigua. We, who were the closest thing to family, were no longer there. When I went back to live in Antigua, I found her alone, and living off bread and cheese, when she was able to get a child to go to the shop and purchase it for her. So I was just—

Pained.

Yes. It stunned me. I realized that she was just one person that I happened to know. Her story would have been multiplied across Antigua. I knew of many women who worked in the homes of the wealthy and who were let go when they became too old to work. I wondered what was their fate.

Is immigration the culprit in this story?

Yes. To a large extent it is. If there had been a continuation of the extended family this woman would have had people around. For one thing, my family had twelve children; we would have all been there, her grandchildren would have all been there, friends of her grandchildren would have been there. But we had all emigrated. The slips of registered mail piled up, but she had no way to get to the post office to collect the money.

Your stories apportion blame in almost equal measure to men and women for the difficulties in their relationships. "On the Gallery" is an excellent case in point.

I never conceived these stories along the lines of gender. It panned out that way because I was writing about what is. And what is reflects this. Regarding men's abuse of women, the questions are: Why are the women there in the first place? Or if they are, what are they doing about the situation?

Some might argue that some women endure these conditions because of economic reasons and cultural beliefs. We came from the Caribbean believing that men are superior to women, that the man is the breadwinner, etc.

I think these are false beliefs. They're definitely not true here. In the Caribbean, then and now, we have had a population in which the women were truly the heads of homes. So if the argument is: I can't leave him because of economic reasons, the real reason is fear of leaving. Mind you, I excuse people for having fear, but I think they ought to name it.

You are so right. At the core it is the fear of finding one's self alone.

Yes. Fear too of reclaiming who they are.

In "Croops, Croops, Croops," the adolescent daughter is able to effect a reconciliation between the parents. And in "On the Gallery," Merine is the catalyst for our understanding of the dual plight of her mother and father.

In "Croops, Croops, Croops," I was concerned with showing the impact of dysfunctional marriages on the children. I felt a strong desire to speak from the child's space and from the ineffectual woman's space, as well as from the space of a woman who chooses to be a mistress, rather than a wife. I was beginning to admire the woman who escapes the drudgery of marriage.

That comes across well in the story.

The man in this story is the least interesting character. He is interesting only for the things we get to know that he doesn't do. He doesn't wash, he doesn't cook—

That he needs a woman to do these things for him.

There are three female characters who are all committed to the well-being of this man.

It's a story that portrays as well something of the mistress-wife binary as well as the qualifications for wifehood.

Yes, because women—even modern women—derive status from being married. It is important that a man has married her. And she demonstrates her gratitude by cooking his fungy [a cornmeal dish] a certain way. There is nothing about what she gets from the marriage.

She's a replacement for his mother.

Absolutely! And she has to work to achieve it [wifehood], whereas his mother doesn't have to work to be his mother. So if the man leaves her for periods of time—and this is probably less true for the modern woman—other women would fault her for not keeping him in place. They'd make statements like, "You are not cooking his food properly otherwise he'd be at home."

Are you aware that the Caribbean stories solve to some degree the gender/marital problems that drive them whereas the two Toronto stories don't? What accounts for the difference?

(Laughter). That's a new observation for me. It wasn't a conscious choice on my part.

In one of the Toronto stories, the woman commits suicide and in the other she leaves.

The shaping of both sets of stories is not one that I ever consciously articulated to myself. I suppose I wanted to show in the case of the second story that women here avail themselves of the choices that exist much more so than do women in the Caribbean. Such choices did not exist in the Caribbean society in which I grew up. The belief systems prevented one from going to a place of suicide. I never knew of anyone who committed suicide while I was growing up in Antigua. I never knew of any woman leaving her husband.

It took my own mother twenty-seven years to leave hers.

When I left mine my mother did not speak to me for a year. She told me it was wrong to leave. My father had three children outside of the marriage, two of whom were born after he was married. For my mother, my ex-husband would have had to be a murderer for her to accept my leaving him. Her arguments were: he never hit you, he worked, he brought home his money, he cooked, he washed, he cleaned—he did all these wonderful things that her husband didn't do—so I had no good reason for leaving him. As far as she was concerned he was a better husband than my father, so I shouldn't have left him. But I had choices my mother didn't have; moreover, I knew I had them—everyone has them; it's just that some people don't know they do, or don't want to know that they do.

It is interesting to me that you made this observation about the differences between the Caribbean and Canadian stories.

"How You Panty Get Wet?" is a story that turns on the vacillation between the innocent cruelty and the immense love that characterize much of Caribbean parenting.

I think that people parent according to the way they had been parented. In that story the mother parents in the way that she knows. The things she says are clichés—I didn't send you to school to learn nonsense, etc. Every Caribbean mother has probably said that to her children at one time or another. It is clear that this is a mother that loves her children, but not in the way the children wanted. She demonstrates that she is a self-sacrificing mother. But she doesn't tell the children I bought you fabric so you can have lovely dresses for carnival. She leaves them guessing and anxious. Such confused situations lead to a lot of anger in children. Cyntie is angry with the adults in her life. She is angry with her father and mother, in a displaced sort of way.

Because she wants to be treated like a person.

Exactly.

In a sense, you are showing a dimension that's missing in the society and that needs to be addressed.

And to be healed. It's a society built on violence, and in that particular story there is violence: emotional violence and physical violence. It's not physical abuse. We don't hear of the child being brutally beaten, but it is violence. The child isn't given the opportunity to explain where she heard the song, or for that matter, whether the child knows what the song means. Remember children sang calypsos because they were always on the radio, without having the least idea what they meant.

Much of this story's force lies in its irony. Irony is one of your powerful devices in almost all the stories. I suppose it's an effective way to reveal the truth that reality hides.

Here's something I've not thought of. I have no conscious bookends. That's a fact. But irony is so present in so much of the reality I deal with in fiction, and so much of what I deal with in everyday life.

"Junice and Stanley" portrays philandering at its most extreme. This story took me back to a statement made by Thorstein Veblen in his turn-of-the-century book The Theory of the Leisure Class . . . *to the effect that in premodern times men measured their status in terms of the number of slaves and women they possessed . . . Comment?*

I think the latter still obtains. It pains me to say that some young men still think that way. These days, they say they're sexually addicted. We had no such term in the Caribbean. There were simply men who were committed to having as many women as possible, and they felt doing so conferred prestige. Because such behaviour is recognized as sexual addiction today, there is prescribed therapy (laughter). It's insecurity. But it's very destructive. It wreaks havoc in the lives of children, in the lives of the women involved, and others close to them. I know that some men valorize themselves that way, and some of their peers look up to them for it. I have finally come to understand that the male psyche matures much later than the female's. Women can look at such behaviour and see that it's stupid and unnecessary, but many men don't.

Or can't. Some men might answer that they cannot fulfill all their needs in a single relationship.

No one can find all that she or he wants in a single person. That's why we have friends, coworkers, sisters and brothers. To me, this is phenomenally stupid. And I call it stupidity because there is a lot of information available that can incite reflection about these attitudes.

By the way, I am not suggesting that this is uniquely a Black phenomenon. My male characters who behave this way happen to be Black because my short stories and my novel deal for the most part with people who are Black. There are men of all hues who do this.

"Miss Amoury's Bathwater" is a subtle contest between science (nursing) and what some would call superstitious belief. So-called superstitious belief wins the contest. Would you like to comment?

Well, you know that there are many Caribbean people who live with both belief systems. The same is true in continental African societies and in the African Diaspora as a whole. And I know enough to realize there are people who believe in one while applying the other: sick people, for example, who would consult a medical doctor and later an Obeah man to find out who set a jumbie (an evil spirit) on them. This dual belief system interests and intrigues me because I believe I have a kind of spiritual-magical acceptance of life, so that I understand that one can have a herbal bath of cleansing, as Miss Amoury does, and also have the antibiotic from the doctor. The story presents both perspectives, but it also speaks to the nurse's dilemma. And it's based on my observations of reality in Antigua when I returned there in 1983. I knew a visiting nurse who was faced with such realities. And there is always the joke about the charlatan Obeah man who abuses people's credulity.

The practice of throwing water at the crossroads has always intrigued me. I was taught by my mother, who didn't believe in Obeah, that I must never walk over water with two pennies in it, at a crossroad. She worshipped at the eighteenth-century Anglican Cathedral on a Sunday but would take us, my sister and me, to a "wayside" church (above a rum shop) where they sang and danced in the service. So in her way, she straddled both belief systems.

Regarding the title story "Ladies of the Night," I must confess that I haven't been able to guess at what the author's own attitude is to Miss Peggy, Miss Olive and Miss Peggy's father. Certainly Miss Olive's commodification of her daughter's body sent shivers through me.

The story deals with some of the experiences I heard about when I went back to Antigua. Regarding my authorial distance, I felt that in the mere presentation of the story, the author makes a commitment to show the marginalized space that the two women occupy.

It's worth writing about.

They are hard-working women. We may not like what they do. The minister doesn't want them to have communion. They were severely judged by the community, and especially so by the men who avail themselves of the services of both mother and daughter. Even though the daughter's father leaves her a piece of property at the end, he'd let her, while he was still alive, suffer the indignity of not knowing who her father was.

He couldn't, given that he was her father, and given that he was having a sexual relationship with her.

He could have stopped.

You have written a novel, Loving This Man, *which one reviewer thinks is autobiographical. Would you like to comment on the genesis of this novel?*

This novel was a gift of the spirit—in terms of no prior planning. The planned part was the rewriting of the Toronto section in the first person, which, I now feel, should have been left in the narrator's voice. Other than that, the rest of the novel flowed out of a deep deep place of spirit. I remember wanting the Toronto section to be stronger in voice, so I rewrote it in the first person.

Interesting. It's true that the omniscient part of the novel is more engaging, but I wouldn't say the second section fails.

No, it doesn't. But in terms of magic, of voice, of engagement, Book I is definitely richer.

It is a different energy.

And what happened was that in Book I, I surrendered totally to the story as the spirit gave it. As I think about it now, Sage's two younger daughters should not have been named. That part of the story is about three girls and three women. Sage's two younger girls are mentioned to show that she had two more children; in other words, that as she had been abandoned by two more men, she descended into alcoholism. It's something I now recognize as symptomatic of a particular stream of thinking, and way of being. Hence Sage is a particular kind of woman—so is Juniper Berry—and Sayshelle is a product of all of that; certainly in terms of her own "Sagelike" experience in Toronto.

I learned a lot about my own writing process while working on this novel. I learned about surrendering to spirit. I learned how to connect with my higher creative energy. I learned to stop working so hard. For the novel I'm currently working on, I am really surrendering. Every time I'm tempted to alter it, I take my hands off. The thing about the story in *Loving This Man* is that it is a period that I know well. I realize that we receive what we know well.

In our arrogance we're not willing to concede that we receive so much. We like to think that we are the creators.

Lawrence Perrine opines that the writer is more of a recorder and less of an inventor.

I too believe that.

The character of Cicero Finley reminds me of Warren Hart, the Black American who spied on Black groups for the RCMP in the 1970s.

Pure coincidence. The difference between Hart and Cicero is stark. Warren Hart was a middle-aged, overweight man who had a curious way of smoking. He'd hold the cigarette in the middle of his hand and pull on it. Hart never had any romantic affiliations with anyone. Indeed, they both betrayed the Black community for personal gain.

Sayshelle has a strong mother and at least one strong aunt and great aunt. She also comes from a family where the strong band together to help the weak. How important are these facts to Sayshelle's negotiating her difficulties in Toronto?

In a sense they are overwhelming role models. Nevertheless they enable her to see how life shapes us. She is unusually independent when faced with peer pressure. She doesn't, for example, join a movement because she thinks everyone should take such decisions independently. At the same time she feels that she should be involved because her parents were involved. Of course, too, she has a strong great-aunt with very firm ideological beliefs. By the way that aunt is modeled on Mrs Johnson of Third World Bookstore. She's my surrogate mother. But I'm not Sayshelle. The role models prepared her for life, but they didn't prepare her to cope with city life.

And certainly not for life with Cicero Finley. In fact, she has to return to Antigua to regain perspective. More important is the fact that she knows that Antigua can be a refuge if one is needed.

There's a place for her.

You told me that this novel is in part a tribute to your father, who suffered because of his integrity. Would you like to comment?

Actually the only character in the novel that isn't strictly speaking invented, that's lifted straight out of life, is Emmanuel, Sayshelle's father. That character is my father, with some modifications. My father was a police officer, he was not half-Carib, he was jet-black; and he was from Dominica. He came to

Antigua at the age of twenty-one. The incidents he deals with in the texts are all factual. He was very disturbed by many of the incidents he witnessed in the police force and many of the political shenanigans he was privy to. I felt as if my father's spirit was urging me to write this book.

Loving This Man *depicts for me the extent to which the country of one's birth always remains home and what "home" means when one no longer lives there. I'm thinking of Sayshelle's return to Antigua to reintegrate her psyche after the experiences of her traumatic marriage.*

The memory of the tree that she had left without saying goodbye is symbolic. I felt that she had left and not really understood that she had left. She realizes that she had left only when she returns home. She may have longed for her family before that, but it's only when she returns that she reconciles herself with having left; and when she leaves the second time, I suspect that she "isn't" going to miss home as much. This time she says goodbye to all that is important. The visit to the gravesites, the grounding with her father—interlinked with Coltrane's music—reveal her integrated self. There's a point toward the end of the novel where she realizes that she understands what's going on and who she is: she remembers and therefore is; she comes to grips with home, her new home . . .

Having grown sufficiently . . .

So that she can live away from home.

In Loving This Man *you turn hair-braiding into a ritual of bonding. Moreover, it is the occasion when Reevah educates her daughter about much in her life as well as oral history. This caught my attention in a special sort of way . . .*

Me too.

Would you like to comment?

(Laughter). I didn't have that type of experience. My hair was braided by someone who lived next door—for a shilling. When I had my daughter, I discovered what a fabulous experience it is for mother-daughter communication! She would be right there with her head beneath my knees, sometimes falling asleep, sometimes dribbling on my knees. Even now, at age twenty-nine, when she comes to visit she wants to feel my hand on her head. She actually purrs when this happens.

That's what that is. It can bring tears to my eyes, the fact that I had never experienced this with my mother. Much later I learned that African women form braiding circles. I wish I'd had that experience while growing up. As my daughter grew bigger and was able to stay awake while I braided her hair, we would talk about all sorts of issues affecting her.

Juniper Berry is an unusual and extremely loveable character. She is perhaps even more liberated than Reevah. Comment.

Way more liberated! She selects her man and insists on one that would allow her her freedom. I regret that I did not explore her spirituality. At the time of writing I couldn't find it.

You kept her at the sensuous level.

I always felt that I cheated that character of something but that I would have another opportunity to correct it; I feel there's a depth there that I didn't fully explore. I know who she is: she is an amalgam of all the women I've always admired who grasped life by the hand, who looked after things, who didn't take shit, and took full charge to themselves.

You have written two very engaging and instructive children's works: How the Starfish Got to the Sea *and* How the East Pond Got Its Flowers. *Both seem to me to fulfill all of the objectives Bruno Bettelheim tells us children's literature should have, especially in terms of making children feel empowered. But beyond that it seems to me that you feel that young children should learn about history.*

During the hair-combing activities with my daughter and while putting her to bed, she always wanted a story. I used to read her a lot of stories but I also told her some stories that I made up. We, her father and I, were always telling her about how Africans came to the Caribbean. One day she asked—she hadn't yet visited Antigua—"So the people who are there, are they the children of those people who came on the slave ships? Are they the same number of people?" Her question motivated me to tell the stories of that period and of the children so that she would get a sense of the children, the older people, etc. Those two books originated in those stories.

There are six books. I have never tried to publish the remaining four. I call them *The East Pond Series.* I realized that if my daughter asked for this information, then other Black children would also need to know. They were the first books I published. They were used very quickly in the school system—the elementary school system—as well as the libraries.

What are your own views about writing for children?

It's the right place to begin writing if one can do it. I think it's the place where we need to start—we are talking about cultural hegemony now—so that children would have visions more appropriate to who they are.

You are the author of a collection of essays, Being Black. *What does the essay form permit that fiction, let's say, does not?*

The essay provides me the space to do what academic writing does not allow. After writing a few academic essays, I realized that I needed to write essays that would reflect what I think. In *Being Black* I ended up having more footnotes than I'd intended.

The informal essay allows me to say what I feel. I don't have to situate my views in the contexts of other views. I can have my own take on things.

How does the essay function as regards audience? I am astounded by the large number of educated people who've told me that reading fiction is a puerile activity.

I'll take a stab at your question. I know that the essay is used in academia a lot, whereas fiction isn't. My motivations don't take audience and market into account. Certainly not while writing it.

Even so, understanding complex fiction requires reading skills that many people lack.

That's interesting. At a reading following the publication of *Loving This Man*, a young Black woman said to me, "I read the first part. I couldn't understand the second part, so I didn't bother to read it." This was said by an aspiring writer. It shocked me.

I found out about such poor reading skills a long time ago.

Someone like her could read the essays in *Being Black* without the problems posed by reading complex fiction.

Where reality adjusts with every new element. Some people don't understand irony.

I live with the criticism for things intended ironically which people interpret literally. Returning to the essay, I think I have fallen in love with the form. I see, too, that it is widely used; and there's a vacuum for such writing in sociology, the social sciences, and the humanities.

James Baldwin's The Fire Next Time *doesn't have a single footnote yet it is one of the most informative and powerful pieces of writing ever done by an African American.*

And there are numerous others.

On the other hand, I remember a remark made by a reviewer of Dionne Brand's memoir, A Map to the Door of No Return*—to the effect that such material was wasted in the essay form. I was puzzled because I didn't see that material used in her memoir couldn't be used in fiction.*

That couldn't have been made by a writer.

It certainly was.

A strange comment . . . One could use anything five hundred times.

How do you feel about the critical response your work has received?

Has it received any? I feel good that it is being read by young people especially. One of my goals has been that I would write a few books, and that people would read them and find them useful. I have met that goal. I still want to write a few more. I don't write to win a Governor General Award—it would be nice—but I would love to see my work translated into film. It is a burning desire. In 1998 the National Film Library bought the rights to *How the Starfish Got to the Sea.* I'm disappointed that it hasn't been done yet.

Most of the books by Black writers challenge the various national myths and are therefore unpopular with White readers. How might we get around the marginalization we receive from Canadian publishers and book buyers?

I did my own, very vigorous publicity for *Being Black*, and also for *Loving This Man.* I did a better job on *Being Black.* I was able to travel all over the country. Also, from my own experience in publishing, I now know how the book market works.

I contacted the universities. I think these are different times when the individual writer has to market his or her books. I called all the high schools. I went to some fifteen high schools over a few months. We have to do some extra things and do them differently. There is no easy answer, no 1, 2, 3, but it has to be done.

Any other issues you'd like to discuss that I've overlooked?

I am very concerned about the Black voice in Canadian literature. I am still reflecting on that. I think many of our writers are now gaining recognition.

Even so some publishers say they won't publish our books.

Yes. I know, but we must still stay focused. I'm not trying to sound "pollyanish." We cannot stop at the obstacles. Just think of the hurdles jazz musicians had to overcome.

Thanks for giving me the opportunity to interview you.

My pleasure actually. It's been a long time since I've chatted this much about writing.

Robert Sandiford

Robert, since your work is set in Barbados and Canada would you, for the benefit of our readers, provide a brief biography regarding your years in Canada and Barbados?

I was born of Barbadian parents. My parents immigrated to Canada in 1958. There are four of us in the family, four children. Three brothers—I'm the third child—and one daughter. In terms of my work, I knew from an early age that I wanted to write. I liked the comics; I enjoyed reading them. A story runs in the family that I taught myself to read. Words came to me easily and telling stories. I first started to pursue writing professionally in 1985, or somewhere around then. My first published piece was in the *Montreal Gazette.* It was a front-page piece about my father in 1988, but it took me a few more years to do more work.

In the preface to your first collection of short stories, Winter, Spring, Summer, Fall, *you state that you want to justify the ways of human beings to one another. How do you see your role as a writer?*

I think that was a little bit of a riff on what Milton had said about what he was trying to do in *Paradise Lost*—i.e., "justify the ways of God to men." If I were to put it into a very tight nutshell, I'd say I write to educate, to entertain and to enlighten, and that is perhaps where the justification for the ways of human beings to each other comes in. We seldom seek to do that, I think. We tear down, but we don't often try to understand.

You see yourself therefore as a writer in the humanist tradition. My impression is that the Black community expects the work of literature to be temple, community fair, and academy. Does this reflect your own experience?

That is a difficult question to answer—I've never thought about it—but I think you are right. Those three elements form a crucial part of Black literature. But, for me, I just write what I write and what I find of interest. It comes from my own experience and background often times. If the church is there, then you'll find elements of religion.

I meant temple in a metaphoric sense, as a place where Black readers find their beliefs, values, and customs glorified, valorized; where they find heroic characters they can live through vicariously.

You can find some of that in my work, but maybe not obviously. I would have to say, "Yes." There is definitely that aspect in there when these stories are from people I know; they're heroic in the everyday sense.

How much do you think of audience when you write?

It depends on the nature of the writing. Probably not very much. Maybe I would be a wealthier man if I did think of audience more. There are those writers who can balance the two. They have a keen sense of the audience but also a keen sense of what they want to accomplish. I admire those writers, and I try to emulate them. But I basically sit down and write the stories I want to write, then I find a market.

But you know Toni Morrison says that every writer begins to write for him—or herself.

That's right. It's like prostitution, you do it for yourself, then you start to do it for others, and then you're doing it for everyone. In fact, I was thinking about her, earlier on today, and about how she has managed to do that. She, obviously, I think, writes for herself, about what she believes in, and then it …

It has a resonance across the Black world—and the non-Black world.

In the introduction to his latest book, Odysseys Home: Mapping African Canadian Literature, *George Elliott Clarke laments what he observes as a tendency by many critics to subsume African Canadian literature under the rubric of African American literature or to elide it altogether. How do you feel about the ethnic and racial labels we put on literature?*

Some of the best Canadian literature is actually West Indian and Caribbean. We were talking before about temple, the academy, and what Black people look for in their writers. I would argue that what Black Canadians look for in their literature is not necessarily the same as what Black Americans look for. So it is important to know what we do and why we do it, especially those of us who are influenced by Caribbean literature and Caribbean reality.

Though I must say that I've been heavily influenced by African American writers and continental African writers. James Baldwin certainly had a strong influence on me and, from Africa, Chinua Achebe.

Definitely. We all are. I think we feed off one another. And, ultimately, we should be helping each other.

Let's turn to your work, to your fiction first. One cannot but notice the imagistic quality of your writing: visual, olfactory, tactile, and to a lesser extent gustatory. This is especially evident in your short stories "Soir d'hiver" and "Pancakes." One feels there's a compulsion on your part to be precise.

There is. It's in the details that we start to recognize and understand what this world is about, what our lives are about. And, I think, oftentimes the details that we don't notice, the everyday details, embody a lot. Someone once remarked to me that hands seem to come up a lot in my stories—are very important—and eye colour. Up until then, I hadn't realized it.

But the physical details extend as well to your use of graphic illustrations in your stories. I was intrigued by why you felt the need to put those graphic illustrations in.

That goes back to what you were saying about having all those elements, the tactile, etc.... I wanted to get the "major arts" into my first book. It opens up with a musical epigraph; the book itself is physical, like a piece of sculpture; obviously the illustrations are the visual art.

A key aspect of your use of detail, I might add, is related to characterization . . .

Give me an example.

The grandmother in "Soir D'hiver." She is a diabetic. The story of her diabetes takes us back to Barbados, to the times she grew up in, the beating that she got for disobedience, etc., her mother's concern, the candy bowl. It all seems initially like digressive anecdote until one realizes that it's germane to characterization, to how culture shapes, etc. These are situations that you're establishing so that we will get to know this woman better.

Writing this story was very intuitive. I knew what I wanted to do, but I didn't necessarily follow a practical structure. So elements like that were there, and I just sort of latched on to them, and I said this is something that I want to explore. In the editing of the story, I became more conscious of the connections.

I think we all do that. We write and throw a lot of stuff out there, and then go back, and pare down or expand.

And interweave. Right. That is how those stories came about. I think what I do in my stories unconsciously defines the characters. Then I play with that, discover other elements that confer complexity, etc.

In "The Touch of Death," your use of graphic detail is less concentrated. I think I know why, but I would prefer to hear your answer. I'm sure you won't tell me it's intuitive.

That was the least intuitive of the stories. It's based on an actual incident. There is another writer—I can't remember his name—who talks about this: about something that happened, and he just had to get it down. And he had to get it down primarily in the way it happened. I'm not saying that the story isn't fictional; elements were altered. But I remember my sister coming across the manuscript and starting to read it and my becoming very upset at that. I said, "What are you doing? This isn't done yet. The story isn't finished." Because the story was still unfolding at the time. It's a very deliberate story, a very deliberate look at death: how you just cannot escape it.

It seems to me that you are doing here what you would later do in your columns for the Nation *newspaper in Barbados. The story is itself a reflection on death, and reflections, because of their philosophical tone, require more abstract language.*

That is very much it. For me, my columns—you call it reflection, I call it meditation, but it's basically the same thing—are thoughts, ideas, and feelings I am trying to give expression to, and it's not always easy to do so. I think I was angry with my sister because she was reading something before it was time; before I had the time to process it, and digest it, and get it out.

Like taking a slice out of the cake before it's baked.

Very much so. In my columns, I try to offer the best reflections on life as I see it. You asked me about the structure of the stories, and what was going on, and how the details function. When I write, what's primary is the story itself. It has to be a story, a narrative, in order for it to be understood. The next thing is I just want to get down what happens, and I'm not looking to put myself into it; I'm not looking to push an agenda or a particular point of view. But I am just trying to describe life as it is, life as it ought to be—because it couldn't be any other way in this context. And that's more or less how I approach my columns and my nonfiction. I don't make a huge distinction.

You seem to leave as well space for the reader's reflection, something especially noticeable in "You Always Promise."

With that story in particular...I don't think I was too sure how I felt about it. It is in some ways a story about abuse. I think I want the readers wondering and free to make up their minds.

It's almost like a cry in the night, and you vaguely know where it comes from, but you don't really know how to do anything about it.

This is it. You see that with the two people in the white parkas, and you think this isn't so bad, but then it's like, Why should they care? And there are several reasons they should care.

And, certainly, the fact that you position the story in the night, where you cannot actually see the characters as clearly as you might after having left a series of stories where you see everyone up close in minute details. This is a story that leaves one thinking, that leaves the reader very uncomfortable, and rightly so.

Which is exactly what I wanted. I wasn't looking to end necessarily on a high with that collection.

How much of your work is the result of experimentation with form?

These days, I realize a lot more that my work is a result of experimentation with form. I always like to give comics their due, here. Some of the best writers I've read have been in comics. In this collection itself, I'm experimenting with form from story to story. The last story is perhaps the most straightforward in that it runs from start to finish without any breaks or sections or anything.

It has a very surreal feel.

Yeah. The experimentation comes in the handling of the material. In more recent fiction, I have gone into magic realism. I find that I enjoy that a bit.

A cursory examination of your stories suggests that archetypes are important in your work. "Soir D'hiver" conforms to archetypal expectations.

The grandmother, the mother, the father, and the setting of the story are incidentally archetypal. But I don't write in archetypes. I think that if it comes up, it is something that comes up.

Oh, but you aren't supposed to. I am sure that when Coleridge wrote The Rime of the Ancient Mariner, *he wasn't thinking about archetypes.*

Having said that, I'll add that if you look at my columns, the archetypes are there. I can't get away from them. I guess all I'm saying is that their presence isn't deliberate. At the same time, what the grandmother stands for, and what Mom stands for, and Dad stands for, all of those other characters—these Black people in particular—what they stand for is important.

I'll add too that tradition, community, family are all listed under what Jung calls the mother archetype. Even the very fact of the story's setting—the room: the warmth and safety of the room contrasting with the cold and the ongoing storm outside—fits the archetypal pattern. This grandmother is well cared for.

She is also respected; there's love and respect. I always tell people there are two basic branches in my work. One is family. I love my family. I enjoy exploring that particular aspect of the human condition. The other branch is the erotic. These are the two themes that constantly recur in my work. The consequences of being an individual might be a third.

Today, it's commonplace to say it all comes down to sex. I'd add—and Freud would bear me out—and violence, too.

And I would agree with that.

There are those who'd no doubt argue that aggression subserves sex: securing the territory, so to speak, in order to enhance mating opportunities.

In my later stories, that does come up. They are often set in the night, and there is aggression that is somehow linked to some sort of sexual undercurrent.

"The Touch of Death" to some extent does not conform to the pattern I was talking about. It occurs in spring—except, of course, you are consciously or unconsciously following the pattern of elegies.

I never really gave much thought to these stories being elegies.

But "The Touch of Death" is an elegy.

Yes, it's an elegy. I'd say that the other stories also are in some ways elegies. I would have to say Edson's recounting of the encounter with his grandmother is an elegy.

A eulogious elegy. "Pancakes," which you put under "Summer," seems on the surface to be showing how the preparing and serving of food could bring out the individual traits in the characters. It is also the one story in which Edson is not the first person narrator.

That goes back to the experimentation we were talking about. I wanted to see if I could write a story, or write Edson's story, in the third person. The other thing that I wanted to do is make it a transitional story. I think that the first time I read a story like that was in the work of Clark Blaise, where it almost seemed like a fragment of a story, and left me wondering. But when I reread it, I realized there was a tremendous shift happening from this story to the next story.

"Pancakes" has to do with the coming of the next generation, being together one more time and also being drawn apart, and how they don't even realize that what is going on in their lives right now.

But it's interesting because the family is breaking up. There are two characters, I think, remaining at home. And that's only casually mentioned.

That is the key to it. It is only casually mentioned. In writing that, in the first half, that fact was even more subtle, but then I thought in my revisions that it was a bit too subtle because this really is a transitional story. That transition had to be clear without beating the reader over the head. It's also the only genuinely humorous story in the book. And I wanted that, I wanted it to be light.

The humour itself is interesting as part of your characterization. Why did you put the story under "Summer"?

I guess because it opens with so much sunlight. I believe it is a summer story; it felt like summer to me, at least. This is why it ends it up there. I was going on about the characters going out there.

That's true, and you can argue that this is one last kick at spring, at adolescence—its fun and frolic—before taking on the responsibility for one's own life.

After that, it's downhill [laughs]. I don't think it's that.

Actually, it could be. "You Always Promise" (or, as I prefer to call it, "Joey's Story") is placed under "Fall." Why?

Again, it is a fall story, but it also has to do with the fall of individuals. We aren't too sure at the end of that story what is going to happen next. *Winter, Spring, Summer, Fall* is supposed to be the first book in a series, and there is a sense, especially after Summer, and after the characters have gone off on their own. . . It is the first time we meet Edson by himself. It's an indication that in the future the focus will be even more centred on him.

In this story, Edson is forced to stand alone; he's forced to make decisions on his own. Is he now prepared—after the grandmother, and the parents, and all his experiences with his older siblings—is he prepared to face the world? Joey seems more prepared, actually, than anybody else, because he knows what his lot is; because he knows his mom will break her promise, and he knows he has nowhere else to go. Edson, fortunately, has choices, but not all of them are going to be easy, and he won't always know how to make the right one. It is the one story in the collection that's built most on tension.

That is a question that arose in my mind. I remember Lawrence Hill telling me that we begin with conflict. This is what he tells his creative writing students. You have written some substantial stories without worrying too much about overt conflict.

Austin Clarke said to me once in an interview that, for him, conventional plotting is neither here nor there. He does what he does. I also like what Neil Gaiman once said: that plot, for him, is anything that gets the reader to turn the page. I firmly believe that. You don't have to have conflict all over the place. If you get in there and the reader says, "Wow, I want to know what happens next," you're fine. It might not be anything that builds tension, per se; you might be just using images, or you might be just using language interestingly. It just might be that the character says it all for the reader. That, to my mind, is accomplishment.

The transmission of cultural traditions is very noticeable in three of the four stories. Given your Barbadian-Canadian heritage, to what extent are these stories an exploration of your own identity?

They are very much an exploration of identity. I'm starting to realize that is what I'm doing. I'm negotiating identity. I'm trying to find the place between Barbados and Canada, if that exists, that I think my family and people of my family's generation came to create. I don't think that they were able to create, to make, that bridge that would have permitted them to move back and forth as freely as they liked—a number of them are here, and a number of them have died here, and some of them have gone back and had to let go of what they had here. So the question is, Can one exist in two worlds? Or, Is there a brave, new world between the two, a hybrid or fusion of the two?

You certainly ask that question quite a bit in Sand for Snow. *In fact, you start off very affirmatively. I laughed reading the initial exultations over your move to Barbados, and waited for . . .*

For the kicker. Right. There has been a sobering effect. I don't know if it's disappointment. I've enjoyed what I've seen and learned.

Your characters speak primarily in standard English, but occasionally resort to nation language. What accounts for your choice of language registers? Audience, aesthetics?

Verisimilitude. It has to do with getting things down correctly, but it's also how one hears it. I have a friend, she is also a writer, and she prefers Austin's spelling for America as he and she understand Bajans pronounce it: Amurca. I hear it as 'Merica.

Doesn't it depend on whether one lives in St. Peter or in Christchurch—regional variations?

Regardless, Austin would spell it Amurca, and I guess, regardless, I would always spell it 'Merica.

Sand for Snow *is a compilation of some of your columns written for the* Nation. *I was struck by the fact that however much you tried to disguise it, you were for the most part directly educating your readers or inviting them to reflect on various social phenomena. Parenting and gender relationships are two of the themes that you addressed, often times by reflecting on your own father. You vaunt your baking skills as well—a skill that won't earn you plaudits from your traditional Caribbean male friends.*

That was the fun thing about writing for the *Nation.* I could do pretty much whatever I wanted along certain lines, about Canadian, Barbadian, North American, or Caribbean relations. So I thought everything was fair game. I didn't necessarily see myself educating people. I knew they would say, "He comes from away and wants to tell us how we should live our lives." But I say, "No; I don't come from so far away. My parents were both Barbadians. I was taught and raised by them. I know things about this island that you don't know because you don't remember them, but I was raised on them." So I didn't feel so far removed. I knew, though, that I was from the outside, a foreigner, as they would say. Again, it just goes back to observing. I was just writing down what I saw.

Were you told that you were a foreigner?

By some people, yes. There was one instance in particular, when John Wickham was complaining about one of my columns to an editor. And I was right there, and I got incensed. He was saying the usual stuff: "These people who come from away think that..." And I just said, "John, if you've got a problem with what I'm saying, just say so." He kind of clammed up, and the editor tried to make peace between the two of us.

Is that the piece in which you give a list of things that men shouldn't do?

It was another piece. I didn't let possible criticism deter me. Although I knew that the article was going to be taken that way, I wasn't setting myself above anybody else. I was just saying, "Take a look at society." That was all there was to it, and then you judge.

You obviously love cake.

Yes, I do, I do. (laughs)

You use your culinary skills to educate. Simply stating that—you and I are West Indians, and we know that West Indian men see cooking as a woman's job—you and . . .

My brothers, Calvin and Patrick, cook.

I don't remember Calvin being mentioned.

No, he isn't, but Patrick is. I believe in being artful in everything one does. So if one's going to cook, one should do it well.

Did people comment on that? Did you get feedback?

One lady called up, saying, "I don't know if I have everything that you have here, but there seems to be something missing." And I said, "You know you've got everything." And she said, "Well, I'll try the recipe and let you know how it turns out." I never heard back from her. So I assume it turned out ok. I did get that call at the newspaper.

Since you compiled some of these columns into a book, quite clearly you must have thought that there was something in them worth rescuing from the ephemera of quotidian journalism.

When I began writing the columns, I knew that I would turn them into a book. There was never any doubt in my mind. I think knowing that helped to keep me honest, because I also knew then that the columns had to be of a certain standard in order to be collected.

You play an active role in promoting the arts. This is evident in your pieces for ArtsEtc, but is also noticeable in the columns you've written on visual and literary artists in Barbados. Do you feel that you have some sort of mission to promote art?

It's about giving back, and it's also about promoting. Writers and artists should engage in promoting their own activity. I'm not only just promoting my work, I promote the good work of others.

This implies that you believe strongly in what you do and that you value what you do. Your piece, for example, "Where's the Next Generation of Barbadian Novelists?" is controversial, inasmuch as you dismiss Glenville Lovell, Cecil Foster et al. You put yourself out on a limb there.

Glenville writes well, but I think his interest is focused still on dramatic pieces. He's still very much concerned and involved with that.

You're saying that he would make a better playwright than a novelist?

Maybe, because his dialogue is really spot on.

Well, I'm not going to put you on the spot by asking about Cecil.

No problem. You can. I've reviewed his work. I think he is a strong nonfiction writer. He may very well be a strong fiction writer, but I don't see that evidence consistently, and that is my reservation.

Well, No Man in the House *is certainly a very interesting and skilfully crafted novel.*

That was his first, and I read that when I was a lowly clerk for a bookseller. I pushed it. I said we have to have this in your bookstores, and it sold. And I was enthusiastic about that. *Sleep on, Beloved,* less so.

It's not a bad novel.

I'm not saying that at all. What I'm saying is that the focus is . . .

Sociological. It is very significant because it deals with the coming of the domestic servants and the legacy of that in the school system. And you are probably saying it is journalism that he transforms into fiction.

Thank you. I think there is nothing wrong with the books themselves, but it's just the handling sometimes. Is it a good book? Yeah, he writes good books. But are they great works of fiction? It is more that that I was getting at in "Where Is the Next Generation of Barbadian Novelists?" Naipaul, for instance: I don't think many people would read Naipaul and say, depending on the work, "Oh, this is more...." I mean, it's very clearly defined: there are the travelogues, and there are the novels. They are not anything else, even if he is experimenting and playing around with the form here and there, or language.

Though in Enigma of Arrival . . . .

I thought you would bring up that one.

It's autobiographical

Yes, it is, but it's well written.

Yes, it's well written.
Does your work as a journalist hinder or help your fiction?

It enriches it. It has taught me to be more concise, to get the maximum effect with the minimum of words, improved my technique.

Don't you worry, though, that you would overload your fiction with what I would call journalistic details? I have seen that mistake made by a lot of journalists who turn to fiction.

Well, that's the other thing I wanted to deal with, because you refer to me as a journalist, but I've never seen myself that way. I'm simply a writer. The first stories I wrote were fictional stories.

But what about your work at the Nation*? I mean, as an editor or associate editor, you do have to put on the journalist's cap.*

Yeah, but that's what happens. I put on the cap, although I don't necessarily separate the two. It's all storytelling, whether it's a painting, nonfiction, a poem—you have to tell the story.

It's true. Austin did some journalism as well.

For the *Nation*, too. All the while that I was doing the journalistic thing, I was still writing short stories, and publishing short stories, and they were clearly short stories; they couldn't be mistaken for anything else.

Have your mother and older relatives seen your erotic comics? If yes, what have been their reactions?

Yes, my mother has seen the prose version of one of them. I think she came across an old draft once, and she said, "Robert, what's this?" (And she has no problems with issues dealing with sexuality.) I said, "Well, it's just another aspect of my work." She said to me, straight up, which I appreciate, "Well, I don't think it is an aspect that I necessarily want to know more about." She is not interested in it. She knows that I publish that stuff, but in terms of promoting it or anything like that, or knowing about or reading them, she's not interested. It's not what she enjoys reading from me.

How do you feel about the critical response your work has received?

As with many writers, I feel it could be more. But I think—if I understand your question—it has been fair. I think people, when they read me, they more or less like it or they don't. It has been a long time since somebody has said something where I had to respond to say you misread me, you didn't understand what I was doing.

You have taken the leap into publishing? Why?

The publishing venture is very much a family venture. It's with my eldest brother, Calvin, but the family supports it. It is to give something back: if somebody didn't take a chance on me, a small press—and our venture is by no means a small press, it's a micro press—I don't know where my books would be today. The publishing venture is founded on the profit from my first book. The schools in Barbados use it.

Most books by Black writers challenge the various national myths and are therefore unpopular with White readers. What implications does this state of affairs hold for the Black voice in Canadian literature?

I am disturbed by how Black Canadian literature seems to be perceived in Canada, in particular by those in the book industry. George Elliott Clarke once told me that somebody told him that books by Black Canadian authors don't sell.

Is it that they don't sell, or is it because publishers don't know how to market them? I'm sorry, but it's easier to say books don't sell and never figure out why they don't sell. Is it because they don't actually challenge the myth? There are very complex books written by Black American authors, male and female, that the entire population will buy and read—or at least recognize as important.

Well, actually, the female authors outsell the male authors.

I recognize that. What I'm saying is that there must be a way to market Black Canadian books. There must be a way to get them out there. Even when a book is considered a sure hit by a White writer or whoever, there is no guarantee it will be a bestseller. Publishers know this. Sometimes, they have a book that they figure isn't going to move. It ends up winning an award, and the next thing you know it's taking off. Or you'll have a book that you are sure will do everything that it should do critically and commercially, and it sits on the shelves. Yet it's a brilliant book that might later enjoy reprinting and outlast that other book that is taking off. My whole thing is that you must put your back into it, in terms of marketing.

Even so. I'm thinking of Cecil's Slammin' Tar, *which was heavily promoted, and I don't think it went anywhere.*

Well, I don't know if it would make any difference, but do they have a lot of minorities—I don't mean just Blacks—working in the PR field?

No, they don't.

This is what I mean: Do they have people who understand that they should go to the community centres and put up a few flyers? Have authors go into the church, give a little bit of a reading after the service maybe and see what happen? They might figure it doesn't take much, it just takes knowing.

Yeah, but White publishers also do a strange thing. They feel it's their role to sell the work to a mainstream audience. They expect Black authors to do the legwork to sell their works in the Black community.

With a small press, that might be a yes or a no. I was on tour with another author: a White author, and we both had to hustle the same way. I was told, "You two are the authors who hustle the most," and this was by a White publisher. I think authors, in general, have to realize that they do have to market their books actively and aggressively. Publishers, too: don't just tell us to go into the community and make the rounds in the churches and in the beauty salons. The publisher's PR person should help with the groundwork to facilitate tapping into that clientele.

I'll be the first to admit that publishers have to be conservative. But then the second thing to do is sit down with your author; sit down and chart a course for the book. I know that has been my experience with DC Books, where we had a meeting to discuss the marketing of *Sand for Snow*. I have no problem sharing the load, but I want to know that we're going to share the load.

Anything else you'd like to add?

No, just that I am what I've always wanted to be, which is a writer, and I feel blessed.

And the paycheck doesn't bother you?

I manage to cobble together a living doing various things. I've been fortunate. When certain things are covered and the Mrs is happy, I can indulge my creativity. And if I didn't write I would be most unhappy.

Contributors

Ayanna Black is the author of two books of poetry: *No Contingencies* and *Linked Alive.* A third book, *Invoking the Spirit,* is forthcoming in 2006. She has edited several anthologies of feminist as well as African Canadian writing, including *Fiery Spirits and Voices* (which combines the earlier anthologies *Voices* and *Fiery Spirits*). She was a founding member of *Tiger Lily Journal,* Canada's first magazine by women of colour, and was its editor. She helped to create CAN:BAIA (Canadian Artists Network: Black Artists in Action) and was its president for six years.

Austin Clarke is known to most African Canadian writers as the dean of Black writing in Canada. He immigrated to Canada from Barbados in 1955. He is the author of nine novels, including *The Polished Hoe* (winner of the Giller Prize); *The Question* (Governor General's Award nominee); *The Origin of Waves* (winner of the Roger's Prize); *The Meeting Point, Storm of Fortune,* and *The Bigger Light* (commonly referred to as *The Toronto Trilogy*); five collections of short stories, the most recent being *Choosing His Coffin: The Best Stories of Austin Clarke*; and a memoir: *Growing Up Stupid Under the Union Jack.* He is a recipient of the W. O. Mitchell Prize. He lives in Toronto.

George Elliott Clarke was born in Windsor, Nova Scotia and grew up in Halifax. He is the author of six collections of poems, including: *Saltwater Spirituals and Deeper Blues* (published when he was twenty-three); *Whylah Falls* (recipient of the Archibald Lampman Award); *Execution Poems* (recipient of the Governor General's Award); a novel, *George & Rue* (recipient of the Dartmouth Book Award); a play, *Beatrice Chancy*; and the literary study, *Odysseys Home: Mapping African Canadian Literature.* He is also the editor of the anthologies *Fire on the Water: An Anthology of Black Nova Scotia Writing Volume One*; *Fire on the Water Volume Two*; and *Eyeing the North Star: Directions in African Canadian Literature.* He is E. J. Pratt Professor of Canadian Literature at the University of Toronto.

Wayde Compton is the author of two books of poetry, *Performance Bond*

(2004) and *49th Parallel Psalm* (1999) (shortlisted for the Dorothy Livesay Prize), and editor of the anthology *Bluesprint: Black British Columbian Literature and Orature* (2001). He is a creative writing instructor in the Writer's Studio in Simon Fraser University's Writing and Publishing Program and teaches English composition and literature at Coquitlam College. He is working on a book of short stories. He lives in Vancouver.

Afua Cooper immigrated to Canada at age twenty-two. She is a poet, historian, and performer of dub poetry. Her poetry collections include *Memories Have Tongue* (a finalist for the Casa de las Américas Award), *Breaking Chains,* and *Copper Woman.* Her several books for children include *Red Caterpillar on College Street*; *The Underground Railroad, Next Stop: Toronto*; and the forthcoming (2007) *The Young Phillis Wheatley and The Young Henry Bibb.* Her latest historical work (2006) is the critically acclaimed *The Hanging of Angélique: The Untold Story of Canadian Slavery and the Burning of Old Montréal.* Her recorded poems are available on the following discs: *Sunshine, Worlds of Fire in Motion*, and *Possessed: Dub Stories.* She holds the Harry Jerome Award for Excellence. She lives in Toronto.

Bernadette Dyer was born in Kingston, Jamaica. She is a poet, fiction writer, and storyteller. As storyteller, she has performed at several venues, including the 1001 Nights Storytelling Series. In addition to her poems and fiction published in many anthologies and journals in Canada and elsewhere, she is the author of *Villa Fair*, a collection of short stories, and a novel, *Waltzes I Have Not Forgotten.* She lives in Toronto.

Cecil Foster has worked extensively in the print and electronic media here and in Barbados, the country of his birth. He is currently assistant professor in the Department of Sociology and Anthropology at the University of Guelph. His fiction has been anthologized widely. He is the author of the novels *No Man in the House, Sleep on, Beloved, Slammin' Tar*, and *Dry Bone Memories*; a memoir: *Island Wings*; and the socio-political studies *A Place Called Heaven: The Meaning of Being Black in Canada* (recipient of the Gordon Montador Award for Best Canadian nonfiction Book on Social Issues), *Distorted Mirror, Caribana: the Greatest Celebration*, and most recently (2005) *Where Race Does Not Matter: The New Spirit of Modernity.*

Claire Harris came to Calgary, Canada from Trinidad in 1966. In addition to her several poems and essays published in dozens of international journals, in English and in translation, she is the author of seven collections of poems: *She* (Alberta Writers' Guild Award shortlist), *Dipped in Shadow* (Guild of Alberta shortlist), *Drawing Down a Daughter* (Governor General Award shortlist), *The Conception of Winter* (winner Alberta Culture Special Award), *Travelling to Find a*

Remedy (winner Alberta Writers' Guild Award and Alberta Culture Poetry Prize), *Translation into Fiction, and Fables from the Women's Quarters* (winner Commonwealth Regional Award). She is a founding member of *blue buffalo* and was its managing editor from 1984–1987, and was the poetry editor of *Dandelion* from 1981–1989.

Lawrence Hill was born in Newmarket, Ontario of US parents, and grew up in Toronto. He is the author of the novels *Any Known Blood* and *Some Great Thing*; the memoir *Black Berry, Sweet Juice: on Being Black and White in Canada*; and the historical works *Women of Vision: the Story of the Canadian Negro Women's Association* and *Trials and Triumphs: the Story of African Canadians.* His essay "Is Africa's Pain Black America's Burden" (Walrus, Feb. 2005) won the 2005 National Magazine Award for the best essay published in Canada. His television documentary *Seeking Salvation: A History of the Black Church in Canada* won the 2005 American Wilbur Award for best national television documentary. He has recently completed *Rainbow Congress*, a one-hour television drama. His novel *The Book of Negroes* is forthcoming in 2007.

Nalo Hopkinson is a Jamaican Canadian. She is the author of the novels *Brown Girl in the Ring, Midnight Robber, The Salt Roads, The New Moon's Arms*, and a short-story collection *Skin Folk.* She is a recipient of the Warner Aspect First Novel award, the Locus First Novel Award, the World Fantasy Award, the Sunburst Award for Canadian Literature of the Fantastic, the Gaylactic Spectrum Award, the Ontario Arts Council Foundation Award for Emerging Writers, and, with Geoff Ryman, Canada's Aurora Award for science fiction and fantasy. She has edited or coedited the following fiction anthologies: *Whispers from the Cotton Tree Root: Caribbean Fabulist Fiction, Mojo: Conjure Stories, So Long Been Dreaming: Postcolonial Science Fiction and Fantasy* (with Dr Uppinder Mehan), *Tesseracts Nine* (with Geoff Ryman). She lives in Toronto.

Suzette Mayr is the author of three novels: *Moon Honey, The Widows*, and *Venous Hum. The Widows* was nominated for the Commonwealth Prize for Best First Book in the Canada-Caribbean region, and *Moon Honey* was nominated for the Writers Guild of Alberta Best First Book and Best Novel awards. Her poetry and short fiction have appeared in journals and anthologies across Canada. She currently lives and works in Calgary.

Pamela Mordecai immigrated to Canada from her birthplace, Jamaica, in 1994, and now resides in Toronto. Her thirty-plus books include: *de Man* (1995), *Culture and Customs of Jamaica* (2000), coauthored with her husband Martin Mordecai, *Rohan Goes to Big School* (2000), *The Costume Party* (2000), *Certifiable* (2001), *The True Blue of Islands* (2005), and *Pink Icing: Stories* (2006). She has edited several anthologies. They include *Her True-True Name* (1989), coedited with Betty Wilson and *Calling Cards: New Poetry from Caribbean/Canadian Women* (2005). She received the Institute of Jamaica's Centenary Medal for Writing and Jamaica's inaugural Vic Reid Award for Children's Literature.

M NourbeSe Philip was born in Trinidad and Tobago. In addition to her numerous publications in journals and anthologies, she is the author of three collections of poems: *She Tries Her Tongue, Her Silence Softly Breaks*; *Salmon Courage*; and *Thorns*; two novels: *Harriet's Daughter*, which was nominated for the Max and Greta Abel Award and the Canadian Library Association Prize, and *Looking for Livingstone*; three books of nonfiction: *A Genealogy of Resistance and Other Essays*, *Showing Grit: Showboating North of the 44th Parallel*, *Frontiers: Essays and Writings in Racism and Culture*; and a play: *Coups and Calypsos*. She is a recipient of the Casa de las Americas Prize, the Tradewinds Collective Prize, the Toronto Arts Award, the Lawrence Foundation Award, the Woman of Distinction Award in the Arts, a Chalmers Fellowship in Poetry, a Guggenheim Fellowship in poetry, a McDowell Fellowship, and a Rockefeller Foundation Fellowship. She resides in Toronto.

Althea Prince is a sociologist and author from Antigua. She moved to Canada in 1965 and resides in Toronto. From 2002 to 2005 she was the Managing Editor of Canadian Scholars' Press and Women's Press. She now teaches at Ryerson University. She is the author of *Ladies of the Night and Other Stories* (short stories), *Being Black* (essays), *Loving This Man* (novel), and two children's books: *How the Star Fish Got the Sea* and *How the East Pond Got Its Flowers*.

Robert Edison Sandiford is the author of two short-story collections, *Winter, Spring, Summer, Fall* (1995) and *The Tree of Youth* (2005); the graphic story collections, *Attractive Forces* (1997), and *Stray Moonbeams* (2002); a travel memoir, *Sand for Snow: A Caribbean-Canadian Chronicle* (2003). He is the coeditor with Linda M. Deane of the forthcoming (2006) *Shouts from the Outfield: The ArtsEtc Cricket Anthology*. He is a founding editor of *ArtsEtc: The Premier Cultural Guide to Barbados*. He has worked as a journalist, book publisher, video producer, and teacher.

H. Nigel Thomas immigrated to Canada in 1968 and now resides in Montreal. His short stories, poems, and essays have been published in numerous journals and anthologies. He is the author of *From Folklore to Fiction: A Study of Folk Heroes in the Black American Novel*; two novels, *Spirits in the Dark* (shortlisted for the Hugh MacLennan Fiction Award) and *Behind the Face of Winter*; a collection of short stories, *How Loud Can the Village Cock Crow? and Other Stories*; and a collection of poems, *Moving through Darkness*. A third novel, *Return to Arcadia*, is forthcoming in 2007.

Works Cited

Biesheuvel, S. "An Examination of Jensen's Theory Concerning Educability, Hereditability, and Population Differences." Ashley Montagu, Ed. *Race and IQ*. Oxford: Oxford University Press, 1999. 108–121.

Brand, Dionne. *A Map to the Door of No Return: Notes to Belonging*. Toronto: Doubleday Canada, 2001.

Brathwaite, Edward Kamau. *Roots. Havana: Casa de las Américas*, 1986.

Elliot, Lorris. *Literary Writing by Blacks in Canada: A Preliminary Survey*. Michael Batts, Ed. Government of Canada Documents, 1988.

Eysenck, H. J. *The IQ Argument*. New York: The Library Press, 1971.

Foster, Cecil. *Where Race Does Not Matter: The New Spirit of Modernity*. Toronto: Penguin, 2005.

_____. *A Place Called Heaven: The Meaning of Being Black in Canada*. Toronto: HarperCollins, 1996.

Hernstein, Richard J. and Charles Murray. *The Bell Curve: Intelligence and Class Structure in American Life*. London: The Free Press, 1994

Huggan, Graham. *The Postcolonial Exotic: Marketing the Margins*. London & New York: Routledge, 2001.

Hughes, Langston. "The Negro Artist and the Racial Mountain." Addison Gayle, Jr., Ed. *The Black Aesthetic*. Garden City, New York: Anchor Books, 1972. 167–172.

Hurston, Zora Neale. "What White Publishers Won't Print." Alice Walker, Ed. *I Love Myself when I Am Laughing . . . : A Zora Neale Hurston Reader*. New York: Feminist Press, 1979. 169–173.

Jensen, Arthur Robert. *The g Factor: The Science of Mental Ability*. Westport, Connecticut: Praeger Books, 1998.

Kamboureli, Smaro, ed. *Making a Difference: Canadian Multicultural Literatures in English* (Second Editon). Don Mills, Ontario: Oxford University Press, 2006.

Laferrière, Dany, *Cette grenade dans la main du jeune Nègre est-elle une arme ou un fruit?* Montreal : VLB, 1993.

_____. *Comment faire l'amour à un Nègre sans se fatiguer*. Montreal : VLB, 1985.

Li, Peter S. *Ethnic Inequality in a Class Society*. Toronto: Thompson Educational, 1998.

Mensah, Joseph. *Black Canadians: History, Experiences, Social Conditions*. Halifax: Fernwood Publishing, 2002.

Morrison, Toni. "Rootedness: The Ancestor as Foundation." Mari Evans, Ed. *Black Women Writers (1950–1980): A Critical Evaluation*. Garden City, NY: Anchor Books, 1984. 339–345.

Philip, M. NourbeSe. *A Genealogy of Resistance and Other Essays*. Toronto: Mercury, 1997.

______. *Frontiers: selected essays and writings on racism and culture 1984–1992*. Toronto: Mercury, 1992.

______. "Discourse on the Logic of Language." *She Tries Her Tongue: Her Silence Softly Breaks*. Charlottetown, Prince Edward Island: 1989. 55–59.

Rushton, J. Phillipe. *Race, Evolution, and Behavior*. New Brunswick, NJ: Transaction Publishers, 1997.

Thomas, H. Nigel. "A Rejoinder to Prospero: An Interview with M. NourbeSe Philip." Kola 8:2 (1996), 38–55.

Ubale, Bhausaheb. *Politics of Exclusion: Multiculturalism or Ghettoism*, 1992. Quoted in Graham Huggan. *The Postcolonial Exotic: Marketing the Margins*. London & New York: Routledge, 2001.

Walcott, Derek. "What the Twilight Says: An Overture." *Dream on Monkey Mountain and Other Plays*. New York: Farrar, Straus and Giroux, 1970. 3–40.

Walcott, Rinaldo. *Black Like Who: Writing Black Canada*. Toronto: Insomniac Press, 1997.

Walker, Alice, Ed. *I Love Myself when I Am Laughing . . . : A Zora Neale Hurston Reader*. New York: Feminist Press, 1979.